Bittersweet Blessings

Bittersweet Blessings

Sweet Highs and Bitter Lows of Life with God

Debbie Huckaby

Deeds Publishing | Athens

Copyright © 2023 — Debbie Huckaby

ALL RIGHTS RESERVED—No part of this book may be reproduced in any form or by any electronic or mechanical means, including information storage and retrieval systems, without permission in writing from the authors, except by a reviewer who may quote brief passages in a review.

Published by Deeds Publishing in Athens, GA
www.deedspublishing.com

Printed in The United States of America

Cover by Mark Babcock

ISBN 978-1-950794-96-6

Books are available in quantity for promotional or premium use. For information, email info@deedspublishing.com.

First Edition, 2023

10 9 8 7 6 5 4 3 2 1

In honor of my family past, present and future.

Contents

Prologue	ix
Introduction	xi
I Myself Began	1
Happy Birthday, Hello Daddy Jay	17
First Kiss, First Love, First Restriction	29
Joy and Jeopardy in Jesup	39
Senior Year Love and Politics	47
A Nurse, Wife and Mother	59
A Warning of Things to Come	69
Athens, Go Dawgs	73
AGH: Great Fun and Great Responsibility	83
Two Incomes, Two Boys	91
How I Got My White Hair	101
Dreams Come True in a Gingerbread House	113
Lord, Please Don't Take My Mother	123
WINGS: An Oconee Christian Women's Group	129
It's Time	145
What's a Wheaton?	161
Parish Nurse, President, and Preacher	173
I Can Rest, Lord, Because of You!	187

It Helps to Have a Personal Mission Statement	193
Personal Mission Statement	195
Candler: The Bride, The King, AND The Lion of Judah	197
Finding Home at Asbury Theological Seminary	201
An Asbury Doctorate and the UMC	205
My Sons and the Daughters They Gave Me	219
Waiting Is the Hardest Part	235
Someone You Need to Meet	239
A Roller Coaster Named Shemitah	253
The Ends of the Earth	265
Doctor Professor	289
An Honorary Master in the Art of Nursing	315
A Doc and a Post	323
A Scene I Have Always Feared	347
His Mustache Was the Key to My Fifty-Year-Old Secret	351
My Family, My Heart	355
The End is a Beginning	371
About the Author	377

Disclaimer

This book reflects the stories of my life, a life filled with sweet experiences and bitter losses. All the events are true to the best of my memory. Some names have been changed and some dialogue has been recreated because I do not mean to defame, slander, or hurt anyone. I share this work for glory and praise to God and in the hope that by reading it you, too, will have a deeper relationship with Him.

Prologue

Write, He Said, So I Did

A few years ago, deep in prayer, I had received an image of a little girl sitting beside God. She had black curly hair, black patent leather shoes, and white lacy socks. She wrote with a big pencil on a tablet propped against her knees. God sat beside her with his arm around her shoulders and talked with her about what she wrote. Well, I was the little girl in the image and "WRITE" was the message that I received.

As I said, that was a few years ago and that message has come a few more times in various ways (scripture, people), but always the same, "WRITE" but what? And for whom? And how? I had many questions and excuses, and besides, I was writing—research papers, assignments, and a journal that I have kept for decades—but still the message came.

Then a friend asked if I would send her an e-mail every now and then just to let her know what God was doing in my life. DAH! That was it! I realized that I am to share my journal—the ways God shows up and speaks to me through life. My friend said, "When you share your stories, I am able to apply them to my life and understand what God is saying to me also." Maybe by sharing my journey, others will see God too, I thought.

A pastor recently spoke about sharing our faith. His words were so clear and profound to me that I squirmed in my seat. "Share your faith! Tell others what God is doing in your life! We learn from each other. Be willing to let others see God through your life!" he said. And quietly, again, I heard God say, "WRITE!"

So, these are the stories of my life, a life filled with sweet experiences and bitter losses. I share them for glory and praise to God and in the hope that by reading them you, too, will have a deeper relationship with Him.

Psalm 73:28 (NASB)

But as for me, the nearness of God is my good:
I have made the Lord God my refuge
That I may tell of all Thy works.

Introduction

Change, Change, Change

Flexibility, like the stretching of a rubber band, is not a natural or static human condition, yet like the rubber band, flexibility is gained in change. In a word, change is the story of my life.

My parents were divorced when I was five years old and both remarried when I was eight, so I had a father and a stepfather, a mother and a stepmother, and three sets of grandparents. I have a brother who is two years younger than I am, a brother who is eleven years younger than I am, and two half-brothers and a half-sister, but I have experienced the deaths of all of my parents and grandparents, my stepsister, and most of my aunts and uncles. I have been married twice myself, which gave me two sets of in-laws. I have been pregnant five times, but only have two living children.

I have moved my residence 28 times. I have attended 17 different schools: four elementary schools, four high schools, and nine colleges or universities, from which I earned six degrees.

I have had two successful careers. A 45-year career as a Registered Nurse and more than 20 years in ministry. In healthcare, I held leadership positions in 17 different departments in five different medical centers and in ministry, I served four churches and a district. In all I have held 32 distinct positions, none of which I initiated. Ironically, the two other positions that I sought, I did not get. I have been a member of four denominations—Baptist, Episcopal, United Methodist, and The Wesleyan Church, where I now serve as an ordained minister.

Although change is inherent in my life, so is God, who has walked with me or carried me like the footprints in the sand through every challenge, yet change, even for me, was and still is difficult. In the midst of the pain of leaving friends or losing loved ones, I learned about woundedness and healing and about grief and hope. I learned about holding on to my wants and desires and then I learned how to bring my burdens to God.

Through these circumstances, I saw God's omniscience, omnipresence, and omnipotence and developed an attitude of acceptance to God's sovereignty. I learned to see life from a higher or eternal perspective. As Karl Rahner noted when describing the receptivity that emerges in childhood, I was highly susceptible to catching a sense of purposefulness in and with God, and through all of this, I came to understand that I must tell of all his wonderous works.

I Myself Began

I dreaded walking into dark places, and I slept with a night light. If I was home alone, I left on the lamp beside my bed all night long and while I would not admit it, not even to myself, I was afraid of the dark. I thought I'd grow out of it, but that paralyzing fear still tormented me even at 50.

The Bible says, "Do not fear," and I wanted to obey, but I just could not. "Help Lord, why am I so afraid of the dark?" For months, I prayed for strength and wisdom to resist. Then one day, while praying in the warm sunshine of our living room window, I saw in my mind's eye a room filled with pitch black darkness except for a sliver of light under the door that I could see from where I stood in my crib. I could hear voices, angry voices in the next room. Momma and Daddy were arguing about me. Momma wanted to leave on the light in my room, but Daddy would not let her. He had put me in my crib, turned off the light and shut the door. I was alone and scared and all I could do was cry.

It was an experience from long ago, but the fear was present and just as real. I gasped for breath. Tears stung my eyes and my heart pounded in my ears. "Jesus, what is going on? What do you want me to know about this?" I prayed. Again, I saw the deep darkness of my room, but there, enveloped in brilliant light, stood

Jesus cradling a baby in His arms. "It will be okay," Jesus said to the tiny bundle, "I am here!" Then the scene disappeared, and with it went my fear of the dark, never to return again.

Macel Nevel Ayers and Jerry Frank Atkins grew up on Sprayberry Road in Newnan, Georgia, and married while they were still in high school. I was born when Momma Macel was just 16 and Daddy Jerry 18. How drastically life must have changed for the beautiful auburn-haired bride and her tall, dark-haired, and handsome groom when the advent of their firstborn changed their fairy tale life. Quiet, gentle, and gracious, Momma Macel joyfully put the lives of others before herself. It would be years before she returned to school. Pondering this and the love of my unselfish Momma moves me to honor her every year on my own birthday.

My first home and the place where I first knew the presence of the Lord Jesus Christ was a second-story apartment on Clark Street, a few miles from my grandparents, aunts, and uncles in Newnan. Momma said she remembered that apartment very well because it was there that she sat in a window to wash it and got stuck when she was seven months pregnant with my younger brother Mike.

Before I was two, my grandparents, Daddy Leon, and Momma Erline Ayers moved to LaGrange, Georgia, where they bought Uncle Eck Presley's motel and a restaurant, a house, and several acres of land at Lee's Crossing. We moved there, too, and lived in a small house on the airport road, but soon moved again to a house next door to my grandparents. When I was five and Mike was three, the storybook marriage of high school sweethearts crumbled under the strain and our parents were divorced. Why? I don't know. No one, absolutely no one, in my family has ever said why, and in all these years since, Momma never spoke a negative word about Daddy and Daddy never once spoke against Momma. The only hint I ever got was from Momma Jiles, my great grandmother and the matriarch of our family, who simply said, "Well, I guess they just grew up."

Divorce to a five-year-old just meant that Daddy was gone. I was my daddy's little princess, so why did he leave me? Had I done something to make him mad at me? Was I not good enough anymore? Years later I would realize that my daddy's absence had bored a deep penetrating wound called abandonment into my soul and caused me to question if God, my heavenly Father, would leave me also.

When Daddy left, he moved to Atlanta, but he visited on my birthday and sometimes on Mike's, but his visit at Christmas was an extravaganza for all of us with his gifts piled high around the tree. Never mind that most were inappropriate and unusable, like the adult-sized guitar and 15-pound bowling ball. What Momma did with that stuff, I don't know. After a few years of this, the excitement wore off as Mike and I realized that Daddy did not know us at all, and his gifts were a poor substitute for his love and presence.

After the divorce, Momma, Mike, and I moved in with Daddy Leon and Momma Erline, who lived with Aunt Josephine Presley and Aunt Pearl Presley in the house adjacent to the restaurant and motel. Aunt Pearl is the one who told me, more than once, that Elvis was kin. "Elvis? Who is that, Aunt Pearl?"

"You know," she would say, "that singer. Your Momma and Elvis are first cousins." At five or six or seven years old, I didn't know, but I do now.

Mike and I slept together in a twin bed in the same bedroom with Momma Erline and Daddy Leon while Momma Macel lived in one of the motel rooms closest to the house with her friend and roommate Wynonna. Mine and Mike's twin bed was pushed up against a front porch window, which provided Aunt Pearl with the perfect opportunity to dress up as Soap Sally Annie and stand outside that window, scratching on the screen to scare us. We knew it was Aunt Pearl, but we would scream and laugh and jump under the covers, sometimes pretending to be afraid and sometimes we really were.

It was there in that twin bed that I met Dale Carnegie and learned to love books. Momma Erline read every night before going to sleep, mostly the Bible, but she had others like Dale Carnegie's How to Win Friends and Influence People. After prayers, Mike would go to sleep, but I would stay awake and read. Dale Carnegie's book is the one I remember the most. I was only in the first or second grade, so I didn't have a big vocabulary, yet night after night I reread every word I knew and added a few more. I still have a copy of that book today.

Every morning before dawn, Daddy Leon dressed in a white short-sleeved shirt and dress pants, tucked his favorite unlit cigar between his lips and crept out of the bedroom he shared with us. He made his way across the lawn and the parking lot to the restaurant just a few yards away. From there he managed the motel and restaurant, bought the groceries and supplies, greeted the customers, and sometimes cooked.

Momma Erline was up not long thereafter. Short, round, and white-haired since she was 30, Momma Erline's days were spent cooking, cleaning, and caring for us kids. Homemade biscuits, eggs, grits, and bacon or sausage, every morning, enough to feed the whole household, which included my Aunt Josephine, her black cocker spaniel, Boots, and Aunt Pearl. As soon as breakfast was over, Momma Erline started preparing lunch for even more. Momma Macel, who worked in the restaurant until 11 o'clock closing, would be there and Daddy Leon would come home to eat and rest. My elderly aunts would set the table and pour the sweet tea and we would all sit down together to say grace and pass heaping plates of fried chicken (the chickens had been caught, killed, and cleaned in the pen behind the house), mashed potatoes, gravy, and green beans, which were my favorites. And there was always a dessert—banana pudding, chocolate cake, or lemon meringue pie.

"Look after your brother," Momma Erline would say, but Mike called me, "Bossy" and I was—after all, he was younger and smaller, so I naturally assumed responsibility for his care and training. We spent our days playing chase or hide and seek in the large front yard and scaring the chickens in the pen out back or swinging in the big swing at the end of the cement veranda that wrapped around two sides of the house, once so high and fast that the swing broke and went flying off into the side yard with me in it. One day when it was raining, Mike and I built a tent in the back yard, and I started a fire inside the tent with matches that I had found beside the wood-burning stove in the center of the house. Fortunately, we were not hurt, but I went to bed without supper for that escapade.

Once a month, Momma Erline rode the Greyhound Bus from La Grange to Newnan to see her mother, Viola Jiles, and we went with her. Momma Jiles was always old, or at least that is the way she seemed to me. She was shorter than Momma Erline and even rounder. Momma Jiles' house had seven rooms, paneled throughout with polished pine paneling on the ceilings, walls and floors, lovingly built before 1910 by my great grandfather, Tim Jiles. Fireplaces, now converted to gas-burning heaters, graced the living room and each bedroom. Large black trunks and chifforobes served as closets in the bedrooms and the foot-pedal sewing machine sat in the wide hall. A Bible lay on the table beside each bed.

Family surrounded Momma Jiles. Uncle J.T. and Aunt Mary Emma Jiles lived on one side of her house with cousins Jerri, Judy, and Joe while Cousin Cordelia and her family lived on the other. It seemed they were always coming in and out, checking on Momma Jiles, enjoying her delicious country cooking at a dining room table that was made for six but often accommodated ten, and spending time together on her front porch.

Uncle J.T. (Joseph Thomas) worked in a factory in Newnan and coached Little League baseball and football teams. Aunt Mary Emma talked loudly and moved either too fast or too slow depending on the state of her manic-depressive disorder. Joe, our youngest cousin, was a miniature replica of his dad and spent every moment at his side. Jerilyn, or Jerri, who was in high school, was bright, attractive, and popular and the apple of her mother's eye, but short, pudgy Judith, or Judy, was alone in the middle. Her emptiness fueled her unhealthy choices. Jerri was furnished with a full monochromatic wardrobe change every season, which I found unusually pretentious for their humble lifestyle and clearly reflective of her mother's erratic moods. Judy found comfort in food and then companionship with boys or men.

Summers at Momma Jiles' were the best, especially August, even though August in Georgia is usually blazing hot with sticky high humidity. Some call those the dog days of summer and we just endure them in anticipation of the blessed cool breezes of fall. Yet that was one of my favorite times of the year. Back then, August meant crab apples, salt, and sweet tea on Momma Jiles' screened porch. Crab apples are small and crisp, but very, very sour when green and that's how we liked them best. Most afternoons, someone would pick a fresh batch from the gnarly crab apple tree behind the old wash house in Momma Jiles' back yard and one by one the family would gather to rock and talk and eat. "Pass the salt please." "Would you bring me some more tea?" "Debbie, you better not eat too many of those, you'll get a stomachache," Momma Jiles always said, but I never did.

From the corner rocker on her screened porch, Momma Jiles reigned as the family matriarch. There she had a wide-angle view of her Sprayberry Road neighbors and easy access to the telephone through the door which opened into the front bedroom. From there, she firmly but kindly had her say about the comings and goings of her extended family. "Watch you char-ACT-ter, Debbie," she once said to me when I was too young to understand.

"Okay, Momma Jiles," I said, but I had no idea what she meant. I've wondered many times in the years since her death if she would approve of my character now.

Little did I know at the time, but those trips to Momma Jiles' house were forming character, mental and moral qualities, deep in my soul. There I developed an understanding of family loyalty and devotion as I witnessed and experienced how my family members supported each other, regardless of the issue. I listened as the adults shared with us their wisdom but allowed us to make our own decisions. I learned to say thank you, yes ma'am and yes sir and how to treat others as I wanted to be treated, and I learned to love and be loved. More importantly, I was loved by people who loved Jesus Christ and shared His love with me.

My family, at least most, attended Love Joy Methodist Church at the corner of Sprayberry and Jefferson Roads just a few miles from the house and gospel singings held occasionally under a big white tent in the front of a large building on Jackson Street. I loved the singings. "Rock of Ages," "The Old Rugged Cross,"

"Victory in Jesus," and "I'll Fly Away" are songs that I learned word for word, and even as a child their messages, although not clearly understood at the time, were transformative in teaching me right from wrong. I remember riding the bus to my first-grade class at Troup County Elementary School and gnawing my fingernails in anguish to rid them of the red fingernail polish I had used because I thought only bad girls wore red nail polish. Why I thought that I don't know; perhaps it was just the culture back then, but the message in the songs had been received; some things were right, and some were wrong.

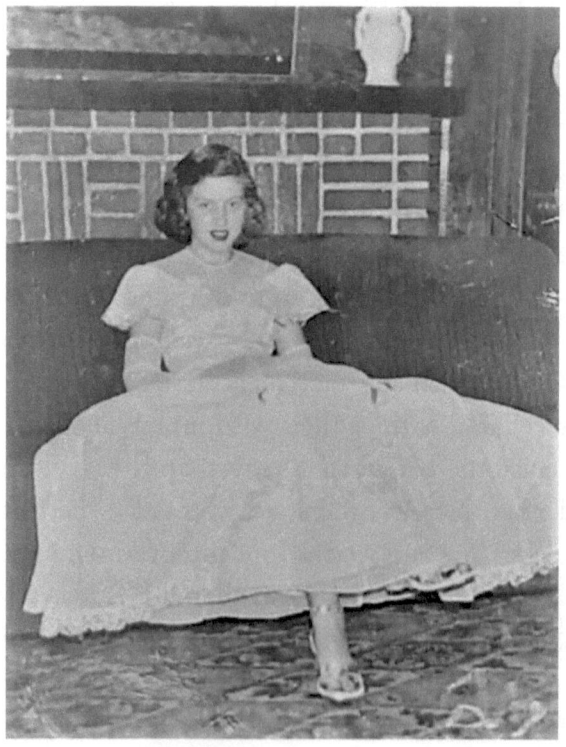

Macel Nevel Ayers

Jerry Frank Atkins

Macel, Jerry, Debbie

Five Generations: Debbie 2 mo. Bessie Hunter, Erline Ayers, Viola Jiles, Macel Atkins

Macel & Debbie — May 26, 1952

William "Bill" Hunter

Elizabeth "Bessie" Hunter & Debbie

Debbie Huckaby

Viola & Tim Jiles

Erline & Leon Ayers

Aunt Maud Elard holding Erline's stillborn son

Four Generations: April, 1968, Viola, Erline, Macel & Debbie

Debbie 5, Mike 3

Happy Birthday, Hello Daddy Jay

Such was life until I was eight, when again my life and my residence changed. It was the first week of March, the week of my birthday, and my mother was not home, which was distressing—in fact, I was mad. What could be more important to her than to be with me on my birthday? Imagine my surprise when Momma came home with the most unexpected birthday present ever, a new Daddy. Momma had married Jay Clennis Kirby, a tall, thin veteran of the Korean War, and came home that day from their honeymoon to introduce him to Mike and me. "What do I call him?" I asked Momma, days later while we were moving into a duplex apartment on Jefferson Street. "What do you want to call him?" she asked. "I think I'll call him Daddy Jay," I said.

Daddy Jay was what people call a bean counter and I believe he did see the world through numbers. We didn't have a car at the time, so every day he walked a mile from our house to the City-County Hospital where he worked as the comptroller. There he kept the books and said he enjoyed chasing down a single penny to ensure the books balanced, and while counting was not too eventful, his weekends on administrative call usually were.

One Saturday in 1961, Daddy Jay found himself in the middle of a potentially explosive situation. A gypsy queen was in critical condition and hundreds of her people came and camped on the lawn surrounding the hospital. Their queen was dying, and they were there to support her in her journey through death. That involved vigilance at the bedside, continuous chants, and a lighted candle placed upon her stomach to guide her way, but the woman was under an oxygen tent and the family refused to allow the candle to be removed. The frantic nurses called Daddy for help. Later that night he explained to us how he had immediately blown out the candle and dared anyone to relight it for fear of death to themselves and everyone else, but that he had also stood by for hours to be sure they did not.

Although our house was only four miles from Momma Erline and Daddy Leon's house, it was within the city, which meant I had to change schools. I started third grade at Southwest LaGrange Elementary School, and it was not long before the teacher informed my parents that even though I had made good grades in the county school, I was far behind her class and that if I could not quickly catch up, I would be demoted to the second grade. Momma and Daddy Jay had met at Perry Business School, where they both learned shorthand and accounting, so every night after supper they drilled me on math and reading, but mostly on writing. My new class was already doing what was we called real writing or script writing, but I only knew how to print. I had to learn and perfect the flowing lines, curls and spacing of script writing and my parents were determined that I learn how—and fast.

"I can't do this," I cried when night after night they made me practice. "You can do anything you want to do, Debbie, if you want to do it bad enough," Daddy Jay kept saying. Somehow, I learned and improved and before long I excelled in writing, but good penmanship was not all I had learned. His words of encouragement stuck in my head. I can do anything I want to do if I want to do it bad enough, I often repeated to myself through the years. It motivated me to try harder and it helped me push through and complete more challenges in life.

* * *

Oh boy, collards! Mom's cooking always smelled so good. Best of all was her fried chicken and corn bread and my favorite, collard greens. I could not wait to dig in! Momma called out, "It's ready," and Daddy Jay, my new stepfather, came into the kitchen along with my little brother Mike, and it was time to eat. Someone asked the Lord to bless our food and when the steaming bowl of those beautiful greens came my way, I loaded up my plate, sprinkled them with pepper sauce and dug in. Ugh! "What is that?" I cried as my mouth turned inside out. "Oh, that is disgusting. What is it?" "Spinach," Mom replied. "It's good," Daddy said, "so eat up." "No, I don't like spinach, I thought it was collards. I don't want it!" I retorted in frustration, but in our meager household a plate of spinach was not to be wasted. "You put it on your plate," Daddy Jay said, "now you have to eat it." And he was serious because we sat there for an hour while I gagged and cried and nibbled my way through that plate of spinach. I still do not like it too much, but that day I learned not to put something on my plate if I was not going to eat it.

Life without Daddy Jerry, then with Momma Erline and Daddy Leon and then with Daddy Jay in just three short years was a lot for one so young to experience. On the surface, so many things were happening to me there was little time to acclimate or accept one thing before it was gone, lost, or changed, but the stress was there inside and showed up in my sleep. I talked in my sleep and walked, too, at least until the night I walked off my top bunk, hitting the table and the goldfish bowl on the way to the floor beside Mike's head. Waking up on the floor with a goldfish flapping on your chest was a shock for all of us.

The Jefferson Street house was a small, green, four-room duplex apartment where a living room, two bedrooms, a bathroom, and a kitchen were arranged in a row, front door to back. In the big backyard was a swing set and a chinaberry tree, both of which I liked to climb, until the day I fell out of the tree on my back onto a rock. Oh, how it hurt lying there struggling to breathe, but it could have been worse. Thank you, Lord, for protecting me all the days of my life.

Jefferson Street was in a great neighborhood to grow up in, especially if your name was Deborah or Debbie. I played Barbie dolls with Debra Wilder, my next-door neighbor, and accidentally swiped a melted marshmallow across her arm one night at a bonfire in her back yard. I spent my first night away from home with my friend Debra Lynn Carruth, who lived in the next house down the street. Well, I did not spend the whole night. As we were getting ready for bed, I saw Debra Lynn's daddy watching TV in his undershorts and it scared me so much that I called Momma to come to get me. Thankfully, Debra Lynn and I remained friends and I learned about kilns and ceramics watching her mother in the pottery barn behind their house.

Another friend, Betty Jean Hicks, lived a couple of houses down from Debra Lynn. At her house, we listened to songs like "Teen Angel" and "Crazy" by Patsy Cline, and I learned about hair spray, rollers, crinolines, and dating from Betty Jean's older sisters. Beautiful white-haired Cecilia White lived in the house beside the railroad track bridge and Kay Bartlett lived on the other side. We were all friends and played together at each other's houses and gathered most every night across the street from my house to play Throw the Stick in the Jackson's big back yard and when someone's parent yelled out their front door, "Debra come home," we all went in.

My best friend was Kay Bartlett, and while I spent nights with Kay, I remember her most for inviting me to go with her to Calvary Baptist Church. Sometimes I walked to Kay's house and rode with Kay and her family or walked the mile to and from the church by myself, and occasionally my parents would attend. I attended Sunday School, learned the Bible verses, and got the gold stars beside my name. I heard and received the Gospel and asked Jesus Christ to forgive me, cleanse me, and make my heart His home. I was baptized in a white robe with weights in the hem in a baptismal font in the beautiful sanctuary as my family and friends watched.

I did not recognize it at the time, but life seemed to change after that. I spent more time at church and with the friends I met there. Along with Sunday morning services, I attended Training Union on Sunday night where I was a member of the GA's, or Girls' Auxiliary, and often participated in church functions, like bobbing for apples at the Halloween Festival. I sang in the choir and read my Bible and when I was by myself, I talked with God. I had a powerful sense that I was never alone and that I was protected and safe with God.

In the fall of 1962, Momma had a miscarriage. "Don't worry. Forget about it. You can get pregnant again next month," people said to her and eight months later she gave birth prematurely to a baby boy who weighed only two pounds. My half-brother, Allen Jay Kirby, spent more than a month in the hospital nursery. People said he survived because doting nurses rocked him day and night and that he is brilliant because he got oxygen for weeks after he was born.

One day when Mike and I came in from school and flew by Momma's bedside on our way to the kitchen, she called us back. "Debbie, Mike, y'all come back. You missed something." "What?" we whined as we reluctantly reappeared at her bedroom door. "Look over there," Momma said, motioning toward the baby crib in the corner, and there, wrapped in a blue and white blanket, was the tiniest, long and skinny, red and wrinkly baby I had ever seen. My baby brother Allen was home, and life changed again.

As our family grew, so did our need for space, so again we moved. This time to a house directly across the street from the hospital, which was a huge convenience to Daddy, who still walked to work, but it meant another new school for Mike and me.

Built in 1903, Harwell Avenue Elementary School was the first high school in LaGrange and the decades of polish on the paneled walls, ceilings, and floors gave the entire building a dense woodsy odor. I was walking down one of those long halls that glistened in the afternoon sunlight when I heard the news that President John F. Kennedy had been shot and just three months later the school was struck by lightning and burned to the ground. A new school again, but this time our entire school moved into Hill Street School, and I finished the fifth grade in half-day shifts. Then sixth grade was in yet another school, my third school in one year.

If ever I needed my church and Christian friends it was then, but the church was too far from our new house for me to walk and my parents did not attend regularly. At the new school I had met Debra Mayfield, a red-haired freckled face girl with an infectious laugh who became my best friend, and Molly Milner who lived on the same street. Both helped me through the chaos.

The transition from the friendly Jefferson Street neighborhood to an isolated house on Vernon Street was rough for us all. The house had a short front yard on a busy street and a large back yard that ended at a frequently active railroad track. On one side of the house was a service station and on the other lived an elderly couple, the Satterwhites, who, other than their Masonic and Eastern Star friends, kept to themselves. If Mike and I played outside it was in the backyard and usually with each other, which was boring for both of us. I turned to the library and constantly read books. Mike played with his border collie named Jip and went to stay with Daddy Leon as often as possible. Momma and Daddy had baby Allen to keep them busy.

We went to Panama City for a week's vacation one summer, camping at Treasure Island, but when a crab pinched my foot and I jumped on my float and kicked frantically to get to shore, I kicked a stingray, and its barb went through my foot. I had to stay in bed in a tent for three days while the park rangers checked on me often for signs of systemic poisoning or infection. That decimated our vacation plans, so we just went home.

One night at home I was supposed to watch baby Allen while he was in the bathtub, but I did not watch him too well and he drank shampoo. I cried and confessed to Momma and Daddy when I saw bubbles coming out of his mouth. Fortunately, for both of us, Allen was fine.

That winter I pretended to be sick to skip school. Momma put the thermometer in my mouth and when she left the room,

I held it up to the heater. Daddy knew immediately what I had done because the thermometer read higher than 105 degrees.

One night I sat alone on the sofa in the living room reading, when suddenly, out of the corner of my eye I saw a hand coming towards my side. Shaking and screaming at the top of my lungs, I ran to Momma and Daddy in the den, hysterically saying, "A hand is trying to get me! A hand is trying to get me." Daddy Jay rushed to the living room and began checking every inch. The front door was locked. The window behind the couch was intact. There was no one under or behind the sofa or chairs.

"Now how did this happen," Daddy asked. "Sit here and show us."

"Well, I was sitting right here on the sofa and reading like this," I said and picked up my book with one hand and wrapped the other arm around behind me to demonstrate.

"Is that what you were doing?" Daddy asked.

"Yes, I think so."

"Debbie, look down," Daddy said. "That's your hand. You saw your own hand. You are so gullible you will believe anything," Daddy Jay said. I have revisited that scene so many times in my life. How stupid could I be, even if I was just a kid. Daddy's proclamation, however, stuck in my head. Gullible, what did it mean? It would be more than fifty years before I would understand.

Macel & Debbie 8 yrs.

Macel & Jay Kirby

Maw & Paw Kirby

Macel in bed after Allen born 1963

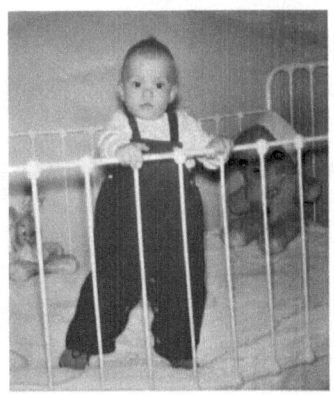

Allen Jay Kirby 1964

Debbie, Jay, Allen, Macel, Mike, 1964

Debbie Huckaby

Debbie, Allen, & Mike

First Kiss, First Love, First Restriction

While the sixth, seventh, and eighth grades of middle school are lamented by most, those were some of my best years. For the first time in my life, I attended only one school, had the same group of friends, and lived in the same house. This gave me the mental and emotional capacity to focus on other things, some good, some bad, but two in particular, boys and money.

In middle school I had friends from different backgrounds, not from different nationalities or races, but with more or less money. Denise Mansour never wore the same outfit twice and her long black hair was always perfectly coiffed with a matching ribbon or bow. Her family owned an upscale department store and friends said she and her older sister took outfits home on trial, removed the labels, and wore them to school before returning them the next day to the store. I had other friends who wore dirty shoes and clothes that were too large or too small. Some friends had new pencils and pens and lots of paper while others needed to borrow everything they used. I was invited to parties at homes that were large and beautiful with swimming pools and smaller homes where once I spent the night with a friend whose bedroom was on a renovated back porch. I attended my first semi-formal dance at the country club wearing a mint green chiffon dress, white gloves, heels, and hose and my first rodeo wearing blue jeans, tennis shoes, and a borrowed cowboy hat.

In many cases, these friends were girls and boys who had known each other since first grade, and I was blessed to be accepted and counted as a friend by all. From these experiences, I learned a lot about people and how to get along with others, regardless of their socio-economic background or interest. I determined that even if I never had a lot of money, I would do my best to be clean and live in a clean home and I learned to share what I had with others because there are always those who have less than what they need.

My two best friends were Debra Mayfield and Mary Francis Neese. I spent many nights at their homes, getting to know their families and their way of life. Deb and I loved to eat French fries late at night, which neither of us needed, but even worse, we ate them with mayonnaise, lots of mayonnaise. I still eat mayonnaise with my French fries and often think of Deb when I do. Mary Francis had several spend-the-night parties where we stayed up late eating, laughing, sharing our make-up techniques, and talking about boys. One night at Mary's we played a new game and I regretted it, almost immediately.

It was a Ouija board and even though we didn't know how to play it, we earnestly tried, and even though it somehow felt wrong to me to be asking things about my future, I played too. Taking turns, with fingers on the edge of a heart-shaped movable plastic see-through indicator, we asked questions about our future and recorded the letters over which the indicator stopped moving. Will I get married? Y E S, the indicator said. What is the name of my husband? First the indicator spelled J O H N, but then it kept moving to G A R. So, we stopped, removed our fingers, and started again. What is the name of my husband? G A R Y. Okay, so it is Gary, not John. Will I have children? Y E S What is the name of my first child? G A R Y. "Oh, this thing is crazy," I said handing the indicator to another, "all it knows to say is Gary."

Years later, I married John Gary Carter and then Gary Huckaby and my first son is named Gary. I didn't know it then, but I now believe that the Ouija board is a form of divination or channeling, which is seeking from occult spirits information that should only come from God. That night, I sensed that playing Ouija was somehow wrong, and I am sure that came from my ever vigilant Lord Jesus nudging my spirit and saying, "No." I wish I had listened and have fervently repented for not doing so.

A few years earlier, I had gotten my first kiss from Steve Martin as we walked home from church, and on Sunday, February 6, 1966, on the steps of the Callaway Education Building, I met my first love. Danny Hollis was a year older than me, with blue eyes and white-blonde hair, which inspired Daddy Jay to call him sheepdog. Danny rode a red Honda motorcycle, which Momma and Daddy forbade me to ride, but in every way, including the Honda, Danny swept me off my feet. He was a freshman at LaGrange High School, and we saw each other every weekend at the Education Building. We often rode his Honda to his house and listened to records in his living room with his parents in the next room. When I was 15 and a freshman at LaGrange High School, we danced every weekend at the Sugar Shack, a teenager hangout with live bands, or double dated to the movies. One night, Danny and I left the dance and parked on a side road. It was the first time we were truly alone in the dark for any length of time. I guess I did not understand, and I did not agree, but the deed was done, and I was changed, forever.

Then, Daddy Jay took a job as the administrator of a small hospital in Franklin, Georgia, in Heard County, 20 miles away. In June of 1967, my family moved. That summer I spent weekends with my grandparents as often as I could and dated Danny while I was there, but that fall, I was a cheerleader at Heard County High School, so our dates dwindled, and our relationship faded. Later I learned that Danny and my very close friend Mary Frances Neese had begun dating.

One day, five decades later, while I was praying about a frequent back ache, this time of my life came into my mind. I understood that Danny and Mary Francis' dates were like a stabbing wound in my back, and this was the pain I still felt. I was led to forgive them both and the pain faded. It has now been many months and that pain has not returned. When I learned through a mutual friend that Mary Francis was in critical condition I prayed earnestly for her recovery and a few months later I was blessed to see her for the first time in 52 years.

When I started at Heard County High School, the news spread like wildfire and the responses were puzzling to say the least. There seemed to be two factions in the school to which the students had already declared their allegiance long before I arrived. I was either warmly welcomed by some, like the basketball team and the cheerleading squad, or roughly rejected by others, with few in between. This became vividly clear to me during change of class one day when a tall, big-boned, and overweight girl body-slammed me across the hall. I hit the wall, dropping my books, and slid to the floor a little dazed, wondering, what happened? Who was that girl and why did she hit me? Later I learned that she was the best friend of the ex-girlfriend of a boy named Randall, who I had recently dated. Others helped me to my feet and retrieved my books and while I had not planned to date Randall again, after that I knew I never would.

My time at HCHS came to an unexpected end in December when Daddy was asked to resign. The hospital board had already hired a permanent administrator who was not able to take the position until January, but they just failed to inform Daddy when they hired him that he was only temporary. When my English teacher learned that I was moving, she asked me to write a short story about the most exciting thing that I had done while attending HCHS. I immediately thought of a Saturday afternoon in late August and wrote the following:

Momma and Daddy had gone to Atlanta to buy furniture and allowed me to stay home with a friend, who had spent the weekend with me. After lunch, we decided to take a ride in Momma's car and drove all the way to Momma Erline and Daddy Leon's house in LaGrange. They were shocked to see me because even though I had just passed a drivers' education course in summer school, I still only had a learner's permit and I had driven 20 miles without supervision. They immediately sent me home. All went well until we were about five miles from home when the muffler fell off the car.

I pulled over and parked and we ran back to grab it, but it was so hot, we could not touch it. Still, I had to get that muffler back to the house. We searched for a stick to roll it to the car, but there was nothing except brittle grass parched in the hot August sun. Finally, we looked in the trunk for a blanket or paper or something to wrap it in but found metal curtain rods instead. Sticking a rod in each end of the muffler, we ran down the road with it between us and threw it in the trunk of the car. That afternoon,

I got under the car and wired the muffler in place with clothes hangers.

When Momma and Daddy came home, my friend left, and Momma drove me to cheerleading practice. On her way back home, the muffler came loose and made a terrible noise, so Daddy took it in to the mechanic on Monday morning and the muffler was repaired. This was the most exciting thing I have done since I started school at HCHS.

I wrote the first draft in pencil and when it was finished, I made a copy in pen. I turned in the paper written in pen and threw the pencil copy in the trashcan in my bedroom. A few days later, when I got home from school, I could tell Momma was upset. She had emptied my trash and read the pencil copy and I was in big trouble. My learner's permit was destroyed, and they said I could not get my driver's license for a whole year, and they kept their word.

Debbie, semi-formal dance

Steve Martin

Debbie Huckaby

Danny Hollis

Debra Mayfield

Mary Francis Neese

Debbie, Deb, Peggy, Mary — Nov. 2019

Joy and Jeopardy in Jesup

We moved to Jesup, Georgia, the last week of December and I started to Wayne County High School after the Christmas break. The school colors were black and gold for their mascot, the Yellow Jackets, which were displayed everywhere. My classes were in the sophomore wing, which was connected to the junior and senior wings by canopy-covered walkways. The warm climate, open hallways, and bright colors were a pleasing change from the stifling and threatening atmosphere at HCHS. The students at WCHS were different also. No divisive factions. Many students were participants on the football, basketball, baseball, and track teams or enthusiastic supporters in the large band, corps of flag twirlers and majorettes, or squad of cheerleaders.

Our house in Jesup was small, but close to the hospital where Daddy Jay worked and close to the high school. My bedroom there was both the best and the worst I have ever had. It was a narrow room with a wall of built-in bookcases, which was great, but the other three walls were painted orange, which I hated. In my orange bedroom, I had a black cat, named Dummy, who quietly sat every night on my bed as I studied, but he also liked to walk on the tops of curtains and jump on people's heads as they walked by. He especially liked to hide and pounce on Daddy Jay, who would swat at him and call him dummy. That's how he got his name.

One night Dummy suddenly let out a screech and began clawing everything in sight. He rolled off the bed and onto the floor and under my bed, still meowing and clawing wildly, and when he backed himself into a corner, I could see froth around his mouth. Daddy and Momma came running when they heard the commotion. "What happened?" they asked.

"I don't know. One minute he was lying there quietly and then he just jumped up hollering and clawing. Why is he foaming at the mouth? Does he have rabies?" I cried. Daddy finally cornered and captured Dummy with his bare hands and found the problem. Dummy had gotten his flea collar stuck in his mouth and was struggling to get free. Daddy laid Dummy on Momma's ironing board and cut the collar, giving Dummy and all of us immediate relief.

Another night, Dummy was my protector. I had gotten into bed and sat propped up studying with Dummy sleeping at my side among the books and papers. Suddenly Dummy's head jerked up, his ears went rigid and straight, and he sat motionless for a long couple of minutes. I did not hear anything or see anything in the window in front of my bed, so I started to study again, but he did that several more times. When Daddy came by to say goodnight, I mentioned Dummy's strange behavior. Daddy didn't say much, except goodnight, but the next day I found out what he did. Daddy knew that the cat could hear and see what I could not, and instead of going to bed, he had gone out the front door and walked quietly around the side of the house in the dark and caught a peeping tom. The 19-year old boy who lived next door was watching me through my bedroom window. How long had he been there? Was this the first time he had done that?

Daddy walked a scared young man home and had a talk with his dad and while it may not have been his first time, it was the last.

I quickly made several friends in Jesup, but tragically lost one. Charlotte Harrell sat beside me in a couple of classes. She was sweet and quiet, and we talked a lot before and after our classes. Daddy knew her father, a radiologist at the hospital. Soon after becoming friends, Charlotte was killed going home from school one day when she pulled in front of a pulpwood truck. She was sixteen and had just gotten her driver's license. She never wanted to drive, but her parents had insisted. Now she was gone, and everyone missed her.

Carolyn was a blue-eyed blonde Christian friend who drove a white Karmann Ghia and introduced me to her friends and showed me around town. Elaine was a local beauty queen and a majorette. Her daddy, Doc Nichols, a locally known pharmacist, allowed Elaine to drive his Model A, even to Jekyll Island, where we often went for the day or the weekend. Once Elaine's mother rented a house on the beach and chaperoned for Elaine and her friends for the weekend. We spent most of the time drinking Hunch Punch, a mixture of sliced fruit, Hawaiian punch and rum on Jekyll's north beach and riding in that old car. Elaine convinced me to enter my first and only beauty pageant. Her dad paid the fee for me, and I wore one of Elaine's dresses. It was embarrassing for me, but Elaine just beamed in the lights of the runway. To commemorate her sixteenth birthday, Elaine's mother commissioned a portrait, but Elaine wanted me to have one too. So, again, Elaine picked out one of her dresses (yellow, which is definitely NOT my color) and her parents paid for both our portraits.

I finally got my driver's license when I turned seventeen, but my privileges were limited. I was only allowed to drive a set number of miles and Daddy checked the car before and after my outings. One Sunday afternoon I had gone swimming with friends in a pool, but we decided to go to the lake instead. That was several miles over my limit, but I went anyway. When it came time to go home, I decided to back the miles off the odometer. I began backing down a dirt road and managed to get some of the miles off the car, but I hit a tree. Fortunately, there was no dent in the bumper, and I made some plausible excuse for the few additional miles. I did not get into too much trouble, until daddy went to check the oil and found the battery sitting on top of the radiator and pine straw in the bumper. Then, he knew what I had done, and grounded me again.

A couple of months after arriving in Jesup, I tried out for cheerleading and made the squad. My junior year was one of the best in my life. I cheered football and basketball and made many friends among the players, band, and auxiliary corps. My dates were usually football or basketball players, as were Elaine's, and we often double dated. I soon started going steady with a senior football player named John Gary Carter. John was short, stocky, and strong with a witty sense of humor. His nickname was Wizard. Why, I'm not sure, but I think it had to do with his ability to do back flips, which his football colleagues frequently urged him to do. We met each other's families and dated every Friday and Saturday. John was a perfect gentleman and always respected and protected me from harm, at least that is what I thought.

The Junior Senior prom of 1969 was held at the County Club. John and I double dated with Elaine and her boyfriend. After dancing a while, many of the couples went out to a place called The Hill to party and drink, and we went, too. On the way to The Hill, we stopped at the Dairy Queen and John got me an extra-large 85-cent cherry coke, poured out about half of it and filled the cup with rum. He put the top on the cup, stuck a straw in it and gave it to me. Now, I had no experience drinking, but it tasted good, and I was thirsty, so I drank fast and through the straw. By the time we made it to The Hill, I had drunk most of my drink and that is about all I remember. I passed out, cold and limp and they could not wake me. It scared them all, so John drove to my house and Elaine and her date helped me to the front door, where I collapsed into my mother's arms. She helped me to bed and later sat with me on the back-porch steps while I threw up. Five years later John, my husband at the time, told me unapologetically that he had intentionally tried to get me drunk that night to take advantage of me. Thank God, he failed.

In the last few weeks of my junior year, the cheerleading squad elected me to be the captain during my upcoming senior year. It was more than I could believe. My little bedroom was filled with 12 sets of pompoms, 12 megaphones, uniforms, sweaters, and letters. I was so happy and so excited I practiced every day and made copious notes of cheers and routines for our cheerleading clinic in August.

Then it happened, the worst I could have ever imagined. Daddy took another job, and we were moving again. "No," I cried, "Not my senior year!" Elaine's parents offered for me to live with them my senior year, but my parents said no, and I cried. John gave me a pre-engagement ring and promised to love me no matter what, and I cried. I turned over all the cheerleading equipment, notes, and uniforms to Kathy Barlow, who became the captain, and cried all the way home. Then we packed and the movers came, and I cried all the way to Douglas, Georgia.

Debbie Huckaby

Carolyn Griffin

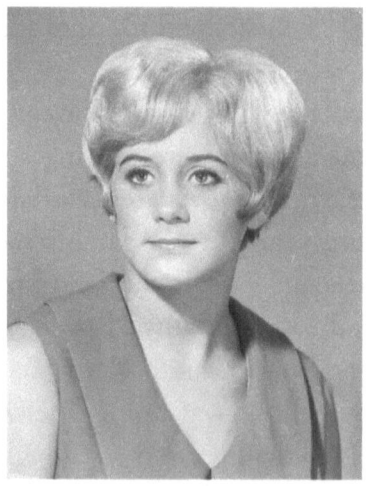

Elaine Nichols

Wayne County High School, Captain of Cheerleading Squad

Debbie Huckaby

Elaine Nichols & Mike Purvis, Jr. Sr. Prom 1969

Senior Year Love and Politics

The movers left our new house in Douglas, but I was so focused on the contents of the box in front of me, I scarcely noticed. All day long, Momma and I had unpacked box after box after box and we were hot because the air conditioner in our new house was not working or not working fast enough to keep up with the August heat and humidity in South Georgia. I sighed, but I didn't complain. The work helped me keep my mind off the fact that I had just moved again. This time away from my home in Jesup, away from my boyfriend, John, and from my best friend, Elaine, and away from the school where I would have been captain of the cheerleading squad my senior year. Tears mingled with the beads of sweat that trickled down my face.

Now only a couple of hours left before dinner and all five of us still had to take baths and put on clean clothes, if we could find them. I showered and slipped on my favorite shirt, a sleeveless red cotton button-up with tiny white polka dots, white shorts, and white tennis shoes. "Good," I proclaimed to no one but myself as I inspected the effect in the floor-length mirror on the back of the bathroom door. The white shorts emphasized the summer tan I had so meticulously created to go with my gold and white cheerleading outfit. "Oh, well," I sighed, throwing up my hands. But my hair was definitely not good! I needed all the time I could get to revive my short, thick, chocolate-brown hair, limp and contorted in the steamy heat.

Dinner would be a cookout at Mr. Allen's house. Jim Allen, the administrator of Coffee Regional Hospital and Daddy's new boss, had invited our family to dinner, which Mom said was a very thoughtful thing to do considering this was our first day in town and after moving all day, she was too tired to cook.

By 6:00 pm, we were all tired, hungry, and even a little nervous when Daddy turned our brown Chevy station wagon into the narrow driveway of the Allen's home. It was a stately one-story brick house that stretched the width of their large lot located on one of the oldest and most distinguished streets in Douglas. The car rolled to a stop as the side door of the house was opened by a man I presumed to be Mr. Allen. His cotton-white hair topped an olive complexioned face punctuated by gray-green eyes that glistened in the late afternoon light.

"Come in, come on in," Mr. Allen called out, welcoming us to his home and waving us inside. First, we met William, Lois, and Carol, who were stretched out on the various sofas and recliners watching TV in the family room, and then followed Mr. Allen down a long hall to the kitchen where we met Mrs. Allen, a tall, slender, blond-haired woman with a warm smile and a throaty, "So glad to meet you," who was tossing a salad at the counter. My younger brothers, Mike and Allen soon found their way back to the family room and TV with the others while I stayed in the kitchen with Momma and Mrs. Allen. Daddy and Mr. Allen grabbed a beer from the fridge and headed outside to manage the grill.

At seventeen, I was not interested in watching TV with the kids, but I could stand only so much of Momma and Mrs. Allen's talk of kids, cooking, and such. "I think I'll go outside for a while," I said after a few minutes of listening, smiling, and nodding to their chatty talk and headed towards the barn-red back door. "Just pull the latch up and push and the whole door will open," Mrs. Allen said.

The Dutch door was new to me, so I followed her instructions, pulling up on the latch, but suddenly the door opened wide with a jerk. Startled, I found myself inches away from full body contact with a person coming in from outside and, looking up, I peered into the most beautiful green eyes I had ever seen in my life. He was a foot taller than me with a lifeguard's tan, wide shoulders, and sandy blonde hair. His navy tee shirt and jeans outlined a lean, muscular body that carried the faint scent of peppermint. Still holding the door with one arm, and looking down at me with a grin, he said, "Well, hi there."

"Um, hi," I replied with what little breath I could muster.

Time seemed to stand still and for a moment, an hour, an eternity, the world around us disappeared as we entered each other's past, present, and future at a depth neither of us then understood. Our moment in time was interrupted with Mrs. Allen's introduction, but our eyes never wavered, nor did our bodies move. "Eddie, this is Debbie. Debbie this is our son, Eddie," she said. "Hi again," he said, raising his eyebrows and widening his grin, revealing a glint of mischief in his laughing green eyes. I took a deep breath and smiled at the face that had just burned itself into my heart.

Is there such a thing as love at first sight? Are teenagers too young to know what love is about? Mom said we were just infatuated with each other, and we were, passionately, but what began that day was love, even though it was not understood or accepted until decades later. I recently discovered a song by Ronnie Millsap that best puts it into words for me.

Our paths may never cross again
Maybe my heart will never mend
But I'm glad for all the good times
Cause you've brought me so much sunshine
And love was the best it's ever been

I wouldn't have missed it for the world
Wouldn't have missed loving you girl
You've made my whole life worthwhile, with your smile
I would not trade one memory
Cause you mean too much to me
Even though I lost you girl
I would not have missed it for the world

They say that all good things must end
Loves comes and goes just like the wind
You've got your dreams to follow
But if I had the chance tomorrow
You know I'd do it all again

Coffee High School was my fourth high school and naturally I made comparisons. CHS had open-air hallways like WCHS, with a garden, called the senior garden, located centrally between three hallways, but that is where all similarities with my other high schools ended. I was too late to try out for the cheerleading squad, but the coach made me a cheerleader alternate, which meant I could join the squad if someone dropped out. I did not cheer for football, but they allowed me to fully join the squad for basketball.

The baby blue and white colors of their docile team mascot, the Comets, echoed the fact that CHS had not won a game in more than ten years, so team spirit was dismal. Many students attended the football games because it was a place to go, to see and be seen, but they never expected the team to actually win. Then, in 1969-70, my only year at CHS, this ho-hum complacency suddenly changed. That was the year of desegregation.

Not long after I became a senior at CHS, desegregation, which had been spreading across the nation for years, prompted racial protest marches in our small town and the Board of Education closed the school from fear someone would get hurt. Many people in the community, including students, took sides and stubbornly refused to budge. The days we were absent from school turned into weeks and when our graduation date was in jeopardy, some students started the plea. I was one of them.

My best friend, Patty Hand, and I became so vocal about the need to return to class that the local radio station WOKA invited us to record a public service announcement. We accepted and wrote and recorded a plea for the local school board, the community, and students, black and white, to return to school peacefully and work together to make Coffee High School better than before. That seemed to help because school reconvened in a matter of days. Then the real work began, bringing together two high schools: students, teams, mascots, and traditions.

The Student Council was charged with executing the change and I was the Girl's Vice President. We surveyed the student body for their preferences. Trojans became the new name for our team mascot and maroon was the new color. In a dramatic presentation before the whole school, the old mascots and colors were put to death in a coffin and the new were raised. Incidentally, I declined the opportunity to be the one in the coffin, but the drama was effectual, and the Coffee High School Trojans class of 1970 was the first biracial graduating class in the history of that town.

A year is a brief time to make friends with a lot of people, but long enough to get to know and love a few, who I believe will be with me through all eternity. Patty Hand and I were cheerleaders and loved to create routines. I enjoyed her large Catholic family and especially dinner around their table with a lazy Susan in the middle. Debbie Minchew was Episcopalian and invited me to go to church with her. I loved the liturgical services so much that I took confirmation classes. Another cheerleading friend was Debra Roberts, whose family were Mormons, and I rode to school with Becky Veal, who lived across the street and whose father was a Methodist preacher. Eddie and his family were United Methodist. Our first date was to a Sunday night church service.

I always connected with Christian friends and was blessed by their friendship, especially one day that spring. Mike, my brother, and I rode home from school each day with Becky Veal and Michelle Mayo. We always took Michelle home first and that day we were a block away from her house when a baby blue Cadillac t-boned Becky's red Mustang on my door. It happened so fast that none of us saw it coming and Dr. Wilson, an elderly retired physician driving the Cadillac, did not see us. Somehow, before we even realized that we had been hit, I was standing outside of the car on Becky's side with her door open. I had climbed over Mike and Michelle, who were in the back seat, opened Becky's door and got out. How, I don't know! We were all amazed, and thankful because no one was hurt and even though my door was dented in significantly with the front fender of a Cadillac still sitting in it, I did not even have a bruise.

My senior year was full and went by fast. It was not long before my parents realized the gray house on Grady Street was just too small and, right before Christmas, we moved to a larger house on the Ocilla Highway. This time moving my residence did not disrupt the rest of my life. Every weekend that year Eddie and I were together. We danced to the Bushmen, the Tams, and other bands at the Rec Center or watched a movie at the theater downtown or at the drive in. He picked me up after basketball games and we spent our evenings riding around talking and listening to music. Nights when we weren't together, we'd talk on the phone for hours. We loved passionately and argued with the same hot fire. Once I slapped him and immediately regretted it. I can't even remember now what he said that made me so angry. We never drank or smoked, but practical jokes were not unusual.

Occasionally we dated in the hospital's station wagon, and one night when it was full of friends, Eddie decided to create a fireworks display. He planned to ignite a bundle of fireworks, jump on the open tailgate, and when he said, "Go," I was to drive away, but I floored the accelerator and the car stalled. Firecrackers went everywhere, blazing and cracking, in and around the car, which rocked with people screaming, jumping, and laughing. Eddie just shook his head and we all laughed until we hurt.

That summer after graduation, our families vacationed together at Fernandina, and I frequented the pool where he was a lifeguard. I was preparing to go to West Georgia College in Carrollton and major in psychology. Eddie was pre-med and planned to attend South Georgia Junior College. Would our relationship survive? It was a chance we had to take.

That fall my parents moved me and a lot of my clothes into the West Georgia College dorm room I was to share with Debra Mayfield, my best friend since sixth grade. One week later I was so homesick that when I heard my mother's voice on the phone I burst out crying, and I missed Eddie terribly too. Calls were long distance and there was a charge per minute, so we could not talk as often or as long as we had before, and the four-hour trip between Carrolton and Douglas meant seeing each other was rare. I convinced him to come to campus one weekend, and I rode a bus home once to see him, but mostly we were apart. After Christmas break, we began to date other people and our relationship suffered. I studied enough to get by, but I partied to forget the longing and despair. By March, I had had enough. I stopped partying and started praying more earnestly than I had in years. I decided to go home and enroll at South Georgia College to become a nurse.

Senior Garden 1969-70

Coffee High School 1969-1970

CHS Homecoming Parade

Debbie Huckaby

Graduation 1970

Dorm room at West Ga. College

Bittersweet Blessings

With college roommate–Debra Mayfield

A Nurse, Wife and Mother

I moved back home and that fall started to work on the 3-11 shift as a nurses' aid at the hospital where Daddy Jay was the Assistant Administrator and Comptroller. I also started nursing school, which I loved and continued to work full time to pay my tuition. The first quarter (yes, colleges were still on the quarter system then), I learned the basics of nursing care: how to make a proper bed, aseptic and sterile technique, how to give injections — intermuscular and intravenous — how to chart or document what is done and, most importantly, I learned to respect my patient. I can still remember my favorite instructor, from Charity Nursing School in New Orleans, Louisiana, saying, "See one, do one, and teach one, that is the nursing way," and that is literally how it has always been for me.

During the day, I went to class, learned new techniques and principles, and then went to work and applied them. There was only one Registered Nurse in the whole hospital during my shift and she was the shift supervisor, so I was allowed to use all my skills and knowledge and work under her authority and license. I was assigned to a 45-bed medical, labor and delivery, postpartum and nursery floor. The shift supervisor assigned patients to teams of licensed practical nurses and nurses' aides and made me the charge nurse over the entire floor. This allowed me to visit each patient and take part in every patient's care as their condition called for and to communicate with the RN shift supervisor at any time. I remember a quadriplegic female patient on a circa-electric bed who got married in her room and the woman who was almost blinded from shingles in her eyes, and I remember assisting at deliveries and checking for bleeding for hours afterwards.

One cold winter afternoon the shift supervisor alerted me to the imminent admission of four burn patients and gave me detailed instructions for creating an emergency burn unit. A family had returned home, flipped a light switch, and their house had exploded because of a leaky gas heater. Two men, a woman and a child were being admitted to our improvised burn unit to be stabilized and then air-lifted by helicopter to a hospital in Albany, Georgia.

The four-bed ward had two patients who were quickly moved to other rooms. Then it was stripped of furniture except for four beds, overbed tables and bedside stands, and everything was quickly cleaned. The windows were closed and sealed with clean sheets and tape. Extra IV poles, IV trays, and bags of fluid were brought to each bedside. Pharmacy brought a code cart with an extra supply of emergency drugs.

Then they came, four bodies wrapped from head to toe in bandages, moaning in pain, yet still, very, very still, each one burned to the second and third degree over their entire body. The minutes seemed like hours as every available nurse, doctor, and EMT worked feverishly to restore essential body fluids, ease excruciating pain, and treat the charred, torn, and blistered wounds. I could see and smell the burned flesh. Finally, exhausted, and helpless to do more, we watched as the life flight team loaded each one into a waiting helicopter and ascended into the night. Did they live or die? I guess I'll never know this side of heaven.

Working 3-11 full time and going to nursing school 6-2 each weekday left me little time for anything else, and even though Eddie and I were in the same town, on the same campus, and occasionally working in the same hospital, we rarely saw each other. I moved out of my parents' home and shared a mobile home with Charlotte Roland, a fellow nursing student during my second year of nursing school, and Eddie went to Berry College in Rome, Georgia.

That year Momma had a total hysterectomy and was a patient on the third-floor surgical unit where I was working. I put a NO VISITING sign on her door to give her the peace and quiet that I thought she needed, but I forgot to mention it to her. She was progressing well but seemed depressed even though her room was full of flowers and cards. She finally said how sad she was that no one had been to see her. I had to confess. I was the reason why. For years, she laughingly told others how well I took care of her in isolation. Maybe it was the current thinking in medical practice at the time, but the removal of her ovaries withdrew her body's needed estrogen, and no hormone replacement medications was prescribed post op. As a result, Momma developed excruciating migraines and deep depression and turned to alcohol to ease the pain of it all. I look back on those years with great regret that I did not recognize her physical need for hormones and that such a kind and gentle woman suffered such pain and helplessness alone. Five years later, she got hormone replacement therapy and let the alcohol go.

Sometime late fall, I got a letter from John, my high school boyfriend from Jesup. He had joined the Army when I moved to Douglas and broke up with him, and now he was serving in

Vietnam. I wrote him back and our correspondence led to the rekindling of our relationship. His tour of duty in Vietnam ended in March and he asked me to visit him in Colorado Springs, Colorado. I had never driven very far by myself, and it had been almost ten years since I had been to Atlanta, and I had never even been inside an airport or flown in an airplane, but I agreed to go.

That weekend in March, I drove my baby blue VW beetle bug to Atlanta following a paper map, found the airport and the concourse. By the time I boarded the plane, a thunder and lightning storm had moved into the area, but we took off anyway. Fortunately, I was seated beside a nun wearing a white habit who noticed my anxiety as the lightning flashed and the plane rocked in the turbulence. She asked if this was my first flight and when I explained, she offered to pray for me, which she did, holding my hand and praying quietly all the way to Memphis where we landed for our first stop. I then flew from Memphis to Denver and landed in a snowstorm so thick that I could barely see, which only added to my fear for the pilot's ability to land the plane. In Denver I changed planes and flew the last leg of my journey to Colorado Springs. John met me at the airport.

The snow of Pikes Peak glowing in the morning sunshine greeted me as I gazed out the window of my room the next morning. Snow piled head high concealed the shrubs and even the trees except for a few barren branches glistening in the morning light. Everything looked fresh and new, clean and white to me, and with a deep breath of crisp mountain air, I promised myself that this day was the first day of the rest of my life, a life of love and happiness and contentment that I had longed for. Before the day was done, I had agreed to spend the rest of my life as John's wife.

Our weekend was short, but the plans we made were long

term. I returned home to Douglas and graduated from nursing school in June. John finished his military obligation and came home in May. I took the state board exam in early July while preparing for our wedding, and on July 14, 1973, I married John Gary Carter at St. Andrew's Episcopal Church in Douglas. My mother was my matron of honor, and our dresses were homemade. Our ceremony was small, but beautiful, and the reception, which Momma and her friends hosted, was simple and tasty. John and I left the church in a shower of rice thrown by family and friends, and after spending the weekend in Daytona Beach, Florida, we returned to our apartment in Jesup.

My first home as a married woman was a small apartment with a tiny kitchen, a living room, bedroom, and bath. I remember piercing the refrigerator freezer with a knife when I was defrosting it, and I remember making a watermelon fruit basket in the summer and a Yule log at Christmas. I also remember the struggles John and I had there.

One month after our wedding John accepted an invitation for us to have dinner with another high school friend and fellow football player, Butch Courson, and his wife, Kay, from California. After supper, sitting at the table having coffee and dessert, John, Butch, and Kay surprised me with an invitation. They had been talking and had something to ask me, but they wanted me to think about it a few minutes before I answered because they had discussed it and all of them wanted me to say yes, but again they said, the decision was up to me. Butch explained. They wanted to have a swap: Butch with me, John with Kay. Would I agree? Well, it did not take me a few minutes to decide. "No," I answered, "absolutely not," but the shock of the proposition did not hit me until the drive home.

Not long thereafter in the middle of the night I woke to the sound of voices and discovered John talking to someone through an opened jalousie window in our bedroom. What was he doing and why did he need to talk to someone through a window in the middle of the night? I had some suspicions and confronted him with them. We argued and he backhanded me across the bed. Fortunately, my face was not injured and, of course, he apologized.

After only a few months in the apartment, John and I moved to a house on Pinebloom Circle, which had two bedrooms, one bath, a living room, kitchen, and dining room. I bought two chocolate-brown AKC registered poodles and named the male Topo Pierre Cartier and the female Mademoiselle Taffeta Cartier, and we installed a fence for them to play in the backyard. I picked vegetables with my mother-in-law, Eloise Carter, and learned to can, freeze, and preserve much of our food, and I dug a flower bed and planted marigolds. John joined the Jaycees, and I joined the Jaycettes, and we attended a convention on Jekyll Island, where I delivered my first speech in the Jaycettes' Speak Up competition.

John worked various jobs with no clear career direction as he struggled to shake the trauma of Vietnam and acclimate to day-to-day life in the U.S. I remember how he warned me not to approach him from behind or near his head or shoulders when he was asleep. To wake him, he said, I should just shake his toe. Well, one morning in my rush to get to work, I forgot. He had just dozed off after working a night shift and I bent over to kiss him goodbye when he reared up with such force that his head cracked my nose. OW! I cried out, but John was already asleep again and I went off to work with a bloody, throbbing nose.

My first nursing assignment at Wayne Memorial Hospital was on the Labor and Delivery, Post-Partum and Nursery floor.

When I reported for my first shift, I learned that the head nurse, who I had met during my pre-employment interview, had had a heart attack while on vacation in Canada and was not allowed to travel, so I had been appointed the head nurse for the three units. I was also informed that the L&D staff had recently experienced a heartbreaking outcome of a breech delivery and were still suffering from that traumatic experience.

My heart went out to the staff who had experienced so much—the loss of their beloved leader, followed by that traumatic delivery, and now me, a new head nurse, all within two months. I set about caring for them by meeting with each one and listening while they introduced themselves and told their story. I wanted to help them care for the patients with the best possible care, but first they needed to know I cared. Then a few months later, perhaps because I was willing to accept a challenge or because there was an RN shortage or both, I was scheduled on several different units and different shifts. In the next eighteen months, I worked medical and surgical and emergency, until one day Dr. Robert E. Miller asked if I would consider working in his office.

Dr. Robert Miller had a very busy family medicine practice which was managed by his wife, Patsy, also a registered nurse. Patsy interviewed me and gave me the position of office nurse. It was my responsibility to greet scheduled patients, escort them to their exam room, take vital signs, document complaints, prepare the needed supplies for Dr. Miller and assist him with their examination. I gave all injections, sometimes on Saturday mornings, if needed, and processed all patient samples through the onsite lab. When the last patient was seen, I cleaned instruments, wrapped trays, and loaded the sterilizer. Every hour was filled with four to six patient visits and some days did not end until 7

P.M., but I respected the doctor and enjoyed working with Patsy, from whom I learned so much.

Such was life until we lost a baby, which I did not even know I was carrying, and the post-partum hormones and overwhelming grief plunged me into a bewildering depression. Who am I? How did I get here? Where is my baby—that I had given to the Emergency Room nurse in a jar after driving myself there because of the hemorrhaging? Was it a boy or a girl? I called John and Momma from the hospital and had the required D&C surgery and I healed physically, but not emotionally.

What did I do to hurt the baby? I am a nurse, why did I not know I was pregnant? I struggled to make sense of my life. You can get pregnant again soon the doctor said, but I did not want to get pregnant. I did not want my life. I did not want John and I did not want to be married. I tried to explain, while making plans to leave. I called Eddie and told him that I needed to talk and that I would be coming to see him. I arranged for someone to take Topo and Taffy, packed my clothes and a few personal things from the house in my car and left.

Momma and Daddy were glad to see me but were very surprised to learn that I was leaving John. I stayed with them for a few weeks while I cried night and day and talked about the baby and the mess I had made of my life. I remember sitting with Daddy on the top step of their front porch one afternoon crying hysterically. "How could I have made such a mistake?" I asked. "I will never be able to trust myself again."

I remember Daddy putting his arm around me and lifting my chin, saying, "Yes you will, child. You will heal and you will be strong again. Yes, you will."

Pinning Ceremony May 1973

Debbie Huckaby

A Warning of Things to Come

I got a job, found a place to live, and contacted an attorney. Then I went to Augusta and spent the weekend with Eddie, a sophomore medical student at the Medical College of Georgia. I sat by his window in the sunshine and pondered my life while he studied. He did not offer advice and I did not ask for any. I needed a safe place to rest, and Eddie gave me that space.

My job was back at Coffee General Hospital where Daddy and Sue Spivey, the Director of Nursing, had decided that the best place for me to work while healing from a miscarriage was in the Neonatal Intensive Care Unit and that is where they assigned me. I worked 12 hour shifts, sometimes days, sometimes nights. I ate and slept, and the monotony gave me the mental and emotional healing that I desperately needed. Caring for those tiny babies was excruciatingly painful, but honestly, I was still too numb to realize it.

Not long after I started working there, a pregnant mother traveling home to Florida went into premature labor and delivered a two-pound baby boy. The mother stayed a couple of days after the birth, but the baby stayed 28 more. Maybe because I needed a baby or because that little baby boy needed a mother, we bonded. That meant I took care of him all day, every day, feeding him, changing his diapers, giving him his meds, holding his tiny hands, looking into his trusting eyes, and praying for his survival. Unfortunately, that also meant when I was away, he cried, which was disastrous for one so frail, so I worked without a day off and spent most of my waking hours with him. Then, when he weighed four pounds, his parents came to take him home and, again, for the second time in just a few short months, I lost a baby.

John convinced me to come to Jesup and spend the weekend with him just to talk and be sure that I wanted the divorce. It was strange, staying with him in his parents' home, married, but no longer a couple, and when I left them on Sunday, I knew I would never go back. The divorce was final in November 1976.

I talked with Eddie a few times on the phone and looked forward to seeing him when he was home. I took an Emergency Medical Technician course and ran a few calls with the on-duty staff, and I transferred to the Adult Intensive Care Unit. I began dating friends I met at the hospital just to have something to do and someone to go out with. One date was with the head of the EMS department, David Fleishman, and another paramedic, Gary Huckaby, took me to their EMS Christmas Party.

Then one night in January 1977, the ICU staff gathered for dinner together at the Pizza Hut where several of the EMTs were hanging out. From there we went to a dance and afterwards four of us went to Augusta, Georgia, for the weekend. We all stayed at Gary's mobile home near Walton Way, and sometime that weekend Gary told me he loved me, and I told him I thought I could love him too. After that weekend we were together constantly. We introduced each other to our families and spent every day off together. We both had four-day weekends every two weeks and used them as mini vacations to go to the Daytona and Panama City beaches.

I was still working in ICU and Gary was working EMS, but he had been accepted to the pharmacy school at the University of Georgia, so that August we moved to Athens. While I was packing the contents of my closet, I discovered that all my pictures and mementos of John and Eddie and Danny were gone. I confronted Gary about it, but he brushed it off. "You don't need them," he said. "You had no right to destroy my things," I retorted, but he refused to discuss it. For him, the matter was closed. Later, I also found out that Gary had called Eddie while we were in Augusta and told him I was now his and not to call me again. Why did I not recognize this as a warning of things to come?

Athens, Go Dawgs

Athens, the sixth largest city in Georgia, is about four hours north of Douglas and the home of the University of Georgia Bulldogs. I had been there once before, a weekend in 1972, when I went for a football game and a date with UGA football player Jim McPipkin, a friend from Jesup. I remembered the city as one of the most exciting places I had ever been, and it still is because Athens on a football Saturday is like none other. Ironically, today as I write, is one of those days.

In Athens on a football Saturday the excitement and energy rise with the sun. That is when a city-county area of 100,000 residents that had expanded in late summer by the influx of 40,000 students, explodes with an additional 90,000 fans streaming into Sanford Stadium for a game between the hedges.

In Athens on a football Saturday the streets are lined bumper to bumper with cars decorated with black and red magnetic bulldog stickers and window banner flags, each jostling for a prime parking spot. The most sought after spots are within walking or shuttle distance of the stadium, but, more importantly, the best spaces accommodate tailgating.

A football Saturday in Athens includes tailgating, which begins early, sometimes as early as breakfast or even the night before. Friends gather together and set up chairs around a table or a grill and talk and eat and throw a frisbee or football for hours. It's all part of the university's century-old pre-and post-game traditions. Drinking, of course, has had a prominent role there as well.

Music is also present, but then music is at the very heart of Athens. Like most college towns, Athens has always reverberated with the sounds of bands and dances, but since the 1970's Athens has been a catalyst for musicians. Kenny Rogers lived nearby and REM lived near downtown. The B52s, Pylon, Widespread Panic, and many more identify with Athens. We once danced to the latest hits in the B&L Warehouse and O'Malley's, played by bands such as The Tams, The Drifters, the Bushmen, and more. Now it is the 40 Watt Club and the Morton Theatre. But every football Saturday for all these years, it is the music of tailgaters that has consistently filled the air above Athens.

Gary's father, Poppa Huck, moved Gary's mobile home from Augusta to Athens and into a mobile home park called Hallmark Estates. It was populated with UGA students, many from our hometown. Gary and Julianne Williams lived there, along with Gary Egan, Ronald and Cindy Johnson and Dale Lott. Gary soon started to school, and I went to work.

I worked at St. Mary's Hospital from 11pm-7am as the charge nurse of a 9-bed intensive care unit. I typically had an LPN and a nurse's aide. Sister Antionette was the director of nursing and Sister Irmgard worked nights and roamed the halls praying for patients, who often reported being startled upon awakening to find a nun in a white habit praying over them.

The work was good, and I learned so much. I remember caring for a man for over a month who had been beaten almost to death with a metal baseball bat. He was broken and bruised from his head to his toes and his plan of care was one of the most challenging of my entire career. I remember one night during a Code 99 (cardiac arrest) how a man came flying into the room wearing a long lab coat that fanned out behind him as he rushed into the room. I assumed he was a lab technician and asked him to leave only to find out that he was a new MD in town. I apologized and introduced myself and asked him to please stay. Thankfully, he did, and we were friends for the next 30 years.

One night we had a middle-aged woman who had just suffered an extensive myocardial infarction (heart attack). Her vital signs were stable. Her heart rhythm was normal, and she was sleeping, but her doctor was worried and came by to see her one more time before going home around midnight. "Call if you need me," he said. I promised I would. I checked her often and she continued to sleep with normal blood pressure, pulse, and heart rhythm, yet I had a growing sense of uneasiness. I checked and rechecked and while everything was still perfectly normal, I was getting more and more anxious, so I called her doctor. "She is stable," I said, "but I don't feel right. Everything is normal, but I just feel like something is wrong."

"I'll be right there," he said. I stood at the foot of her bed and prayed and watched. In just a few minutes, as her doctor stepped through the main door to the unit, she flipped into ventricular fibrillation and with two or three steps of his long legs he stood at her side and gave her one of the hardest and most perfectly placed pre-cordial thumps I had ever seen. Immediately she converted and breathed on her own and opened her eyes. WOW! What a recovery! Thank You, Lord Jesus and thank you, doctor.

One snowy night in February 1978, the unit was full and several patients with pain, peritoneal dialysis, lidocaine drips, and abnormal heart rhythms were requiring constant attention. Mr. Gunter, a jovial older gentleman in room 9, however, was quiet and resting peacefully when suddenly his heart rhythm became erratic and he arrested. I rushed into the room, hit the code button, and started mouth-to-mouth resuscitation while code team arrived. Everyone knew their place and their task. CPR, backboard, medications, oxygen, and intubation were routine and after a very few minutes, Mr. Gunter converted back to normal sinus rhythm and opened his eyes. The code ended and the emergency response team left when Mr. Gunter's vital signs and heart rhythm stabilized. I stood beside his bed charting. Occasionally he would open his eyes and I would reassure him that he was doing better. Then he spoke. "I saw you," Mr. Gunter said. "I was watching you and I saw you kiss me and I'm gonna tell my wife."

I was amazed at the clarity with which he spoke and the confidence he had in his statement. Mr. Gunter was critically ill and arrested several more times that night, but he survived and somehow he remembered his out of body experience and even told his wife. Mr. Gunter recovered completely and was discharged. Then every February for the next seven years Mr. and Mrs. Gunter came to see me again and thank me for helping him live.

Although work was good and I was growing in my leadership abilities and learning something new every day about the practice of nursing, home life was not so great. That first fall together in Athens, Gary and I attended all the home games and hosted family and friends for the game weekends. Drinks and food were always abundant in our tailgate gatherings, but Gary tended to drink rather than eat. Instead, he spent time trying to figure out ways to sneak liquor into the stadium and drink it without being seen. Sitting in the hot sun for several hours and drinking continuously often led to him being inebriated and the outcome of the game determined his mood and behavior afterwards.

One weekend when UGA lost in the final minute of the

game, Gary went ballistic. He jumped up, angrily pushing past people, and rushed out of the stadium. His father and I trailed behind in the dense crowd, but when I finally made it to the parking lot where we had parked, Gary and Poppa Huck were nowhere in sight. He had left me in a UGA parking lot all alone and without a phone. I stood there mad, hurt, and confused. What to do? We had only lived in Athens a few weeks and I was not even sure of our address or how to get there if I had to walk. I waited and paced and when almost all the cars were gone, Poppa Huck drove up. He had gotten to our house and found out what had happened and came back to get me. The climate in our home was cold for days and I told Gary how I felt about him leaving me, but he never acknowledged his behavior or offered an apology.

A few months later, on a Friday night, Gary did not come home. He was working an internship with Ed Kilgore at Rhodes and Kilgore Pharmacy in Union Point and should have gotten off around 5 or 6 P.M. at the latest. I watched the clock and consoled myself with excuses and paced. Hour after hour there was no sign of Gary and no call. Where could he be? Why had he not let me know something? Was he dead on the side of one of those back roads? I called the police and asked if they knew of any wrecks. "No, none that we knew of," they said. I went to bed but did not sleep. I tossed, turned, cried, and fumed. Finally, about 5 A.M. Gary came in and got in bed. "Where have you been?" I demanded. "Are you alright? Why didn't you call?" Questions poured out of me, but he offered nothing in return. He simply went to sleep.

The next day he said that he and Ed had gone to the Chelsea's strip club in Atlanta. So, while I was at home, alone, and worried sick about his safety, he was drinking and looking at naked women in a club in Atlanta. How and why I dealt with that, I do not know. I did not leave, and he did not apologize. To make matters worse, I was preparing for our wedding, which was less than six months away.

Gary and Julie Ann Williams, who lived near us in Hallmark Estates, became our closest friends. Gary Williams was also a pharmacy student and he and Julianne had two little girls, Cody and Rebecca. Julianne was a seamstress and made my wedding gown, her matron of honor gown, and all the bridesmaids' gowns. Our wedding was on September 2, 1978, Labor Day weekend, in the chapel at the United Methodist Church in Douglas. It was a typical wedding on a small budget, but our honeymoon was like none I have ever heard of before.

Our honeymoon was a double date. Gary's idea, of course, and although it was somewhat disappointing that my new husband would not want to be alone with me, I went along. Julianne's brother, Jack Tanner, was getting married in Buffalo, New York, so our honeymoon was spent with Julianne and Gary touring the states and historic sites between Athens and Buffalo for a week before the wedding and a week afterwards. We stretched our money by eating breakfast at McDonald's and eating lunch in rest areas and state parks from our cooler full of cold cuts and a stash of fruit and snacks. Dr. Stegeman had given us a wedding gift of a bottle of Moet and Chandon Champagne that we used to drink a toast at each state line when we crossed it. That is, everyone except the driver.

After the wedding in Buffalo, the wedding couple asked us if we would transport for them some of the leftover liquor from the bar, which they wrapped and tucked under the seats and luggage section of our station wagon. We were so close to Niagara Falls that after the wedding we decided to take a day and go there. We toured the U.S. side and crossed the border into Canada to have lunch and walk behind the Horseshoe Falls.

At the border, the crossing security guard asked Gary W., who was driving at the time, to declare if we had any of the following articles in our car and he began to reel off a list of items, including liquor, firearms, fruit, vegetables. To each, Gary W. said, "no" and after each no I kicked him under the seat. Yes, we did have a pistol under the driver's seat. Yes, we had enough unopened bottles of liquor to be selling it and yes, we had a cooler full of fruits and vegetables. After they waved us through, Julianne, Gary, and I all bombarded Gary W. with the obvious and began to consider what we were going to do now. We were in Canada, and we did not know their laws and we could not just dump the stuff, which could be worse if we got caught. What could we say if they found out? Would we be arrested? Would we be able to call our parents for help? The dilemma put a huge damper on our day and the anxiety just got worse every minute we were in line to cross back into the U.S.

It was the 1970's and drugs were rampart in the U.S., so the border guards were literally taking apart every other vehicle, looking under the seats, searching through luggage, even looking in and under the engines. I prayed and prayed and prayed, "Lord, please, please let us get through and we will never do this again." Finally, after more than an hour in line, we neared the crossing guards and watched as they searched the car in front of us and held our breath when the guards turned towards us. What were we doing in Canada, a guard asked? How long had we been out of the U.S. Where did we live? Where were we born? Finally, he waved us through without inspecting anything. Oh, the blessed relief! Thank You, Lord. We rode in complete silence. Physically and mentally exhausted from the strain, we skipped supper and almost crawled to our beds in a nearby hotel. I remember that Gary and I lay perfectly still in the dark for hours as our muscles slowly relaxed and our minds found peace. Never was I so glad to be back home in the USA.

AGH: Great Fun and Great Responsibility

In January 1979, I resigned from St. Mary's Hospital (STMH) and started to work at Athens General Hospital (AGH). I had worked at STMH on the 11pm-7am shift and then 3pm-11pm and, finally, on 7am-3pm, as the shift charge nurse in ICU. I was always learning as much as I could about the patterns and practices of the patient care, doctors, staff, and the hospital in general on that shift. 11pm-7am was my least favorite shift for my personal health and social life, but it was the most challenging and rewarding professionally. 7am-3pm was best for me personally, but it was the dullest shift professionally. 3pm-11pm was my favorite. It was the best of both worlds for me.

In the nursing profession at the time, there were two distinct tracks, the clinician track, and the management track. After having worked clinically in most every department of a hospital, I decided to pursue the management track. I soon learned that all the head nurse positions at STMH were filled with long-time employees or nuns and my chances of getting head nurse position there were zero. So, I inquired at AGH and was hired by the associate nursing director, Mrs. Joyce McCrudden as the 3pm-11pm supervisor.

I started to work at AGH on January 29, 1979, with Mary Ellen Mealor, who had been a supervisor there for a long-time, and Jan Honnaker who covered the 7am-3pm shift. Frankie Lee and Connie Tippett, both long-time supervisors also, covered 11pm-7am. I was to work with Dot White, the other supervisor on the 3pm-11pm shift who would orient me to my new job. However, just two weeks after I started working with Dot, she was put on complete bed rest for a pregnancy that was damaging her spine. That left me with no one to orient me and no one to relieve me for a day off. Ms. Lee lived in the apartments behind the hospital and was willing to take a call from me anytime I needed it and Connie was willing to give me an occasional day off, but mostly I worked alone, and I worked a lot. It was the best job I had ever had, and I loved it.

One day after Mrs. Mealor gave me report, she pushed her chair back from the desk, crossed her arms over her expansive chest and stared at me. "You think you are something else, don't you?" she said with a smirk.

Bewildered I asked, "Why, what do you mean?"

"Well, you come in here and you work by yourself without any relief. You act like you have been here for years. You just think you are something else, don't you?" I was stunned and speechless. I was not acting at all. I loved my job and was just doing the best I could, by myself, without any help. When she finished, I thanked her for her constructive criticism, which must have been what she wanted to hear because after that day she was one of my biggest advocates.

I was responsible for the patient care anywhere in the hospital from 3pm to 11pm. My years of nursing and leadership in many different areas of the hospital had prepared me with a diverse knowledge of patient care and staff leadership principles that came together in the supervisor role. I made rounds on every unit at least twice, getting and giving report on all patients, potentially as many as 365, coordinated staffing for every nursing unit, and managing any crisis with patients, staff, physicians, visitors, or others. Every day, I collaborated with professionals, such as physicians, nurses, therapists, and technicians about their plan of care for the best possible outcome for each individual patient, given their unique conditions and situations. There was never a dull moment, but one day was more exciting than all the rest.

That day, not long after Mrs. Mealor and Jan left, my pager sounded a Code 99, which meant that a patient was suffering a cardiac arrest. I raced up the stairs to the fourth floor and into the patient's room. A nurse was performing cardio-pulmonary resuscitation, or CPR, while another nurse wheeled in the red code cart with the emergency drugs and equipment. Code team members from all over the hospital, including respiratory therapists, lab technicians, emergency medical technicians, ICU nurses, and any available physician came in and began their pre-assigned tasks. As supervisor, I assumed oversight of the emergency proceedings until the first physician arrived. After updating him on the patient's diagnosis and situation, I relinquished the lead to him and did what I could to help the nurses, communicating with the attending physician, finding and informing family members, and facilitating the patient's transfer to the ICU.

When the transfer was underway, I made my way back to the first-floor office, gathered my reports, and headed out to begin my rounds. It was 4:35 pm and I hadn't made it to the first unit yet and my pager was ringing again. Code 1000! Multiple victims. I threw the papers on my desk and ran as fast as

I could to the ER. The wide-eyed look on the faces of the staff as they rushed to gather supplies and set up extra equipment told me this was not a false alarm. A school bus had wrecked, and kids were being transported to us. How many? They did not know!

In what seemed like seconds, ambulances began pulling up to the dock and wheeling in gurneys with kids! I was expecting high school, middle school, and elementary kids on a school bus, but these were little 4- and 5- and 6-year-old wide-eyed crying children. The school bus was a day-care bus returning from a field trip. Thankfully, their injuries were minor cuts, bruises, and a couple of broken arms, but the real issue was trying to identify the children and notify their parents.

"What is your name?" I asked.

"Bobby."

"Bobby what is your last name?"

"Bobby."

"Well Bobby, what is your Momma's name?"

"Momma."

Some knew their names first and last, but many did not, and every child needed constant attention, which meant calling staff from the upstairs units and disrupting their workload. With help from the day-care workers, we eventually treated 34 children and three adults and reunited the children with their parents. A cardiac arrest and a disaster before supper—what could happen now? I should not have asked.

I collected my reports and grabbed a candy bar from the office and headed to the units. I decided to start at the top and work my way down through the units, get something to eat, and start out again making my last rounds for the shift. Riding the elevator to the sixth floor, I breathed a sigh of relief. The units were quiet. I had gotten a few calls but, so far, the situations and requests were not stressful. The psych unit was always locked, so I rang the bell and pushed the door open when the buzzer sounded and waited for the charge nurse coming down the hall. I offered a quick apology for my delayed arrival and an assurance that all or most patients were calm and stable.

Out again and down the stairs to the fifth floor, a 40-bed surgical unit. Pam Glass, the charge nurse, was on the phone. A patient, just out of surgery, was being wheeled into the room across from the nurses' station, a room appointed for the more acute patients. The unit secretary said the new patient had been slow to wake up from the anesthesia so he would be monitored on telemetry and close to the station for frequent observation. Pam gave me a quick report on the new patient and others who were fresh post-ops, all stable, no known complications at present.

Good, two units down, nine more to go and the beeper was ringing again. It was probably the operator and an outside call, I thought. Hopefully not a call out for 11-7 because I did not have time to sit in the office calling people and asking them to work on their day off.

"Hi, this is Debbie." I said, answering the page.

"Debbie, we have a Code 6."

"A what?"

"A Code 6."

"How much time do we have?"

"An hour and a half."

"Ok, I'll be right there." I raced down five flights of stairs and down a hall to the switchboard office. Maggie had received the call. A bomb was set to go off at 8:00 pm. We didn't have much time.

I grabbed a phone to notify the administrator on call. It was Mr. Drew, the CEO, and he answered on the second ring. "Mr. Drew, this is Debbie Huckaby at the hospital. We have a bomb threat. Maggie took the call. It's set to go off at 8:00pm. I'd like to call a Code 6."

"Go ahead and I'll be right over," Mr. Drew replied. "Call as many administrators as you can. Meet me in the nursing office."

I instructed the switchboard operators, Maggie and Rachel, to page a Code 6 and to page me stat if the bomber called back. Grabbing the list of administrator's names and numbers, I headed to the nursing office, the control center for hospital-wide codes. Hearing beepers going off in the halls and seeing others hurrying to their departments propelled me to run. What would a bomb look like? Could someone set it off accidentally while searching? The hospital is so big with so many places a bomb could be stashed and there are so many people here. The hospital was full of patients, staff, visitors, doctors. Dear Jesus, help us! So many thoughts swirled through my head.

I called Ms. Lee first. She was closest. Then Joyce McCrudden, acting Director of Nursing, and the VP of Finance. The CEO arrived first and took command of the search. From the first floor to the sixth and from the ER to the ancillary buildings, the hospital was searched. At 7:45 we gathered again in the control center. Nothing anywhere and no suspicious activity was seen by anyone, so the CEO and the vice presidents left. Yes, at 7:55pm they left the building! Wait, are y'all seriously leaving? What about going down with the ship? Yes, they left and probably watched the building from the parking lot, but I watched the clock and waited and listened and prayed.

Thank you, Lord, no bomb, no explosion, and the patients and staff were safe. A cardiac arrest, but the patient was still alive in ICU. A bus full of children wrecked, but only minor injuries, and a bomb threat, but no bomb. So much to be thankful for. Thankful this was not a typical day.

Two Incomes, Two Boys

Gary graduated from UGA Pharmacy school in 1981 and took a position at St. Mary's Hospital on the 3-11 shift. We both wanted him to work at Athens General with me, but AGH administration would not let him because we would have been working the same shift and that was not allowed at the time. Also, as supervisor, I would have been ultimately responsible for his work and that too was not allowed. Ironically, not long thereafter, I transferred from 3-11 to 7-3 and took the position of Director of Medical Nursing. Finally, we had two incomes.

That meant I could buy groceries without restraint and that I no longer had to stretch a pound of ground beef to make four servings. It also meant a new car. Gary sold my Toyota, without telling me, and bought me a new 1980 Buick Park Avenue, with gold exterior and gold velveteen seats. It was huge compared to my little Toyota, but it had the latest bells and whistles, including electric seats and windows, and while that was incredibly nice, it wasn't the biggest surprise.

We had not discussed it, in fact, I did not know Gary was even thinking about it, but one day, he announced that he had found us a house, and everything was arranged. Fortunately, he showed it to me before he signed the papers. It was a redwood two-story three-bedroom house with a gambrel-roof and an unfinished basement on five acres of land, 20 miles from Athens, and we loved it. The driveway was dirt, but the water was cold and crystal clear from a very deep and high volume artesian well and it was quiet, so quiet you could hear the birds singing during the day and the owls and coyotes at night, which always scared me when I heard them.

Every football weekend, friends and family came from all over the state to spend the weekend with us, tailgating, going to the game, and to dinner and dancing Saturday night. We often had as many as 25 people at a time, so as soon as we could afford it we tackled the unfinished basement, creating two rooms and a bathroom with UGA red carpet, white walls, a grey stone fireplace, and black bookshelves. One room had a pool table and a built-in bar, the other had a white sectional sofa, card table, and TV. It was perfect for entertaining! Yet when I think of that basement and the fun we had there, I also remember a hurt it brought.

A few weeks after the basement was finished, I came home one afternoon from work to discover a crowbar lying on the floor in the kitchen. Someone had broken into the house! Were they still there? I didn't know. I didn't hear anything, but I didn't wait long to find out either. Backing out of the house and racing across the yard to the neighbors, I called the police and Gary. "We've been robbed. Come home. There is a crowbar in the kitchen." Shielded from the road by the house and woods, thieves had apparently picked the lock and entered through the basement door at the back of our house, which was located on a corner of a main county road in front and a dirt road to one side. My jewelry box was emptied, and the microwave, VCR, and several pillowcases were gone. Our home had been invaded. I felt vulnerable and violated and tried not to think about evil people rifling their grimy hands through my clothes and looking into my cabinets. Would it happen again? I prayed and listened and kept watch.

Many times, Gary and I sat on the front porch and talked late into the night, sharing our dreams for our home and family that we thought would be sometime in the future, but it happened sooner than we planned. In the first year in our new home, I suffered two miscarriages. The doctors said, Oh, don't worry. You can get pregnant again in a month. I took three days off from work, had a D&C and did not look back. That is until many years later while I was receiving healing prayer at Francis and Judith McNutt's Christian Healing Ministry in Jacksonville, Florida. Imagine having two people pray for you and with you for three whole days. The revelation and subsequent healing were remarkable.

During the second day of prayer, somehow the miscarriages came up and the ladies asked me how I grieved for the babies I had lost. "Grieve?" I said somewhat shocked, "I guess I didn't. I had the required surgery and went back to work as soon as possible and thought about getting pregnant again."

"Well, you suffered in your body, mind, and spirit the loss of a part of you and even though you set it aside at the time, there is still a hurt that is not healed. Those wounds in your spirit are like fragments, which keep you from being whole." Along with my own losses, I shared that my mother had had a miscarriage and my grandmother had had a stillborn baby. So, the generational grief and my own wounds became the subject of that day's healing prayer.

"Do you want to ask Jesus for the names of your children," they asked.

"Can I do that?" I replied startled at the possibility.

"Yes, you surely can," they answered and enveloped me in

their loving prayers, while I asked Jesus if He would reveal to me the names of the babies I had lost. Stephen, John Mark, and Susan were the names I understood in my spirit. Then I was given some time and space to consider each child, what he or she looked like, who they are and what kind of life they might have had, and when I was ready to release them, the prayer ministers led me to place each child in Jesus' arms. Somehow, I knew He had healed the grief and knit together fragments in my spirit. I look forward to meeting my three children one day when I join them and Jesus.

In 1982, I was the Director of Medical Nursing, which included four medical units and I was working on implementing an Oncology unit. I was also pregnant again but, at five months, I started bleeding. I was terrified that I would lose still another child. I prayed earnestly, "Lord, if you will protect this baby and let him be born healthy and whole, I promise I will raise him in a Christian home," and after a few days' bed rest, I was released to return to work.

During my last regular doctor visit, the ultrasound showed my baby boy was in a shoulder presentation. The obstetrician said that could be dangerous if my water broke because the cord could drop through and he could die, so if that happened, I was to get to the hospital as fast as I could. What a cruel thing to tell a pregnant woman ready to deliver, I thought. Gary was working 3-11 and we lived 20 miles out in Madison county, so I tried to get my doctor to admit me, but he would not or maybe he could not admit me early according to the admission criteria, but that did not make me feel any better. Besides I was miserable with what I thought was Braxton Hicks contractions, so I stopped by the grocery and got six chocolate covered devils food donuts and that night I ate them all.

The next day was my due date, and my co-workers brought donuts for breakfast to celebrate. For lunch I had a slice of lemon meringue pie, and the 4-East staff gave me a chocolate chip cookie-pizza for an afternoon snack. I finished rounds and gave report, but instead of going home, I went to the Labor and Delivery suite. I had decided that I was staying, whether they admitted me or not, but keeping me was not a concern after all, because when the nurses checked me, they paged Dr. Smith stat. I was five centimeters dilated and two little feet were completely palpable. That meant my son was standing up inside of me ready to slide out, feet first. They lowered my head and raised my feet, putting me in a Trendelenburg position and called the operating room crew to perform an emergency Cesarean Section.

Gary was working an internship in Royston and left as soon as he got the call, so we waited, while Dr. Smith, my obstetrician, and Dr. Pylon, my anesthesiologist, paced back and forth outside my door. They soon decided that they couldn't wait any longer, and off to the operating room we went. Gary came in just as Dr. Smith was ready to make the incision and was present to see his first son, Walter Gary Huckaby II, born healthy and safe.

Two years later, however, the story was quite different. I got pregnant again when my son, Gary II, was just 10 months old. That pregnancy seemed to fly by with no complications and I was admitted to the hospital the night before the scheduled C-section. Momma had come to spend the week with us and was at home taking care of little Gary while I read magazines and rested in my hospital room in anticipation of the birth of our second son the next morning.

On the morning of April 3, 1984, I got up early and showered, fixed my hair, and even put on a little makeup. I was relaxed and happy and ready to hold my second baby boy. My husband

Gary was with me in the OR and when Dr. Smith and the crew were ready, Dr. Pilon started the anesthesia. I could feel myself fading away, like I was fainting, but everything was not black, it was brilliant white. I could hear the nurses and techs scurrying around, putting me in Trendelenburg, opening the IV fluid, and ambuing me. As a nurse I knew what was happening. I was dying, but I was not afraid. In fact, I was peaceful, and while I did not see Him or hear Him say anything, I knew I was in the presence of the Lord Jesus Christ, and I was permeated with incredible warmth and love. "But what about the babies?" I asked and immediately the light, the warmth and love were gone, and I succumbed to the anesthesia.

Later Dr. Pilon explained that he had given me the same dose of anesthesia I had been given when I had my first C-section — a dose that was perfect for a tired, anxious woman amped up on sugar, but apparently too much for me then. "You have a super sensitive liver," he cautioned, "so always be careful about what you take or what someone else gives you." Years later, I remembered Dr. Pilon's words and realized that my super sensitive liver was why the smallest amount of alcohol would make me pass out and why a Drixoral allergy pill essentially paralyzed me for almost eight hours.

Dr. Smith delivered Benjamin Andrew "Andy" Huckaby and tied my tubes. Gary said that baby Andy had heart decelerations and they had to give him oxygen and stimulate him to cry, but he was soon pink and perfect. I do not know if that caused it or not, but Andy cried for the first 11 weeks of his life. He seemed hungry, and took his bottle, but promptly and with force vomited everything back out. We tried every kind of milk, including goats' milk with the same results. My brother, Allen, was attending the University of Georgia and living with us. He still talks about how

I would call him to stop on his way home and bring yet another kind of milk.

Finally, a friend gave me the recipe for the old fashioned Karo syrup and Carnation milk formula, which Andy loved and retained, but he still cried. Finally, Dr. Hendrix, his pediatrician, suggested giving him a half dose of Benadryl to break the cycle of anxiety. I was so anxious about sedating my child that I could not give it to him, but Gary did and thankfully it was what he needed. My little baby boy stopped crying and slept peacefully for about four hours. By then, I had lost 53 pounds and was down to just 98 pounds, and Gary had lost 25 pounds. Together we lost 78 pounds in almost three months, and I gave thanks every day that I had had my tubes tied!

A man once asked me if I was in church the day before. "Yes," I said. "Well, I didn't see your hair," he countered. Sounds bizarre, right? But that is an example of how people have located or recognized me for years. You see, I once had dark chocolate brown hair, but it began to turn white when I was only 37 years old. I think it is hereditary as Momma Erline once told me that she had had white hair since she was 30, but I know that work and my two little boys contributed a lot to my transformation.

First Home — Madison County, Ga

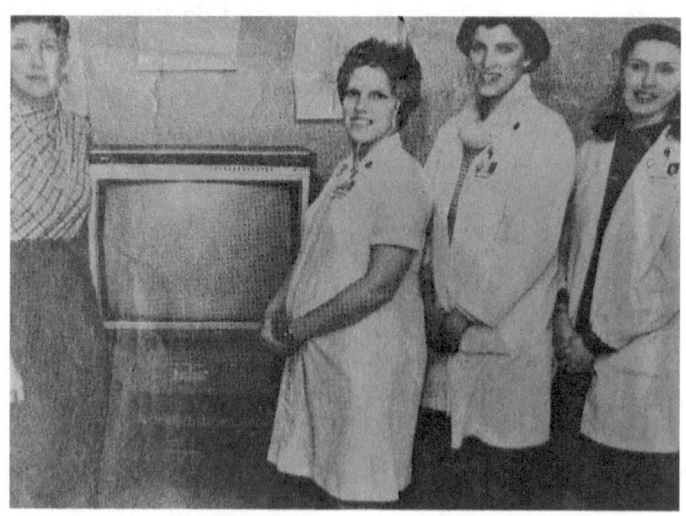

Ga. Power Women Donate TV to Oncology Unit, Dir. Medical

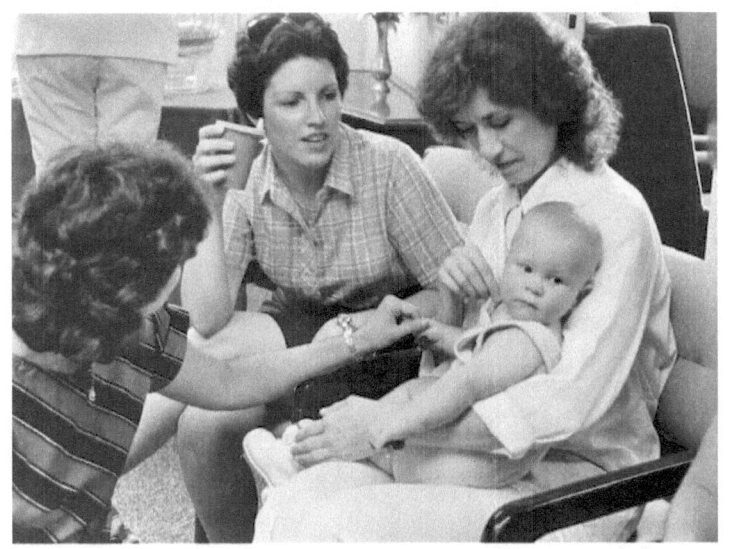

Debbie, Dot White holding Gary II

How I Got My White Hair

While Gary II was little, Gary worked 3-11 and I worked days so there were only a couple of hours a day when he needed a babysitter. How blessed we were to find Trudy Walker, who lived a few hundred yards down the road, to be his babysitter. Her young daughter had just started to school that fall, and Trudy was the perfect doting babysitter for my precious toddler and for me, his anxious mommy. When Andy was six weeks old, we put both boys in Jack-N-Jill Daycare center. The owner, Mrs. Clara Wilbanks, adored Gary and Andy and treated them as her own grandchildren. In fact, Andy entered the infant room beside her own six-week-old grandson, Matt, and the two boys have been good friends ever since. Over the next forty years whenever I saw Ms. Clara, even when she was ninety, she always asked how her boys were doing. Thankfully, they grew up, but many times I wasn't sure they would make it.

When the boys were toddlers, their table antics were so disruptive, Gary and I decided going out to dinner with them was not worth the effort. So, we stayed home for at least two years. Finally, when Andy was three, we ventured to take a vacation, actually just a weekend. Gary had a pharmacy conference on Hilton Head Island and got a condo for us near the meeting location. It was our first time on the island and the first overnight trip we had taken with the boys, other than to my mother's. I had bought swimsuits, floaties, and beach toys in anticipation of fun times with the boys on the beach, but it rained, buckets, continuously day and night. After five hours in a car, we waded through ankle-deep water, carrying little boys and luggage into the condo for some much needed rest in our home away from home, only to have those hopes dashed in the foyer. Like the effervescence of uncorked champagne, Andy broke into a run the moment his wet foot touched the tile floor and racing across the condo foyer tackled a large decorative urn sitting against a glass wall. That condo, decorated in white carpet, purple walls and glass tables and valued at over one million dollars, was definitely not a haven of rest with two little boys in a rainstorm. I was so glad to get back home to rest from our vacation.

Between 1985 and 1988, Gary and Andy had four ER visits, three surgeries and a two-week bout of salmonella. It seemed like I was always taking Andy to the emergency room for stitches. Two times he jumped from one twin bed to the other, cutting open first his ear and then his eyelid. Once when the boys were playing with a bicycle turned upside down and turning the pedals to watch the chain and wheel spin, Gary told Andy to stick his finger in the gear, which he did, and back to ER we went to have the end of his finger and fingernail sewed back on.

When Gary was just three years old, he had acute appendicitis and an emergency appendectomy, and when he was about four, he was in the hospital for two weeks with salmonella after picking up a turtle in the yard. He said he washed his hands, but now he confesses he didn't. That was a hard way to learn to wash your hands.

Andy had tubes in his ear when he was 10 months old and

then had his tonsils and adenoids removed when he was about two. When he was four, he was playing ball at Athens Christian School Pre-K and got hit with a ball in the groin. I knew something was wrong when he came to the car crying, barely able to put his foot on the ground and when I found out what had happened, I rushed immediately to the ER again. The jolt to his groin had twisted one of his testicles and surgery was required. Thankfully it was successful and today, decades later, he has a precious little girl and boy as proof.

Gary has loved golf since he was a child and played every chance he could get. He even took golf clubs on our honeymoon and hit balls across the Susquehanna River in Pennsylvania where we stopped for lunch, so naturally he introduced his sons to golf. When Gary II was just barely sitting up, he got his first Izod golf shirt in Master's green, of course, and while the boys were still little, Gary bought them each a set of Hogan golf clubs. One afternoon, I watched Andy boisterously swinging his club over and over again and shouting. I couldn't understand what at first, but he was absolutely proclaiming it with passion, so I got closer. "I am Andy!" he was shouting with each swing of the club, "I am Andy I am Andy," over and over again.

Parents need to cling to each other when their children are going through a crisis and Gary and I did, at least once. When Gary II was being wheeled into the operating room for his emergency appendectomy, Gary and I stood in the hall and held each other helplessly and cried, but stress did not usually bring us together.

Just before Andy's surgery for tubes in his ears when he had yet another earache, I was rocking him when I heard a bump or knock near the basement door below our bedroom window. I was home alone because Gary was working 3-11 at St. Mary's

Hospital and apparently working late because it was well after midnight so, holding Andy, I went downstairs to investigate. The living room, kitchen, and dining room were quiet and dark except for the lamp beside Gary's chair, but then I heard voices in the basement. I laid Andy on the orange shag carpet in the dining room and crept to the basement door. The voices I heard when I opened the door were clearly male and female and as I walked down the stairs, there was laughter and the sound of someone shooting a pool ball—that is, until they saw me.

Gary was there, playing pool and drinking with another man and two girls. I didn't speak, I couldn't! I immediately turned and retreated upstairs to take care of my sick baby. Apparently, he had a date or had picked up a girl in a bar after work and had the audacity to bring them to his own home where his wife and two small boys were sleeping. Of course, he just brushed it off. No explanation. No excuse. No apology. It was not a problem to him. To this day, forty years later, I still don't know who they were in my house that night or how that scene was contrived. All that was enough to give anyone white hair, but my life at work was just as hectic as home.

In 1984, when our new Vice President of Nursing, Martin Sparks, asked me about my career goals, I told him that I wanted to pursue the administrative versus clinical track of nursing. As a result, he offered me a position as the director of Nursing Information and Finance, a new department that he wanted created. He then tried to find a particular consultant to teach me the Hospital Corporation of America's (HCA) financial productivity system for nursing, but when he could not find her, he arranged for us to make a two-day site visit to an HCA hospital in Encino, California. I learned all I could, but it was overwhelming. Ironically, soon thereafter, Martin found the very consultant he had been looking for right here in Athens. June Somers had been diagnosed with multiple sclerosis and was no longer working but was getting her PhD in Philosophy at the University of Georgia. Martin hired June to teach me the system, which she did for the next 12 months.

I continued to develop and direct the Nursing Information Department, which grew over the next ten years to seven people responsible for staffing, scheduling, budgeting, and reporting of nursing financial and productivity information. With June's help, we created a staffing system that detailed the hours per patient day for each patient population (medical, surgical, nursery, critical care) and calculated the number of hours required for registered nurses, licensed practical nurses, patient care assistants, and unit secretaries by shift and for every possible census level. The master staffing plans were used each shift to call in more staff when census increased and downsize staff when the census decreased. Since the staff were paid for their hours worked, that data was used to project budgets for the upcoming fiscal year and to report expenditures as compared to budget as the year progressed.

During those years we also designed and implemented a timekeeping system in keeping with the staffing and scheduling parameters and automated all the procedures through a software system called OneStaff. After speaking about our comprehensive system at a national OneStaff conference, I was invited by healthcare leaders in New Zealand to come there and lecture about our system. My expenses were paid by New Zealand while Athens Regional and the OneStaff Software Company paid for Sandy Rooks, our OneStaff system administrator to accompany me.

The flight to New Zealand was 17 hours long and I will always remember the refreshing feeling of a warm, damp cloth given to me and every passenger by the flight attendants as we prepared to depart our plane in Auckland. The presentations were well attended, and the people were sincerely interested in learning how to use the staffing plans and budgeting processes we had created. Late afternoon on the second day of our presentations, Sandy and I were included in the dedication ceremony of a new wing of an Auckland hospital and given a tour of the hospital. I was astounded to find that their neonatal intensive care unit was located in a wooden house adjacent to the hospital. We entered through a front door that opened directly into the unit from the outside and there, wearing street clothes and without any admonitions to wash my hands or put on a mask, I was permitted to approach and even touch the tiny fragile babies in their open incubator beds. I decided then that I would never again complain about the copious rules and regulations to which American hospitals must adhere.

After the presentations were completed, our New Zealand hosts provided us with a day tour of the north island. We visited a Māori village and walked around bubbling hot geysers in Rotorua and even rode in a boat on an underground river to see the Waitomo Glowworm Caves. There we saw the amazing orange, green, yellow, blue, and purple hues of the fluorescent glow worm larva attached to the ceiling and were reminded to keep our mouths closed since larva occasionally fall into the boat or an open mouth. I did not have to be told twice. Later I fed a tiny white lamb with a baby bottle, saw trout jumping in a stream, and watched kiwi in a nature reserve. We ended our trip with supper in a rotating restaurant high above Auckland and flew over the most beautiful black beach as we headed home.

In 1990, Dr. Marion Ball, professor at the School of Nursing at the University of Maryland at Baltimore invited nursing informatics directors from across the nation to participate in a week-long conference/project where they taught and then interviewed us for seven days. The data from three such conferences (1990, 1991, 1992) were used to develop a master's degree and subsequently the Doctor of Nursing Informatics degree. Today, the school of nursing at the University of Maryland at Baltimore is rated the number one nursing informatics program in the nation.

During the 1991 conference, we toured several medical centers, including Johns Hopkins and Princeton, and learned about the electronic medical record or clinical information systems. I was so convinced of the value of such systems that I made a presentation to our hospital's administrators in November of 1991 asking them to endorse a feasibility study. The President and CEO, and all six vice presidents approved my request and made me the leader of a team to research and identify the best technology/software company to implement a data repository and an electronic medical record.

We called our team the Strategic Healthcare Information Project, or SHIP team, which included three vice presidents and a representative from each division of the hospital. Over the next four years, this team made multiple site visits across the nation evaluating consultants and systems to fit Athens Regional Medical Center, our patients, physicians, and staff. My best and worst memory about the SHIP team was the crazy way we had to travel. Because the team included the chief operations officer (COO), the chief financial officer (CFO), the chief nursing officer (CNO) and directors from eight of the largest and essential departments of the hospital, I had to coordinate our travel in two separate planes, vans, or cars so that the COO and the CFO, the CNO and I and the directors of the two largest departments, laboratory and radiology, were never in the same vehicle together.

The team concluded its work in 1994 with a recommended software application but the expected purchase was put on hold until the health system's HMO could be implemented.

The work of the SHIP team revealed the need for ARMC to have a Chief Information Officer. Since I had been on that path for ten years, I applied, but so did my good friend and colleague Tim Penning, the radiology department director. Tim and I agreed that we would remain friends and that whoever did not get the position would work for the other. Well, Tim got the position, and I kept my word. I re-engineered my NIS department in 1994-95 and transferred to the position of Applications Service manager in Tim's Information Services department (IS). Working in IS between 1995 and 1997, I managed the implementation of hospital-wide software systems, which included order communications, automated budgeting and OneStaff, the staffing and scheduling system.

In June of 1995 on a trip to Princeton University with the SHIP team, Gary Phelps, the COO, asked if I would create and direct a new department that would function as an internal consultant to all departments of the medical center as well as collect and report comparative data. I agreed and left IS in 1997 and created Quality Support Services with 23 employees from across the institution. Beth Warner was my QSS performance improvement manager and Elizabeth Nufrio was my QSS data reporting manager. Linda Thompson, the hospital's JCAHO coordinator, was also assigned to my department and Lynn Nagy became my administrative assistant and right hand in everything. Together we introduced, implemented, and facilitated two performance improvement initiative teams in all 85 departments, provided administrative support to a quality council, implemented and facilitated a system for root cause analysis of untoward medical outcomes, managed databases and reporting on internal and external comparative data systems and assisted ARMC in scoring a perfect 100 on the Joint Commission on Accreditation of Healthcare Organizations (JCAHO) survey.

One day Dr. Miller stopped me in the hall. Frowning and pointing to my hair he asked, "Why do you do that to your hair? Why do you streak it like that?"

"I didn't do anything to my hair, Dr. Miller, you did. You and this place and my boys!"

Gary Andy Debbie at Stone Mountain

nurse whites until 1985

Bittersweet Blessings

Visited Rodeo drive while in California

ARMC Boss of the Year

Dreams Come True in a Gingerbread House

I promised God that I would raise my sons in a Christian home so when they were just little ones, I dressed them in tiny three-piece suits and took them to Central Baptist Church. They loved Sunday School and children's church, but not so much the suits. Gary started to school at Athens Christian School in kindergarten and accepted Jesus as his Lord and Savior when he was in the first grade. I am eternally thankful for Mrs. Wynn who shared the gospel with my son. Andy attended Pre-K at Athens Christian and it was there he got hit in the groin and had required surgery.

When the boys started school, so did I. The CEO of ARMC, announced that all department directors must be masters prepared. Since I wanted to keep my job and I didn't want to climb the clinical ladder, I decided to get a master's in business administration (MBA), but I needed a bachelor's in business administration (BBA) first. I enrolled at the University of Georgia and began taking night classes, usually one subject a quarter. After a couple of semesters, I sensed God saying, "Are you going to do this? If so, you need to get going." I also found out that UGA did not have an MBA curriculum for night students, so I transferred to Brenau University (Brenau College at that time) and finished my BBA in 1991 and graduated with an MBA in 1993. It was such a proud day for me to have Gary I, Gary II, and Andy in the audience for my graduation, but it was a rough day for Gary who had to entertain two little boys all day. It was also the only one of my graduations Gary would attend for 24 years.

Since we became a two-income family, Gary's love language has been buying me cars. He never consulted me about the kind or color, but his choice of Lincoln Continentals seemed to be my choice, too. Every two years, he leased a new Continental. One year, I think it was 1988-89, he brought me a Lincoln Continental Fiftieth Anniversary series. With heated seats, automatic dimming lights, and electronic windows, I laughingly said it could do almost anything except cook supper.

Just one month after I got that dream car, I totaled it. That morning, I dropped the boys off at school and headed to work. While merging onto the 10-loop from Highway 29N, I was rear-ended by a vehicle going at least 50 mph. My car rammed into the car in front of me and a few more cars in front of it. The impact made an accordion out of the front and rear ends of my beautiful vehicle, but, thankfully, the passenger compartment was untouched. I, however, was not. The airbag had deployed and peeled the skin from my face and the seat belt constrained me so well that it bruised my ribs, but otherwise, I was uninjured. Years later, I learned otherwise. As soon as I could, I called Gary with the news of my accident. He never asked, are you alright? Are you injured? His only concern was the car.

In 1991 we built a house in Oconee County, and I enrolled the boys in Oconee County Schools, however, the house construction was delayed by a couple of months and the principle of the Oconee County Primary School said they could not attend his school unless we were living in the county on the first day of school. So, the boys attended a Madison County elementary school that year. The trauma of three different schools in three years was not the legacy I wanted to give to my boys, but it was beyond my control. Thankfully, the excitement of moving into a new house muted the school disruption.

Our new house was a custom designed Queen Anne Victorian home with all the Victorian details, built by Ted Williams, the brother of our neighbor Bill Williams. It was truly my dream home come true. Like a picture in a history book, the blue and white gingerbread house was graced by a three-story five-window turret, broad front steps and a wide porch that wrapped around two sides of the house. Many who passed by were drawn by a sense of nostalgia to stop and gaze at its beauty. On the porch, white rocking chairs and big green ferns and whirling ceiling fans invited all who came to visit to sit a spell and enjoy a glass of iced tea on scorching summer afternoons.

Upon entering our gingerbread house, one found themselves in a two-story foyer, with an elevated staircase in the center, a parlor on the left, a dining room on the right, and a view of the entire ground floor. The parlor was elegantly appointed with a black Kwai baby grand piano filling the five-window turret and flanked with Queen Anne wingback chairs. Balloon drapes completed the Victorian era parlor décor.

I had always wanted to play piano, so on my 40th birthday, I bought the baby grand and enrolled in lessons through UGA continuing education classes. I knew I would never be a concert pianist or even play very well, but I had had piano music in my bones since the days of outdoor singings and I longed to play and sing the old hymns. Surprisingly, Andy and Gary were able to play many songs by ear, especially Andy, whose musical ramblings were beautiful melodies which, unfortunately, he could never recreate. He took lessons and even played in church a few times, but his extemporaneous music far exceeded his learned expertise.

The formal dining room was beautiful with periwinkle blue carpet, a large, polished brass chandelier, a table for eight and a matching hutch, but, honestly, it was used more as a shortcut to the kitchen than for dining. In fact, I only remember one occasion when we actually ate there. What I remember most about that room was the Christmas tree with its pink and white lace angels, and strings of pearls that I put in the front window each year.

A 30-foot "keeping room" included a living room, breakfast room, and kitchen. The floors were hardwood, which shined in the afternoon sun and showed the week's accumulated dust bunnies. The sitting area included a fireplace, and the breakfast room had a bay window with an exterior door to a deck, but the kitchen was the best room in the house to me. For once in my life, I had enough storage. Stained wood cathedral cabinets surrounded the stove, refrigerator, and sink on two walls and covered, floor to ceiling, an 8-foot expanse across another wall. It was pure joy to put up the dishes and groceries in that kitchen. That room was the setting the day I brought the family a huge surprise.

My surprise began around noon one day. I had a meeting in the glass classroom on the third floor of the hospital. I was the first to arrive and took the extra minutes to review my schedule and to-do list. Soon, Tammy Kemper came in and took a seat directly in front of me and without so much as a hello, Tammy said, "Do you want a weenie dog?" What? I could hardly believe my ears. Gary and Andy had been asking for a weenie dog, a Dachshund, for months and time after time Gary had refused. Never mind that he had his cats, once as many as 25, but he would not even discuss allowing the boys to have a dog. How they became fixated on a weenie dog, I don't know, but that was what they wanted. How could Tammy know? Did I have a wanted sign on my forehead? Tammy didn't know, but God knew. "Well, I guess I do," I said to Tammy and that very afternoon I went to Tammy's house and picked up Paco, a short-haired, one-year-old red Dachshund.

The boys were ecstatic when they got in the car after school and met Paco, but I warned them that Daddy might not like him. We went home and deposited their school stuff and the bag of dog food Tammy had given us and went on to Walmart to buy Paco a bed and toys. Gary came home, in the meantime, and saw the dog food, but just thought I had bought dog food instead of cat food. Laughing and grinning from ear to ear, the boys took turns holding Paco and playing with him all the way home, but my stomach churned with anxiety at what Gary might say or do.

When we got home, the boys took Paco and I gathered up the supplies. They put Paco down inside the back door and that is when Paco introduced himself to Gary. Gary was sitting in his favorite chair in the far corner of the living room, and Paco raced as fast as his short legs would go and jumped squarely into Gary's lap. What a shock. He didn't even know we had a puppy, and suddenly one was in his lap. Well, never a cross word was spoken for it was love at first sight. Paco was home and the whole family loved him, Gary included.

Like the first home, our gingerbread house had bedrooms and baths upstairs and a basement below. The blueprint showed the basement as one huge unfinished space, but I worked with the builder, and we configured a guest bedroom, bathroom, office, and an L-shaped gathering room, which included a kitchen, a living room with a fireplace and, of course, the pool table. My favorite part, second only to the office with walls of bookshelves, was the five-sided boxed-seat turret, which I envisioned as a reading nook filled with comfy pillows, focused lighting, and scattered ottomans. Another special touch by our builder, Ted Wilkes, was a cedar-lined closet. What a treasure that was for storing ski suits and winter coats.

The first fall after we moved into our beautiful home, my high school boyfriend, Eddie, and his wife, Susan, and their daughter, Lauren, came to our new house for a gathering after a UGA football game. Eddie had graduated from med school, completed a residency in gastroenterology, married an ICU head nurse from Savannah, Georgia, served four years in the Air Force, and settled in Gainesville, just 30 miles away. It was strange seeing him there with our families, and yet after all those years, it was okay. There were enough people that we had no awkward moments or even the slightest personal interaction. It was good to know that he was successful in his career and had a family. I felt that a chapter of my life had closed, and I could put that behind me, and focus on relationships in my here and now.

Sadly, the most important relationship in my life was also the one that needed the most work. Life had been busy—a new home, new schools for the boys, and graduation in 1991 and 1993 for me. Mine and Gary's relationship was gradually getting worse. He had gotten into the routine of going to work and going by Jennings Mill Country Club (JMCC) before coming home. Sometimes his after-hours time there was spent playing or practicing golf, but mostly he spent the time talking, drinking, smoking, and watching golf on TV with the other golfers.

Since he joined JMCC in the late '80s I had come to passionately hate golf because his golf life did not leave any time for me and the boys. Gary was there playing golf all day Saturday and Sunday as well as most every afternoon during the week. Sometimes he even took off on Wednesday and/or Friday and played 18 holes. Golf became a third person in our marriage and a hindrance to our family.

Somehow, I decided that I needed to do better and be better. I needed to be a better homemaker and maybe if our home was more pleasing, Gary would spend more time there. So, I cleaned relentlessly and decorated every room, but there was no change in his routine. Maybe I needed to be a better cook I thought, so I worked harder on recipes and dishes I thought he might like and produced elaborate meals. I even had the boys dress for dinner, but Gary didn't come home to eat with us, and I was even sadder for the effort. I wondered if I needed to look nicer, prettier even, so I bought more clothes and had my hairstyle changed. All to no avail. I even bought him an azalea flower for his birthday and had it delivered to him at the hospital. I don't think he noticed.

Finally, I decided I should take him away for the weekend and devote all my attention on him. I made reservations at Callaway Gardens to see the Christmas lights and spend the weekend together, and while the decorations in lights were nice, the drive there and back and the rest of our time together was conspicuously quiet and honestly boring!

When I had done all I knew to do to be and do better with absolutely no response, I decided to openly address our impasse. "Why?" I asked. "Why don't you want to be with me and the boys? Why do you never tell me you love me?" It had been 15 years since he had said those words. "Why?" And when there was no answer, I sobbed. "Why won't you talk to me?"

"I don't know," was all he said.

Queen Anne Victorian Gingerbread House

Old Mill Chase in the Summertime

Keeping room—Andy warms by fire

Breakfast room to garage door

Lord, Please Don't Take My Mother

It was in 1993 that I also sensed the Lord calling me to draw nearer. I began reading my Bible every night before going to bed and reading books about faith that I purchased at the Carpenter's Shop in Athens. It was also in 1993 that my sweet, gentle mother found out that she had lung cancer. We had taken the boys to Disney World in Orlando and stopped by her house on our way home. It was then that she told me. I was devastated. I cried and cried, "Lord, please do not take my mother," but in 1995 my mother died.

I had spent as much time with her as possible those last two years of her life. It was not easy, but she courageously fought for as long as she could. She drove herself to Valdosta every day, a two-hour round trip for radiation, but suffered so much from the burns to her esophagus and chest that they said no more. She was the manager of a Cato store, one of the chain's leading producers, and loved it, so she continued to work at least part-time until the pain became too intense. She had volunteered with the Cancer Society for years and was afraid of chemotherapy. From the cases she had seen, she believed that the side effects were worse than the benefits. "Debbie," she once asked, "isn't there anything else they can do?" I did not know of anything else medically available for lung cancer, but I did not try to find out either. That is something I have regretted till this day.

About a month before she died, when the pain was unbearable, she agreed to have chemotherapy but first she asked to see her only granddaughter, Heather Kirby, who was just a few weeks old. As she expected, the side effects were severe. I think she gave up the day her hair fell out in such clumps that her head looked like a badly plucked chicken. I asked Daddy, Mike, and Allen what Mom had said about her wishes. No one knew anything. No one had talked with her about it. It was left up to me, so one afternoon two weeks before she died, I sat on the corner of Mom's bed and, putting my heart aside, asked my mother about her wishes. What did she want done? Where did she want to be buried? In her humble and selfless way, she only had one request and that was to be buried in Douglas. Then she was gone.

One day twenty-five years later, while praying and asking God if there was a lie that I was believing, the day I sat on Momma's bed and asked her about her final wishes popped into my head. I had always looked back on that day with such pain. How could someone ask a dying person where they wanted to be buried? I believed all these years that I was hard-hearted, but, in my heart, Jesus said, "What a selfless thing to do." Thank you, Lord. You heal all my hurts, even those that I do not even realize I have.

I learned so much from my mother that it would be impossible to write it all. She read voraciously—fiction, cookbooks, and magazines—from which she gleaned cooking, housekeeping, and beauty tips that she often shared. She taught me to dry my hair starting at the roots and then decrease the heat to dry the ends. She had an eye for traditional or classic styles and taught me to mix and match clothing to expand the wardrobe while staying in style. She taught me to peel potatoes, because, as she said, she could not afford to serve potatoes if I did not learn better. She always had a to-do list and a grocery list and a recipe she was trying to master in a steno book lying nearby. A flan was the recipe she was working on when she became too sick to cook. Ten years after her death, I was again looking through her steno book and found this verse from Isaiah 41:13 inside the cover: For I, the Lord thy God will hold thy right hand saying unto thee, Fear not, I will help thee.

She never accumulated things, never set any records. She never really devoted her life to anything outside of caring for family and friends. She was loving, happy, gentle, funny, and smart. My mother was a true southern lady and she loved me unconditionally. I thank God for her often, but especially on my birthday.

That year was so hard. Gary II cried for his grandmother. Andy had a dream where Momma came to him and told him she was okay and that it would be alright. Two weeks after her death, Gary told me sternly that I just had to snap out of it. "After all," he said, "You have me and the boys." I didn't know what I was doing or not doing. I just missed my mother terribly and grieved deeply for her. I was also so busy at work, the boys were involved in sports, and Gary spent all day long every Saturday and Sunday at Jennings Mill Golf Club, playing golf, drinking, smoking, playing cards, and talking to other golfers.

By October, I was miserable. I was alone and lonely. One night, I sat in the middle of our bed and talked and talked, trying to tell Gary how I felt. His answer: he turned over with his back to me and went to sleep, snoring while I was still talking. I cried out, "Lord, I want to leave. I want a life. I want someone who loves me and wants to be with me. I married Gary but in his heart he has not married me. Can I please get a divorce?"

"No, some daddy is better than no daddy" is what I understood God to say.

"Ok, I'll try," I said, and try I did.

Macel & Jay Kirby

Macel & Jay Kirby and Momma Erline

Daddy Jay, Momma Macel, Debbie, Allen, Momma Erline, Mike

WINGS: An Oconee Christian Women's Group

The Tuesday after Momma's funeral I led a SHIP team to visit Princeton University Medical Center. While traveling the COO asked if I would create and develop a new department to serve as an internal consulting and a comparative data reporting service for the hospital, physicians, and board. I agreed, and in 1997 Quality Support Services (QSS) was born. It was my favorite department. I truly enjoyed working on the diverse initiatives with such a creative and intelligent staff and apparently the relationship was mutually enjoyable because in 2000, I was named ARMC Boss of Year based on their testimonies.

One week stands out more than others when I think of QSS. ARMC had embraced the concepts of performance improvement and the administrative team (CEO, COO, CFO, CNO, etc.) asked all 85 departments to develop two performance improvement initiatives each. That meant we needed 170 teams across the institution, so I was sent to a facilitator training course and asked to train my staff and others to facilitate those teams. After some internal department training, we developed a seminar about facilitating performance improvement teams to be held for three days in September 1999. There would be 23 participants taught by a team of seven leaders. Monday and Tuesday of that week we worked to prepare. We gathered supplies and handouts and I wrote and rewrote the working agenda. The many weeks of preparation paid off because the seminar was excellent, absolutely excellent. By Thursday evening, pleased with the progress of the seminar, the quality of teaching and the enthusiastic response of the participants, I settled into bed early for some bedtime reading and extra sleep.

I had been reading Good Morning, Holy Spirit by Benny Hinn, an autobiographical testimony of his conversion and moment-by-moment relationship with the Holy Spirit. That Thursday night as I finished the book, I sensed a deep longing for such a meaningful life. I got out of bed, knelt, and prayed, "Lord, I want a moment-by-moment relationship with You. Help me know You, Holy Spirit, the way Benny Hinn knows You. I invite you, Holy Spirit, to fill me and use me. Teach me to hear you and obey you."

The next morning, I woke with such excitement, I literally bounded out of the bed. Wow! I thought, maybe God could really use me today. "What are we going to do today, Lord?" I asked. Mid-morning a participant asked me about my church and Sunday school class. I thought, this is it. This is when I can be a meaningful witness. So, I answered her questions and invited her to join us and thanked God for the opportunity to share with someone that day.

It was Friday, the final day of the seminar, so I asked the teaching team to sit with me at lunch so that we could "be on the same page of the hymnal" for the afternoon role-play exercises. The restaurant dining room was filled with round tables and white tablecloths, a banquet table filled with food, and many more people besides the seminar participants. I sat down to establish a location for the teaching team and waited for them to get their plates and find their seat with me.

Randall, our waiter, was someone I knew from the hospital. As he filled the water glasses, I asked him about missing the hospital. He said he didn't miss the hospital but that he did miss some of the people, although he got to see several old friends every month when they attended a Christian women's meeting there at the restaurant. "Oh really," I said, "That's good to know because I am starting an Oconee Christian women's group." Well, my mouth said those words, but they had never entered my brain. I honestly and truthfully had never had those thoughts in my entire life. I had never had one thought about a Christian women's group, but there it was, spoken out of my mouth. I looked at Beth, my friend and colleague, sitting beside me and in shock at what had just happened, I said to her, "I wasn't going to do that!"

Beth said, "I know." Well, I began to shake. What had just happened? How did I speak something that I had never thought of before? I was speechless and confused and I knew I was going to cry. I said to Beth, "Please take over, I've got to get out of here!" And out I went—walking and crying. I walked the streets of downtown Athens, praying, "Lord, what happened? How did I say that or how did You say that with my mouth? I never thought of such a group before. What kind of group? What do you want me to do?" For almost three hours I walked and prayed. By the time I returned, the seminar was over, and Beth and the other leaders were cleaning up. I must have looked like a wreck!

That night was a high school football game, and Andy was playing. At the concession stand, I saw an old friend. "Debbie," she said, "I haven't seen you in so long. Let's get together and do some Bible study." As we were leaving the game another lady came by me, hugged me, and said how she would love to get together with me for some prayer time. I was amazed. This went on for the next two months. During that time, 23 women approached me about getting together to study the Bible, pray, have lunch, and go to Christian conferences. I did not approach them. I did not tell them about the September 24, 1999, 12:15 PM event in my life. I just prayed, "Lord, what do you want me to do?"

Finally, after two months, I wrote a letter to those 23 women, inviting them to join me on Dec. 6, 1999, at the local library for a meeting to discuss a possible Christian women's group. That Thursday night, I shared the story and told them the truth that I still did not know the purpose of the group or exactly what we would be doing. I asked them to pray and if they were led to join me, together we would seek to understand and obey God's leading. Of the 23 women who were present that night, 12 joined me in January and then only seven in February, but that group of seven became known as Wings of Hope and met two hours every Monday night for the next eight years.

My WINGS sisters and I met first at the Oconee library and then at one of our houses, but most of our meetings were held at Dr. George's dentist office. We prayed, worshipped, studied, and shared our spiritual journeys using John Wesley's accountability questions, such as, how is it with your soul and what temptations have you had this week? We learned to hear God's voice and share our hearts, good or bad, but always in love. We called it Holy Spirit School because the focus of our meetings was led by the Holy Spirit. Once Cindy looked at me across the room and said, "Debbie, when I look at you, I see a fish, with a mouth stuffed full or words."

"What? Do I look like a fish?" I laughed and said, yet the

thought of having a mouth full of words resonated somewhere deep inside me.

We focused on worship and hungered and thirsted for even more opportunities to gather and worship at churches and conferences locally and nationally. We spent years growing in our understanding of healing prayer. First, we learned about the Order of St. Luke and then from the Christian Healing Ministry of Francis and Judith McNutt in Jacksonville, Florida. Peggy and I went there for a workshop and Cindy and I spent three days there receiving healing prayer from their trained prayer ministers. Later we studied John G. Lake's teaching on healing and, somehow, I became one of the prayer ministers in the J. G. Lake Healing Rooms of Georgia. With them, I prayed for the public once a week for nine months. Not long after that we learned about Ed Smith's Theophostic Prayer Ministry and Peggy and Cindy took the classes and taught the rest of us. We determined to learn and grow as much as we could through all these experiences and always to keep the Holy Spirit as our guide.

We spent a year on spiritual warfare with author and ministry leader Elizabeth Greer acting as our mentor. After a few months of instruction, Elizabeth invited the group to her house for teaching and prayer. Elizabeth and her husband, Bill, operated an affluent interior design and decorating business that served wealthy clients across the southeastern US, so naturally their own home was filled with exquisite fabrics and décor, but things were not the heart of their home. Both Bill and Elizabeth (E) had been called and equipped to minister repentance and deliverance in the power and leading of the Holy Spirit to God's hurting people and that is what they so lovingly and painstakingly taught us.

That night at their home, E and Bill poured out their hearts in prayer over each WINGS sister. With my eyes closed and my heart open to the Lord, I prayed to receive all and only what God had for me. Soon, I felt hands lightly resting on my shoulders and head as E anointed my forehead with oil and prayed, but what she prayed I don't know because, after only a few sentences, I grew warm all over and seemed to melt from the inside out. The next thing I knew I was lying on the floor. I could hear E praying for another but didn't have the energy or interest in opening my eyes. I knew God was working in me and I was content to receive.

That was also my thinking when I learned about speaking in tongues or what we chose to call our prayer language. I studied scripture and read diverse teachings on the subject, but most of all I prayed, "Lord, if this a gift from you and you want me to have it, then I am willing to receive. If it is not your desire for me, then please keep me from it."

In the fall of 2001, several of my WINGS sisters and I attended a Women of the Word Conference to hear Fuchsia Pickett speak. That night while worshipping, my heart was so full of praise I searched for another word or song or way to express to God my overwhelming love and gratitude. With tears streaming down my face, I raised my face and hands to God and opened my heart, which poured out through my mouth in words I have never heard before and could never intentionally repeat. It felt like my mouth was moving 100 mph while an incredible peace permeated the rest of me. I don't know what I said, but the sweet sense of God's presence assured me it was pleasing to Him and that is all that really mattered.

Bittersweet Blessings

In early 2001, we (WINGS) were led to bless pastors' wives. After a few months of prayer, discernment, and preparation, we held a pastors' wives social at Cindy's house on Saturday, March 24, 2001. The purpose was to create a safe environment for pastors' wives to relax and enjoy themselves as a way of honoring and thanking them for their role and ministry in the body of Christ.

WINGS worked well together putting the finishing touches on the food and decorations and then we sat down to praise and pray. Soon our invited guests arrived, along with a guest of a guest. Karen brought a "friend" named Chris. We ate and talked and afterwards gathered in the living room for a little time of fellowship.

Our program was simple and included only singing and a devotion and prayer for each guest, but it did not get off to a good start. During the singing, Karen and Chris left the room and went into another room at Cindy's house. Pam went to check on them and then came to get me saying Karen and Chris were upset because we had not invited the Holy Spirit into the service. I apologized for causing them to be upset and assured her that we had prayed for almost an hour before she came. She was, however, not forgiving and said some harsh words in response. I thought the issue was resolved, but when we rejoined the group, she prayed and boldly asked God to forgive us for not praying first. When she caught her breath, she then asked those who wanted prayer to come aside to her. Very soon, some of the guests left, but Karen continued her loud and long prayers for any who would receive.

I had been blindsided by the rebuke and by Chris taking over the event. I was devastated that WINGS had received a public rebuke and that our guests were made to feel so uncomfortable. Finally, everyone left, and WINGS gathered in a depressed huddle in Cindy's office. I was still shocked and almost speechless, but desperately tried to process the situation and help WINGS find comfort and peace.

That evening, after walking in the neighborhood, I was still so upset that I stood in the vacant lot at the top of a hill and poured my heart out to God. I was the leader of the group/event and yet someone else had come in and had taken over the whole agenda and our safe environment had not been safe for our guests or for us. People were hurt and, somehow, I was responsible. I had not caused the hurt, but I had not stopped it either. I cried and prayed and cried some more and when I was numb and empty, a quietness settled over my being. I sensed the Lord drawing closer as if He were walking towards me and, with every step, the sense of His presence grew stronger. My whole being grew alert and every nerve seemed to stand on end. I literally tingled all over and, at the same time, I was overwhelmed with such a peace and joy that I had never known before.

In an instant I knew that I was standing before the Lord. I could not see Him, but I felt Him. I was consumed in love. I felt love over me and around me and through me. A love so deep, so brilliant, so intense that I was consumed. Completely undone! Enveloped in liquid, burning love. Unconditionally loved! Eternally loved! I understood, it would be okay. I would one day be home with my Lord and until then, it would all be okay.

As WINGS met faithfully each week, studying and praying together, our bonds grew at a heart level, and I came to trust each woman as a 3 A.M. friend—one I could call at 3 A.M. for anything. That trust was needed, for God had plans and we needed each other to walk it out.

In July 2001, Sarah had been studying Ezekiel and believed she had gotten a leading from the Lord that God was going to give us land. In prayer, Wings individually and collectively caught a vision from God to purchase land and build a city of refuge. God even gave me the name. "Betheland with one l," He said. Bethel means house of the presence of God, so we understood that Betheland would be land with a house of the presence of God. It would be a non-denominational retreat for spiritual rest and restoration.

The house or main building was to face east according to Ezekiel 37 and the land would have water of different levels. There would be gardens, a chapel, and places to sleep, like a dorm and individual cottages. The central building, perhaps, like a lodge, would accommodate groups for classes and conferences. It would have a library and a café where area pastors and ministry leaders and Christians could come to study and fellowship. There would be a walking trail with benches for contemplative time alone. A location in Oconee County would be easily accessible to people across the southeast and, through Atlanta, internationally.

It would be a small taste of heaven, for those who felt pressured in their jobs and overwhelmed by their busy lives. The Lord would make His presence known to those who have arrived with aching hearts, suffering over a marriage breakup, a rebellious child, a lost job, or financial crisis. As they wait in the presence of the Lord, praying and receiving healing prayer and counseling, they will experience release from bondage and new freedom in Christ. It was such a clear and compelling vision that we all prayed about how and where such a place would be.

Sarah was led to take maps of Oconee County and, starting at Watkinsville, sketch out a path according to the verses in Ezekiel. She understood that the different levels of water described in the verses were different bodies of water. For example, a creek could be ankle to knee deep, a lake could be loin deep and a river could represent the waist deep water. The next step was the courthouse.

Sarah, Peggy, Pam, and I met at the Oconee County Courthouse and, using Sarah's map, we examined the plots of land on the eastern border of the county near the Oconee River and found a plot of land that seemed to resonate with each person. Again, we were blessed with God's grace in discovering differing levels of water on the land. There were springs (ankle deep) that flowed into creeks (knee deep) and there was a large valley, which would be perfect for a lake, and the eastern boundary of the land was the Oconee River.

Over the next few weeks, we prayed and often walked the land together praying for God's presence and provision according to His will. We studied the history and ancestry of people who had once lived there. We prayed for repentance and healing of the wrongs done to the Native Americans who had lived on the land. We built a small altar of 12 uncut stones and anointed it with water and oil and prayed for God's blessings on the land and on whomever was led there.

Spiritual words of encouragement continued to come from others, which strengthened our faith and trust that God would bring it to pass in His way and in His timing. Was this the plot of land God wanted us to have? Where would the money, projected to be almost two million dollars, come from? We had so many questions but few answers. Over time the encouragement from God and other believers and trips to the land dwindled, but Betheland is in our hearts even today and only God knows when or where it will be.

Over the next 22 years, Elizabeth poured her teachings into me and her prayers over me. Many, many days we sat and talked for at least three hours. She had an intense gift of discernment and a passion for repentance, about which she wrote eight books, and a gift of prayer, especially for healing. Once while we were praying for someone to be healed, I said, "if it be your will."

Well, E stopped praying immediately and scolded me. "It is always God's will to heal," she said. "Pray for healing, knowing it is God's will to heal, even though not everyone you pray for will be healed the way you ask." So, that is what I did, and soon I was given the opportunity to test my conviction.

In late September 2001, I was asked to remember David, the spouse of my colleague, Kaye , in my prayers. David was on a liver transplant list and not doing well at all. I had also asked E to add him to her prayer list and she had but said that in prayer she had seen his liver, which was black. That morning, I understood God's leading for me to go and lay hands on David, anoint him with oil and pray for his healing.

Now, praying with someone I didn't know was quite scary to me and I had never directly spoken to Kaye about her husband's illness. I didn't even know if she and her husband were Christians. I had lots of reasons why I shouldn't go, but I sensed the firm insistence of the Holy Spirit. So, finally, I called and explained to Kaye what I wanted to do and asked her if she would talk with David and let me know if and when I could come. All day I waited and prayed and fasted and when evening came without word from her, I honestly breathed a sigh of relief.

At 7:50 PM she called and asked if I would come, so I went. I took David a copy of Elizabeth's book on repentance, anointed him, laid my hands on his head, and prayed. It was after 9:00 PM when I got home. "Thy will be done, Lord," I said and, as Elizabeth had instructed, I left his healing in God's hands.

The next afternoon, my son Andy sat down with me in the swing to tell me about his day. At a friend's house that day after school, Andy had met a man who asked if he was my son. When Andy answered yes, the man told him that he had been sick, very sick, but that today his test results had come back negative. "That is good, honey," I said, "What's his name?"

"David D. . Do you know him?"

"Yes, I know him. I work with his wife," I quietly replied, but my heart was bursting with praises to God. Not only had I been given the opportunity to pray for someone's healing, but God had so graciously sent me word that my prayers had been answered. David lived another 20 years and died in 2021.

One day, while we were having lunch together, E suddenly started shaking all over. She grabbed her lapel in her left hand and raising her right hand to heaven and staring wide-eyed off in space cried out, "Oh Lord, Lord." Just as abruptly as it started, it stopped. Elizabeth's body relaxed. She wiped her eyes, running with tears, and looking into my eyes said, "I saw you. You were radiant. Covered in glory. You will see God's glory."

Gradually E grew weak from heart disease and after open heart surgery, she suffered painfully from congestive heart failure. "I won't be here when He (meaning our Lord Jesus Christ) comes back, but you will," she said. Then she gave me her wishes for her funeral and, in a few weeks, she was gone.

We buried Elizabeth on a hill on a cold windy day in January 2020. Bill's face was drawn and exhausted and his eyes downcast in grief. He had been by her side, night and day, through the worst. Now she was at rest. Better still, E was with Jesus, which is right where she always wanted to be. Many times now, I think of her sitting with Jesus, watching and waiting until we can all be together again. Will she come with Him when he comes to get us who remain? Will we see each other in the sky?

I will forever be grateful for Elizabeth's counsel, especially regarding Gary. She was determined to love him and pray for him regardless of what was happening in mine and his relationship, which was no small feat considering Gary's response to me and WINGS. "Religion is something that you keep private and don't talk about out in the open," he said, but it was his behavior that showed me how deeply perturbed he was. He refused to sit with me at the coliseum for Gary II's graduation. He said he came, but how could we know? He never interacted with me, Gary II, or Andy. He didn't even speak to us. He got up and went to work without saying a word and came home, watched TV, and went to bed in silence, yet I sensed his frustration with me and WINGS was bubbling just below the surface.

WINGS started meeting at our house on July 9th and by July 16th Gary was volatile. He had been drinking, a little more than usual, and when everyone left after our meeting, he erupted. He cursed me and God and WINGS. He said I got up too early and I stayed up too late. He slammed the bedroom door and knocked my clock off the table while spewing hurtful, ugly things from his mouth. Finally, he said that he couldn't live with me and my religion anymore.

"Well, if that is your decision," I said, "but I am not giving up my quiet time in the morning or reading my Bible at night." He then tried to argue theology with me, telling me Jesus was not God, but I didn't take the bait. I just stated emphatically, I believe in God the Father, God the Son, and God the Holy Spirit and that Jesus is the Son of God, and that Jesus is God. It was shocking to see and hear, but every time I said Jesus, he became even more agitated. Somehow it seemed his voice and his face changed. I knew that God was with me and held me close because through it all I had the most incredible clarity, peace, and calmness. I spoke, but the words were God's. I was not weak with fear or trembling. When Gary's barrage was over, he stomped out, slammed the door, and slept in the guest bedroom.

In the morning, my peace began to be interrupted by periods of foreboding, almost to the point of nausea. I clung to the peace I had known the night before and prayed continuously, but I felt I was holding on by my fingernails. My lack of sleep and memories of the night before made it almost impossible to concentrate enough to work. I went through the motions.

That night, I asked Gary if he wanted to talk, which, of course, he refused, but neither of us could sleep, so I talked, and he listened. I opened my mouth to speak but all of the pain and hurt from the past 23 years of our so-called marriage poured out. I sobbed and sobbed with every word and all the while he never said a word. Finally, exhausted from the pain and the tears, I curled into a ball on my side of the bed and slept.

Gary was waiting for me when I got home from work the next day. He put his arm around me, and we sat side by side for an hour in silence. How did I get here, I wondered, and where can we go from here? After about an hour, Gary spoke. "I want you," was all he could say. "That's fine, Gary, but what do you want me for?" I replied. "Can you live with me and Jesus?" I asked.

He simply said, "Yes."

Well, for the next few weeks he did give it a good try. He came home by 6:30 PM and did a few things around the house, like taking out the trash. He took me out to dinner or cooked something special on the grill. He looked at me and actually acknowledged my presence. Then, one morning about a month later, like a light switch had been flipped, he woke up, went to work, came home, watched TV, and went to bed again, without speaking a word to me or the boys. He had retreated back inside his wall of silence. A wall, God once showed me, that Gary had built around himself as wide as Jericho. A wall I knew I could never conquer, but God could, and that would be my prayer.

It's Time

The boys and I attended Briarwood Baptist Church, where they were baptized. Poppa Huck and Granny Vicky came, but Gary would not attend. That was very disappointing to me, but I am sure it was even more so to the boys. They were active in the youth group and grew spiritually under the teaching of Rev. Mike Ricks and John Messara.

I taught Sunday School, sang in the choir, and served as the choir librarian with my friend Pam Brown, served on the Constitution committee, and the HR committee and did a term as the Director of Discipleship training. I also began taking Precept Bible Study Classes with Carolyn Rogers who, after a few courses, said she thought I was called to be a teacher and convinced me to take the Bible Study Leader course on the Precept Ministries campus in Chattanooga, Tennessee.

Late one night in 1997, while sitting on the floor beside our bed studying my Precept lesson, God said, "Feed my sheep. Tend my lambs." What did that mean? I did not know. I knew it was from John 21, but I did not know what it meant for me. His words were so strong that I immediately prayed to be obedient.

"Lord," I said, "I don't really know what that means, but I will do whatever you lead me to do. Help me understand." Well, I didn't notice much at first, but I gradually I became voraciously hungry for God's Word. I read any chance I could get, but I just could not get enough. I started getting up an hour earlier in the morning and I ate my lunch in the car with my Bible. I continued with Carolyn's classes, but I also enrolled in Calvary Chapel Bible College, where I attempted to take eight classes in one semester while working full time. I felt that I would starve to death if I did not consume more and more of God's Word.

In November 1998, I got the chance of a lifetime. I traveled to Israel and toured for ten days. Just a month before our travel date, fighting in the Golan Heights caused travel to be banned and two-thirds of our group canceled. Only ten of us were left when the ban was lifted, which was an unexpected blessing because we moved so much faster than other groups that our guide added additional sites to our itinerary and took us to places that could not accommodate large numbers of people.

We toured Jerusalem, Bethlehem, Masada, the Dead Sea, Jordan River, Jericho, Galilee, Tiberius, Capernaum, Caesarea Philippi, Dan, Nazareth, Carmel, Caesarea, and Tel Aviv. One night in Tiberius, we toured a diamond factory where I bought a Jerusalem cross with a Solomon stone. In Jerusalem, I bought a Scripture necklace of Judges 6:16, "I will be with you." We stayed in 5-star hotels and ate amazing Mediterranean meals of meats, breads, fruit, nuts, olives, figs, and dates. On Thanksgiving Day, we were in Bethlehem, touring the Church of the Nativity, and at the creche our guide asked me to read Luke 2 out loud to the group. It was a breathtaking moment for me, and I fought tears to speak the words.

The most memorable and life-changing experience of my trip, however, was at the Holocaust Museum at Yad Vashem. There I walked in silent prayer before pictures of emaciated and naked men, women, and children, piles of shoes and relics of lives long gone, until I reached the Children's Memorial, an underground cavern illumined by a canopy of twinkling lights, dedicated to the 1.5 million precious Jewish children who were murdered in the Holocaust. I sat for what seemed like hours and listened as their names, ages, and countries of origin were recited. No words can describe the horror and pain inflicted by evil upon so many innocent people and their families. I knew that I had been changed and that I would live with those sights and sounds and stories forever, and many times since that day I have recalled their suffering and wondered what it must have been like to be in those horrible situations. How could people do such things to other human beings, especially to children? Evil had become real to me there that day.

Briarwood Baptist was a great church and Gary II, Andy, and I felt we had a true church home. The boys enjoyed the youth group and their retreats to the beach and snow skiing. I enjoyed singing in the choir and worked hard on finding and keeping the right note. Me, singing in the choir, was especially funny to the boys who had heard me sing in the car for years and had even begged me to stop. I prayed a lot about my singing, especially asking God to help me not damage the sound of the many beautiful voices around me.

One Sunday in the spring of 2000, while sitting in the choir loft, I had the strangest sensation. Scanning the room of beloved people, I became grieved, almost to tears. It was as if I was seeing them for the last time. Was I about to die? I had never had such an experience, so I searched the room again with my eyes, lingering on the faces of ones who were so dear. If this was the last time I would see them, I wanted their memory engraved on my mind.

The next Sunday, Clarence Pope, a guest preacher, was bringing our message. I don't remember his topic, his text, or much about his message, but one sentence I will never forget. Walking around on the chancel, he stopped and, looking back at the choir, said, "Someone has been called to step out, but is afraid it is not time. God wants you to know it's time." Like a dagger his words pierced my heart and sent shock waves through my body. Was I called to step out? What did that mean? I knew God had said feed my sheep and tend my lambs, but where and how? I wanted to know more. Was there anything else Pastor Pope could tell me? So, I visited him in his ministry here in Athens. "Trust the Lord" was his message. "You may not understand how, but God will get you there."

I sometimes forget that life happens one step or one choice at a time and only when we look back can we see the path we were walking. That is what happened to me that summer. After months and months of work, Pam and I finished organizing and cataloging the choir music. Then my term as Director of Discipleship training came to an end and I turned over all the materials to Carolyn Rogers, who took the position. Soon thereafter, the Constitution Committee finished its work, as did the HR Committee. I still sang in the choir, but we were taking the summer off. So, over a couple of months' time my hectic schedule of church service dwindled and literally disappeared.

At about that time, my secretary, Kathy, said, "Debbie, you have to come to St. James and hear our Pastor, Kent Reynolds." So, Pam and I went, and Kent was not there, but I sensed the presence of the Lord so strongly that I could barely breathe or even open my eyes. A pastor from Scotland was preaching from Matthew 14:28 about Jesus walking on water and Peter getting out of the boat and walking toward him. God's message to me was profound. "You can't walk on water until you get out of the boat."

Again, Kathy encouraged me to come to SJUMC and again there was a visiting preacher. This time a professor from UGA was speaking on healing prayer and, again, the sense of God's presence was overwhelming. So, the third time Pam and I ran away to SJUMC, we heard Pastor Kent Reynolds and decided that instead of running away, we were actually running to SJUMC, our new church home.

I met with Pastor Dan Fuller at Briarwood Baptist Church to let him know that I would be leaving Briarwood, not because I was upset with him or anyone, but that I was moving to SJUMC because I believed that was where God was leading me. Although I didn't know it then, I know now that I was leaving the Baptist Church because God had created me to be a preacher. The Baptist Church at that time did not recognize women leaders and certainly not women preachers, but the United Methodist Church did, and God moved me to a place where I could accept and grow into the preacher God had created me to be. That journey, which began there, would take the next twelve years.

Matthew 12:34b records Jesus saying, "Out of the overflow of the heart, the mouth speaks." My friend Beth says sometimes things pop up and out of your mouth like a beach ball you try to hold underwater. Well, both of those axioms proved true for me one day in a meeting with my vice president, Larry Emmelhainz, when I spoke from my heart and not my head. Larry was giving me my annual evaluation, which was very good and talked about a substantial raise that I would get. He summarized his assessment by saying he hoped that I would never leave my position. It was such a kind but odd thing to say that I laughed and said I loved my job and would never leave it unless I was called into full-time ministry. What? I couldn't believe I actually said that to my V.P. I had never seriously considered that God would take me away from ARMC and into full-time ministry. Yet, that is exactly what was about to happen.

Because of my ten-year experience with the concepts and technologies of the electronic medical record, I was asked to be the QSS facilitator of a clinical information system team, which was composed of many former SHIP team members. By the fall of 2001, it was evident to the team and hospital leadership that ARMC needed a Clinical Information Services department, and I was asked to be the director. So, in March 2002, I transitioned my QSS department into the hands of my friend and assistant director, Beth Warner, and formed a new department called CIS. It was my responsibility to lead the CIS team department to identify and select the best electronic medical record system for ARMC and direct the CIS department to implement the selected system.

Through demonstrations, site visits, and testing we worked for over a year to understand how the software capabilities of three different systems fit each department's functions. Finally, the team and all but one of the clinical departments selected Cerner as the best system for their service, but, unfortunately, our decision was overridden by the CFO, the medical director, and a few members of the administrative team, who chose Eclipsys based on financial benefits rather than clinical functionality. Implementation of the Eclipsys system meant learning and programming the software functionality to execute and augment each clinical department's procedures, which could take four to five years. It was my dream job, the opportunity that I had worked for and waited on since 1991, but in 2002 when I finally had the position, the staff, the financial provision, and the leadership support, God said, "It's time."

It was Saturday, Sept. 19, 2002, and Pam and I were in Kansas City at The International House of Prayer. IHOP was having a conference on harp and bowl worship and the prophetic gifts. Thursday night and all day Friday we soaked in the worship and teaching and prophetic sharing of Mike Bickle and the IHOP teams. Saturday's teaching was focused on the harp and bowl. Corey led us in worship and then taught for a few minutes about catching the fire of God and developing an unquenchable hunger and thirst for Jesus. As we practiced singing Scripture and worshiping in the harp and bowl manner, our sense of the presence of the Holy Spirit grew steadily. It seemed that God was speaking to all of us, leaders, and participants alike, and soon Corey just sat down under the tangible weight of God's presence and worshipped with us.

I found myself repeating "nevertheless, nevertheless"—from Ps. 73. Nevertheless, I am always with you...earth has nothing I desire besides You Lord. My flesh and my strength may fail, but God is my strength and my portion forever. Nothing matters– only God!! I could hardly stand up under the weight of God's presence. I was singing in tongues and tears were streaming down my face and I heard myself saying over and over again. "Lord I do not know how You are going to do it but just go ahead and do it..." as I came to the realization that God had said, "It is time...time to follow me" (into full-time ministry) and my being had bowed to His will.

Pam and I went to the bookstore after the session, and it seemed that every book that I picked up confirmed what I had heard so I just sat down and cried. I could only imagine telling Gary and I thought about how this would mean leaving ARMC and how after 12 years of working towards the purchase and implementation of the electronic medical record, a vendor had been identified and now—NOW, God was saying, it is time.

How I was to go forward, I did not know. I sensed that telling Gary, my husband, was the first step, but listen and wait was what I heard from God. At home again, I entered a liquid fast that lasted 10 days and helped me keep my focus on God and helped me keep my mouth shut. Then one day about three weeks after my IHOP experience, I was sitting on our screened porch praying when Gary came home early and sat down across from me and just looked at me. "Now Lord? Now? I silently prayed ... Yes, now! I knew it was time to tell Gary so somehow I did, and I assured him that although I did not know how, I knew that God would take care of us.

With the vendor decision and contract negotiations, my work at ARMC took on a frantic pace. In early November, the CEO of ARMC, was discussing the major implementation of the EMR at a meeting with board members, physicians, and directors. I listened as he accurately shared the details and gave the names of the implementation team members, but, somehow, he did not mention my name, although there I sat, the director of the department and the leader of the team. Oh, well, I guess he just assumed everyone knew me and my position, I thought.

Then it happened again. The ARMC leadership retreat was at Stone Mountain Park and included 85 directors and department supervisors because the EMR implementation was the primary focus of strategic planning for the next year. I was rooming with Beth and she and I sat together about three rows from the stage where the COO, gave his kick-off presentation. He began with thanking the EMR team for the excellent work completed in the past year. He called each team member by name, but to my utter shock, he did not say my name. What, Lord, was that about? I am the leader of the team. I am the director of the department. I met with the COO regularly about the status of the EMR. I gave updates to those directors regularly at department head meetings. He and the whole leadership team knew my position. Why was my name not included? As soon as I could, I fled to my room where I cried and poured out my heart to Beth. She had also realized that my name had not been mentioned. Had any of the others noticed? Why? I was sitting right in front of him. He looked right at me. Am I invisible?

Yes, I must have become invisible, and that was just the beginning of such occurrences. First, the CEO, and the COO, and then the CFO, and the CNO, and right down the chain of command, I was somehow ignored, missed, left out, and forgotten by each one of them in presentations, emails, announcements, and meeting notices. Apologies were sometimes given when an oversight was made known, but God did not allow me to complain. Still, I was confused and hurt and prayed Col. 1:9-10 constantly for wisdom and spiritual understanding.

All day long, the last Tuesday in February, I calculated numbers as I compiled personnel data for a software purchase contract. Needing yet another report from HR, I hurried down the hall to Janie's office and, although she knew I was coming, she was already on a call. Laughing, she soon hung up and said, "My husband! Since he started to seminary, he thinks the whole world is happy." Well, the word seminary hit me like a ton of bricks and I'm still not sure what happened, but, in that instant, with a smile on my face and a hello still in my mouth, I began to sob! Tears gushed from my eyes as a deep ache rose from my chest to my throat. What? What is this? I screamed in my head as Janie stared at me in wide-eyed confusion. Somehow, I choked out an embarrassed, "I gotta go! I'll come back later" and rushed out of her office.

"Lord, what was that all about?" I prayed as I entered my office, locked the door behind me and fell to my knees, "Oh Lord, DEAR LORD! What was that all about? Am I going to seminary?" Shaking and weak from the roller coaster of unexplained emotions, I sat still there on the floor, dazed, and overwhelmed, and prayed, "Lord, I don't know what just happened, please help me understand."

The following Friday, I traveled with three of my close friends to our church retreat a couple of hours from our hometown. Staying in a cabin with several other women meant that any quiet devotion time would be somewhere else. So, early Saturday morning, as the sun was coming up over the nearby mountains, I crept outside and sat on the porch. Somewhere amid my Scripture reading and prayer, I distinctly heard the word wheaton. Wheaton? What was a wheaton? I wondered. I had never heard the word wheaton and I finally decided that I must have been mistaken in my thinking or hearing.

Later that day, I asked someone if they had ever heard of wheaton...Wheaties yes, wheaton no. But the next morning was Sunday and as the guest preacher was being introduced, I heard it again. Wheaton! He had graduated from Wheaton. Oh no! Was I going to Wheaton? Where and what was Wheaton kept rolling through my mind. Monday, at work again, a search of the internet produced the answer. Wheaton was a college in Chicago. Dear Lord, if I am going to Wheaton, you have to make it clear.

All week long I prayed, "Lord, if you want me to go to Wheaton, in Chicago, you must make it clear, very clear." I knew that going to Wheaton would change my life. How could I go to Chicago? Would I have to quit my wonderful job? Finally, after 12 years, I was doing exactly what I had wanted to do—implementing the electronic medical record. I had the highest paycheck and the best job I had ever dreamed of. What would Gary say? What about my sons? Still, I knew if this was God's direction, I would do it. I must! "Lord," I prayed and prayed, "You have to make this clear!"

By Thursday, I had prayed that prayer hundreds of times. I drove home slowly, wondering what to do, but then suddenly I knew. I was the first car in the intersection, sitting at the red light, mindlessly watching the cars on the four lanes in front of me when a semi-truck approached directly in front of me—WHEATON clearly displayed across it in giant letters. A WHEATON moving company truck. WOW! Lord! I laughed, "Ok, Lord, I'll go. Thank you, Lord, I'll go."

I applied to Wheaton in May and received my letter of acceptance in less than two weeks. That weekend, May 16-17-18, we hosted a harp and bowl prayer conference at St. James UMC, my home church, and during worship that Saturday night, I understood the Lord to say, "Things will be radically different soon." Now soon is relevant to the situation. If I say I am going to bed soon it may mean a few hours or if I am planning a trip soon it may be in a few days, weeks, or even months. I had no idea what soon meant to God, but I found out. Over the next three weeks, my life changed more drastically than it ever had. Thankfully, as my world crumbled around me, I held tightly to God's words in my heart.

First the CIO, warned me "to watch my back" and told me that there had been a meeting a few days before and that the CFO and another VP, were making critical remarks about me and my staff. Then I had a meeting with the CNO, and another V.P and a director that was not pleasant either. Their issues involved a communication committee, which was not even my responsibility, but it was not what they said as much as the way they acted.

Finally, one of my staff called to tell me that the clinical medical director, had called my staff together and met with them after work hours at someone's house. They were all upset, some were crying, thinking that their jobs and our department were being eliminated. In fact, according to one staff member, they were specifically told to get their resumes ready. That night I called my VP and told him what I knew. Then I called each staff person and apologized to them for the MD's behavior and reassured them that I would do the best I could for them and our department. The next day the CIO and I talked, and he suspected that I was being black balled.

Psalm 23:5 says, "You prepare a table before me in the presence of my enemies" and that is a good description of my meeting on Monday with the two V.Ps. Like Meshach, Shadrach, and Abednego in the lions' den, I too sensed the presence of God surrounding me as vicious people (animals) threatened to tear me apart. I had prayed for strength and clear thoughts along with concise and articulate speech. I also prayed that I would not be emotional and that God would prepare them for what I had to say. God answered my prayers in an incredible way. My voice was strong, and I did not blink a tear. I was honest to the best of my ability and tactful and before it was over my VP even praised my behavior and tactfulness.

It had been nine months since God had said that it was time to go into full-time ministry and began moving my life in that direction and it had been three weeks since God said things would be radically different soon. I had watched from an eternal perspective the events as they unfolded and experienced them in conversation with Jesus. I had been accepted to Wheaton College and knew that I could not attend Wheaton College in Chicago while leading the EMR implementation even in the best of conditions, which I certainly did not have. I knew that it was time for me to resign my position and I was ready, but I still did not know how.

I knew Gary had not married a minister and did not understand God's leading so there was a possibility that he would leave me. I did not know if my sons would think I was crazy, leaving the position, the work, and the salary that I had worked so long to achieve. I talked it over with Gary, late into the night, and gave him the freedom to leave if that is what he wanted.

The next day I met with Human Resources about a staff nurse role in the Resource Utilization Department where Cheryl Wunsch was director. I would be taking a $60,000 cut in pay, but it was better than outright resigning with an immediate $100,000 cut in pay. On Wednesday, I met with COO, and told him that I would be stepping down from my position due to lack of support from the two V.Ps and that I would not be sharing that publicly but wanted him to know.

Over the next few days, as my resignation became known, several people shared their suspicions of things that were going on and promised to keep me in their prayers. The Clinical Medical Director said that I was a good person and that there were some things going on that I did not need to be involved in. He also said another M.D. had resigned from the implementation committee for the same reason. I handed in my resignation on Friday, June 13, 2003, and made the announcement to hospital-wide leadership at the department head meeting on June 17, 2003. People cried and hugged me, gave me devotion books, and even bought me flowers, and, after 24 years, Thursday, June 19th, was my last day in leadership at Athens Regional Medical Center. From September to June, nine months, God had made the way. What an amazing journey.

My VP had written on my last evaluation that I had been in the blender this past year and that is how I felt, and since my first course at Wheaton was not until July, I took four weeks of vacation during which I walked, prayed, worshipped, rested, and healed. I got news from my stepfather, Daddy Jay, which was not good. He had an esophageal tumor which was cancerous and an aortic aneurysm the size of a small grapefruit, and my stepmother, Betty Atkins, wrote that my stepbrother Kevin Atkins, had intestinal cancer.

I returned to work at Athens Regional Medical Center in the Resource Utilization Department. I no longer had a high-profile leadership title, department, or role. I no longer had a six-figure salary. My office was now a desk in a room with nine other people that, ironically, faced the trash dumpsters and receiving docks below the VP office windows. How often I looked out that window and prayed, "Dear Lord, this is hard, but I trust you to carry me through," and every day I prayed to forgive each of them. The COO once said that when he looks at us, the group of ARMC department directors, he sees a flock of swans floating quietly on the surface of the water but whose feet are moving so fast underneath. That would be a good description of me that year. Held in God's arms on the surface, I seemed to be quietly moving through my day-to-day life, but underneath I was moving so rapidly that my heart overflowed into my dreams.

Now I guess I dream a lot, but rarely do I remember what, so when I do recall a dream, I pay attention. Is God trying to tell me something? Lord, what do I need to know about that? One dream I had had that past year disturbed me more than any other I had ever had in my life. In that one I had lost my pocketbook and was frantically searching everywhere and crying for help. Maybe I was being careless with my purse, I thought, so I became more vigilant. Then I had the dream again. In fact, I began having that same dream every few months, different scenarios but essentially the same dream. Each time I woke myself up searching frantically for my lost pocketbook. What was so important with my pocketbook? I had the usual credit cards and driver's license, so I wrote the account numbers and put them in a safe place along with the telephone number to call if I needed it, but the dreams continued.

Finally, one night Jesus gave me the answer. I dreamed that I was sitting at a small kitchen table with Jesus who was teaching us a Bible Study. While Jesus was speaking, I got up and went behind him and started looking in the cabinets and drawers—for my lost pocketbook. Jesus said, "Debbie, do I need to get up from here?"

"Oh, no Lord," I said with a shock as I rushed back and took my seat in front of Jesus.

"What's so important in your pocketbook," he said, "is your identity!" Then I understood. My heart was crying out through my dreams for a lost identity. For almost 30 years I had been the "director" of something at ARMC and now, without that title, without that role, I didn't know who I was. Through that long year of transition, I had lost my old identity, but God was giving me a new one.

What's a Wheaton?

A week after starting my new staff job in RU, I was off to Chicago and Wheaton for my first weeklong course intensive. I flew into O'Hare and took a taxi to Wheaton College in Wheaton, Illinois, on a Sunday afternoon. I did not rent a car because I had arranged to stay on campus in a dorm room and planned to eat in the cafeteria or at the Stupe Café in the student center. The taxi left me and my luggage in front of the campus security office where I had been told to come to get the key, but no one was there. In fact, no one seemed to be on campus at all. I didn't see any students, or even a car for hours. So, I sat on a picnic table in front of Elliot Hall, enjoying the afternoon sun and the peace and quiet of that hallowed campus and waited.

Wheaton College! Why Wheaton, Lord, I pondered? It is so far from home. Weren't there any colleges and universities closer that I could have attended? I didn't like what I had seen of the north when I was leading the SHIP team on site visits to places like Hershey, Pennsylvania, Princeton, New Jersey, Ann Arbor, Michigan, and Chicago, and I certainly didn't like the cold weather. What was it about Wheaton that God wanted me to know and experience?

I had read that Wheaton was a premier Evangelical Christian

Liberal Arts College with a long history of coalescing academics and faith and saw that dedication, "For Christ and His Kingdom" boldly displayed on a wall at the entrance to the campus. I knew that Jim Elliot and Billy Graham had graduated from there. I also knew that "The Stupe" had recently been renamed for another graduate, Todd Beamer, who, with other passengers, had died saving the White House on September 11, 2001, by diverting the hijacked United Airlines Flight 93. I was awed to be on the very campus where such esteemed men had walked and studied and grew into such illustrious Christians. I didn't know what was ahead for me, but I was humbled and thankful to follow their large footsteps.

Finally, I connected with a security person, who was definitely not expecting me and even admitted he didn't know what to do with me, but after a few phone calls he took me to a room on the second floor of one of the Terrace Apartment Buildings. He gave me a key to my room and a key to the building, which I thought was odd, until I realized I was the only person staying in that very large and very empty building.

Later that evening I discovered the college cafeteria was closed during the summer months and that the Stupe was only open for lunch on weekdays, which meant I would not have any food, at least not until noon the next day. Fortunately, I had a few granola bars and a couple of apples I had brought for snacks, but that would not last the whole week.

My class was in the Billy Graham building and during our first break I found vending machines that supplied coffee and a honey bun for breakfast. I also heard that the Stupe was closed for the summer. So, by Tuesday, I was beginning to get hungry for some real food and began to consider walking the few blocks to downtown Wheaton. What an amazing surprise. That next morning a small grocery store/café opened across the street from my apartment building with egg and sausage biscuits, lunch sandwiches, yogurt, fruit, snacks, and beverages. I do not remember praying for food, but I was certainly giving thanks. Just another way my Lord, Jehovah Jireh, showed me that He knew my needs and was able to provide for me in a way far beyond anything I could have thought or asked.

My class that week was Theology 101, the first course of a Master of Theology degree, and I loved every minute of it, but I honestly didn't know what you did with an MAT. I even asked a couple of pastors and fellow students, who looked at me with knowing grins and, smiling and shaking their heads, said, "Don't worry, God will show you when He's ready." I knew by the Wheaton truck that I was where God wanted me to be and just assumed that degree was my way into full-time ministry as God had said. So, I settled my mind to wait and prepare four more years for the ministry God had planned for me.

Life, a blur of work, courses, Wings, and family, was pleasantly interrupted in March 2005 by an unusual invitation. Sandra Glass, the wife of Roger Glass, one of Gary's best friends, asked me to go with her to Jackson, Tennessee, to meet a pastor from Mozambique. Why she thought of me, I still don't know, but for some reason, she believed I was to meet Surprise (Supressa) Sithole, who was coming to stay with her missionary daughter Paula and son-in-law Leon Hoover and their family.

In his book, *Voice in the Night*, Surprise tells the story of when he was fifteen years old, sleeping in his father's home, and a voice woke him in the night saying, "Surprise! Get out of the house! If you do not leave, you will die." Surprise obeyed and after walking with his friend Gafar for two weeks through the jungle, they were met by Mr. Lucas, a Christian man who told them that God had told him to take care of them. Now Surprise didn't know God because the members of his family were witch doctors, but Mr. Lucas led Surprise and Gafar to the Lord. A few days later they learned that all of Surprise's family had been killed by a rival group of witch doctors. He was the only survivor. Surprise's conversion transformed him into a passionate soul-winner for Jesus and since then he had been a conduit of God's miracles, including eight resurrections, multiple healings, food multiplications, and the ability to speak several languages, including English, that he had never studied.

So, Sunday March 20, 2005, Sandra and I made the seven-hour trip to Jackson. We arrived just in time for bed, which was a blessing since the road trip fatigue was great enough to quiet the butterflies in my stomach that took flight every time I thought of meeting Surprise the next day.

Leon met Surprise's plane in Nashville, and they arrived home mid-afternoon. After quick introductions, Surprise, exhausted from an 18-hour flight, lay in the middle of the living room floor for a couple of hours' rest. That evening, Paula and Leon, and four of their five children, Sandra and I, a local pastor and Surprise sat down together for dinner. Leon asked the blessing over our food and our time together and then began making introductions. Before Leon could get more than my name out of his mouth, Surprise gave me a startled look and said, "Haven't I seen you before? I know I have seen you before."

I said "No, I don't think so," but Paula just laughed and said, "Surprise, you probably saw her in a vision." To this he agreed. Then, when Leon explained that I had been called into ministry, Surprise fixed his eyes on me across the table and bluntly asked, "So what is the delay? Why delay?" I explained I was in school getting a degree, but I didn't think that met with his approval.

After supper, Surprise laid hands on my head and spoke prophetically saying, "God has given His word into your mouth, prepare, He will give you the nations. Go to destroy, go, and take it. You are called to the ends of the earth. You will speak the tongues of many languages and see great healings." Then along with Surprise, Paula, Leon, Sandra, and the local pastor prayed for me, asking God for an open door and a straight path, and wise use of resources. Known as the Smiling Apostle, Surprise explained that to birth something where there is nothing is an apostolic anointing and he confirmed that I too had such an anointing. Then he asked if I would come to Mozambique to speak. I was shaken to the core and could say nothing more than yes, but, like Mary, I have pondered all these things in my heart.

My work in the RU department was monotonous and anything but fun. Cheryl assigned Naomi Palmer to orient me to my daily routines, which included reading charts and calling insurance companies, government agencies, and physicians about coverage for patient hospitalizations. The daily pressure to complete the assigned number of patient reviews and convince the payers to approve the hospital days was perhaps the discontent that inflamed the profuse cynical and profane commentary by most of the RU staff.

There was a silver lining, however, in the midst of this darkness. Her name is Donna Yates McPipkin. Donna was my best friend when I was the new girl at school in Jesup, Georgia. I remembered spending the night with Donna and going to the movies with her family and, sadly, I remembered that her high school sweetheart and fiancé had died in Vietnam. Like me, she had become a nurse and married and came to Athens while her husband was in pharmacy school.

I had not seen Donna for the past 30 years and, by then, she was married for the second time and had two daughters. Sarah, the youngest was quite ill. She had been diagnosed with leukemia when she was just three years old and had been in remission for a couple of years but relapsed not long after I joined the RU staff. Donna and I talked when work permitted and I prayed for Sarah daily, but Sarah's struggle was immense and after many treatments, she died.

That January Sunday morning, Donna called early to ask me to come. Sarah had been at Egleston Children's Hospital in Atlanta for a couple of weeks following a stem cell transplant, but at 4 am that morning she had had a massive stroke and was non-responsive. Donna wanted to take Sarah off the ventilator and wanted me to be there with her and Jim when that was done.

I talked and prayed with Donna and Jim at Sarah's bedside as soon as I arrived. I remember most how content and peaceful they both were. "No regrets," Donna said. They had fought for Sarah in every way they could and now, if this was the end, they were at peace. We reverently watched as the vent tube was disconnected and the machine was removed. Silence enveloped us as we held our breath and waited. Sarah's breathing was sporadic, more like gasps than actual respiration, yet her 10-year-old heart was strong. Minutes turned into hours and still we stood by her bed, sometimes crying, sometimes singing, mainly caressing her little arms, and watching her baby face. Late that afternoon, January 15, 2007, Sarah Victoria McPipkin died, surrounded by love and prayer and the presence of God. This is the message I gave at her funeral.

> *We came here today to celebrate the life of Sarah Victoria McPipkin and, because you were a part of Sarah's past, I want to assure you that Sarah is also a part of your future.*

Bittersweet Blessings

As we each remember Sarah in our own way, I know that we all agree that Sarah loved life and she lived every moment to its fullest. Everyone who encountered Sarah or even just heard about her was touched. In her few short years, she lived with an intensity that few ever enjoy, regardless of their age. I believe that, in her heart, Sarah knew her destiny. Yet, she dared to desire. She gave herself to the desires of her heart. She dreamed of life in many roles. She played the parts; she took her place on life's grand stage. She answered the call. Sarah could have embraced her disease. It could have become her role model. Instead, she chose to live each day her way.

Family and friends have shared their precious memories of Sarah. I encourage you in the days and weeks ahead as you are reminded of Sarah and that special something she said or did—do not just look at that moment in time and put it back on the shelf of things past. Consider how that memory touches your heart. What part of you stirs to meet that call? Like Sarah, we are all made for a purpose.

In God's word, Jeremiah 29:11, the Lord says, "For I know the thoughts that I think toward you, thoughts of peace and not of evil, to give you a future and a hope."

We are all born with a destiny. But you do not need to write out your purpose statement with its goals and objectives. God has written the secret of your life in the desires of your heart. We humans are made in the image of God—that is not just a fact—it is our vocation. It means we are to reflect into this world the creative and redemptive love of God. It means being made for each other—to love and encourage each other to be all that we can be. It means to look after and shape our world and to love and worship our Creator. Ask yourself what stirs your heart, what makes you alive. Not what you have to do or what someone else wants you to do but what is your desire. Then take a lesson from Sarah and dare to live your life to the fullest.

Yes, desires are the roadmap, but we were never meant to travel alone. I believe that God strategically places us in the families and in our particular locations where we'll receive exactly what we need to reach our goals. If you are part of Sarah's family, friends, or just an acquaintance, she loved you—you were important to her. You made an impact on her life. You helped her find that joy and hope which gave her the strength to fight for the life she loved. But we are the truly blessed because we knew Sarah. As we celebrate the life of Sarah McPipkin, reflect upon how knowing her and loving her has made you who you are today.

God created Sarah to be a bright joy in our lives. She came to shine the light of God's love into the lives of those around her. I believe that Jesus walked with Sarah through every trial and every pain. I pray that Jesus—the true Light of the world—will continue to shine in your life through your memories of a precious little girl.

As Sarah left us on Sunday she was surrounded by love. We watched and prayed and took turns whispering our thoughts and love into her ears. Sarah's body was no longer able to respond, but I know in her heart she understood. And not only did Sarah hear our prayers that day, but our Heavenly Father heard every word and saw every tear. I stood at the end of the bed. Jim was on one side of Sarah and Donna was on the other. I closed my eyes and prayed. Dear Lord, what can I do? What can I say? "Just pray" was all I understood. So, I prayed. I prayed for Sarah to rest, to have comfort and no pain, and I prayed for strength and peace for Donna

Bittersweet Blessings

and Jim and all the rest of us. Minutes turned into an hour and then two. Suddenly, in the depths of my prayers with my eyes closed I saw a shaft of light. It was tall and very bright. Then I noticed another shaft of light, it was shorter, and very dim. As I looked, the shorter light moved and went into the taller light and I knew then that Sarah had gone into the loving arms of our God.

I know now that Resource Utilization was not just a place to work while I was in graduate school. It was a divine appointment to minister Jesus' love and salvation to my friends, Donna and Jim, and their precious daughter, Sarah. It was also a place to be in full-time ministry. You see, the RU department and the nursing units' nurses, physicians, and staff were my ministry. Many a day I was blessed to answer questions about what I was doing and why, which gave me an opportunity to tell each inquiring soul about Jesus. Sitting side by side reviewing charts, I was able to share my story and pray with those who shared their hearts. When I started RU, the language of the staff was coarse and profane, but by the end of my time there we had developed a habit of praying together in a circle in the middle of the department, in the basement of a busy medical center.

Four years of studying, writing, and traveling were finally coming to an end. A Wheaton College master's degree in theology was just a test and a ceremony away. Four years of work coming down to a comprehensive final exam. Words cannot describe the relief I felt when that three-hour test was done. Yet, I could not ignore a strong sense that this was not the end of my journey. More needed to be accomplished; as Robert Frost wrote, and as I have often quoted, "miles to go before I sleep, miles to go before I sleep." My path was still not clear. Are we there yet, Lord? What are the next steps? These were the blurry thoughts that I brought into my prayers the afternoon after the exam.

Quiet and still...hands open, palms up, head bowed. "Come, Lord Jesus, come, I prayed. Cleanse me of my unrighteousness. Create a clean heart and renew a right spirit in me. Help me know your will." I sensed the joy and peace of the Lord's presence and acknowledged that I was content to stay there for eternity. Suddenly, even while my body was still and my mind at peace, my spirit soared. I became aware of holding another's hand and that I was walking on the very edge of the rooftop of a tall building, looking out across a vast city and down at the streets below. Streets filled with ant-sized cars and people going about their appointed tasks. We, my companion and guide and I, walked as casually as you would walk in your yard, stepping easily from one rooftop to the next without a glimmer of fear or concern. Instantly, my spirit flew, and the scene changed.

Beside my companion, arms stretched out to the sides and front, I flew! I, well, my spirit, soared effortlessly, yet rapidly through the air towards a large stately building with a wide lawn, rapidly moving towards the front door of that somewhat familiar white building with the beautiful columns. Then, in the shock of recognition, my sight and my senses cleared as I realized I was flying—flying into The White House, THE WHITE HOUSE in Washington D.C.

WHOA! My spirit was overwhelmed and responded by coming to an abrupt halt and immediately rebounding backwards and up, ascending high in the air. Had I willfully aborted God's revelation? Or had I seen and experienced all that God planned for that time? "What was that all about, Lord?" I prayed, as I came to my full senses. "Your wilderness is the city and the state," He said.

I graduated from Wheaton College on Saturday, May 4, 2007, and even though I was surrounded by thousands of people, I was alone. None of my family were there to witness and celebrate my accomplishment. After the ceremony, I lingered in the Alumni House, perusing the papers, desk, and wardrobe of C. S. Lewis, because I didn't have anywhere to go or anyone to be with. Yet, I wanted to do something special to celebrate. I was staying at the home of the college registrar, but she was occupied with family activities, and made some suggestions for food and activities. A Macaroni Grill restaurant was somewhere I wanted to eat and there was one close to the college. I decided I would go to dinner by myself and that is what I did, only I didn't eat alone. As I was being seated, I saw Jesus standing by the empty chair at my table. He was smiling as he took the seat across from me. All around me, small groups of people were celebrating graduation with laughter, stories, food, and fun. I sat quietly eating and talking heart to heart with Jesus, my Lord, the King of Kings, the Lord of Lords, and the most amazing dinner date anyone could ever imagine.

Parish Nurse, President, and Preacher

That January, while finishing my last class at Wheaton, I realized that I had never attended a service at Willowcreek, which was just 40 miles away. So, when I got home, I searched online to see what I had missed. Much to my surprise, I found that Willowcreek had a medical ministry. I had never heard of a medical ministry in a church, so I called the director to learn how it worked.

A few days later, while searching other sites for medical ministry, I saw "parish nursing" and I had never heard of parish nursing either. It was at a little church in Minnesota. I decided that it was just a local church function, but not long after that I saw a "parish nurse" training course in Florida. The tuition for that course was high and there would be travel expenses, and even though it was certainly interesting, I was retiring, and knew I didn't have money for that kind of expense.

Then one night a few weeks after my retirement, as I was sitting in bed reading The Advocate, the UMC Newspaper, I opened to a half-page picture of Linda Bailey, a parish nurse at Duluth First United Methodist Church. WOW! Three times in such a short amount of time. Okay, Lord, I am listening. Toward the end of the article was information about a parish nurse course at Gwinnett Medical Center in Lawrenceville, just 30 miles away, for only $750 in June. Three times the Lord had brought me face to face with parish nursing and now He had resolved all my objections. Immediately I signed up.

The Gwinnett Medical Center Parish Nurse course was held at St. Ignatius House, a Jesuit Retreat Center, a beautiful setting overlooking the Chattahoochee River in Atlanta, Georgia. There were only 12 students but scores of instructors teaching multiple topics in the weeklong course. I learned that parish nursing was a specialty practice of professional nursing that focuses on mind, body, and spirit health of people of faith. From the first day of instruction, I was astounded. Like the pieces of a puzzle, I could see the disparate stories of my life coming together and making sense. The knowledge of whole person health, mind, body, spirit that I have received from my training and experiences in healthcare was expanded into a much richer and deeper understanding than I ever imagined existed. I was giddy with joy.

One of the students in the course was Lori Floyd, a former military nurse, and a foot care specialist. Lori and I connected as friends and shared several meals together that week, talking about how we might be involved in parish nursing in the future. We also were dismayed that parish nurses across the state of Georgia seemed to be independent contractors, without any formal connection, except for those few nurses who were affiliated with GMC. Little did we know then, but one day we would work together to change that.

The summer of 2007 was a blur except for a St. James UMC Women's Conference that I attended at the Georgia Baptist Center in Toccoa, Georgia. I never enjoyed women's retreats. Besides, I knew very few women in my church anyway. Since going to St James UMC, I had worked full time while attending graduate school, which left little time for church activities. But when I was invited to give the morning devotion at the retreat, I decided to attend.

The day was packed with teaching sessions, worship, prayer ministry, breaks, meals, and fellowship. During worship, women lifted hands in praise and prayer and cried out to God for more—more love, more power, more of God. Send your fire, Lord, we sang. Send your fire to heal, renew, and restore, we prayed. Send your fire, Lord.

My roommate, Anitra, who I had just met for the first time, and I retired to our rooms and spent a little while getting acquainted. Pregnant with twins in the first trimester, she soon fell asleep, but I had not finished my devotion for the next morning. I finally turned off the lights about midnight.

At 2:10 AM, the fire alarm jarred us from our beds, and we frantically fumbled for our robes and the lights, which would not come on. Where was the fire? We opened the door and by the hallway light, with hands over our ears, we examined outlets, the bathroom, and the hall nearby. We did not see fire, nor did we smell smoke, but the alarm in our room would not stop.

Anitra and I stood in the hall, expecting other women to come pouring from their rooms and for firemen to run down the hall. Seconds became minutes. We stared at each other. Are we the only ones hearing this alarm? How do you turn off a smoke alarm and where was the fire department anyway?

As I went to search for the building manager, a fire truck pulled up to the building and four firemen rushed down the lighted hallway and into our room. They searched with infrared monitors for smoke and flames. Still the alarm blared. They deemed the room smoke-free and tried in vain to reset the alarm.

Each man took his turn, but none could stop the noise. They took apart the alarm and even took it off the wall. It still rang. Now even the firemen were wide-eyed with wonder. Finally, they cut the wires and thankfully the noise stopped. Quiet at last, yet my body still vibrated.

The firemen left, the lights in our room came back on, and we settled back into our beds, too hyper to sleep. I stared into the darkness and prayed and in the quiet of the night I heard Him say, "Well, you asked me for My fire!" With a giggle and smile, I whispered, "Thank you Lord, good night!"

That fall, I began taking classes again—this time at Candler School of Theology at Emory University. I had entered the United Methodist Church ministry discernment process in late 2006 and learned that my Wheaton theology degree was not enough. The UMC ordination process required a total of 10 classes from an approved school. Seven of those ten classes, I had taken at Wheaton, but I still needed to take three UMC-specific courses—history, theology, and polity—from a UMC college or university. Candler was one of those 12 approved universities, and it was in Atlanta, so two days a week I made a three-hour round trip to Candler. Fortunately, theology and history are two of my favorite subjects because the Atlanta traffic was my worst nightmare. Ironically, Candler's fall break week coincided with a Parish Nurse Coordinator's course held in St. Louis at Eden Theological Seminary and, somehow, I had the money, so I took the course. "Okay, Lord, now I am a parish nurse coordinator, but I don't have any nurses to coordinate," I said, knowing that He already knew. Then I waited to see what God would do.

Following the break, I received disturbing news. Candler would not accept my Wheaton classes, which meant I now needed a total of 10 classes to meet the UMC ordination requirements. I was NOT happy! Why, Lord? Why did I have to go all the way to Wheaton, in Chicago, in the snow, when I could have just gone to Candler instead? Then I began to doubt. Was God calling me to ordination? Did I really need to have more classes? I was frustrated and full of questions that tormented me throughout the whole month of October. Finally, I stopped arguing with God and said, "Okay, Lord. What's a few more classes and another year or two if that is what you want me to do." Then I accepted the idea of commuting to Atlanta to get it done.

A few weeks later, when registration opened for Spring semester, I requested a full load of courses and when I got my schedule, I had gotten them all. I was enrolled in all the courses I wanted, with the professors I wanted and the times that I had needed. I was elated and took this as confirmation that I was proceeding according to God's will. But that assurance did not last long.

Two weeks before the semester began, I received a notice that if my tuition was not paid in five days, I would be dropped from enrollment. Well, of course the tuition needed to be paid, but I did not have the money. In fact, I had not even thought about the money. I assumed that since I needed to take the additional courses and since I had gotten the perfect schedule, that the money would be forthcoming, but it was not and it did not, so my courses were dropped. The perfect courses, with the best professors, at the exact times I wanted them, gone! Now what? I was speechless.

While I was trying to recover from shock over the dropped classes and figure out what to do about school, a friend called to tell me that Carol Jelke, RN, and Director of Home Health at Athens Regional Medical Center was interested in parish nursing. We had both worked together at ARMC for years, and I did not really know her well, but I contacted her, and we made plans to get together. Just before our first meeting, Carol had surgery for a broken patella, so when we met, she was weak, pale, and in pain. Still, we talked for hours, sharing our passion for parish nursing. Weekly we met to pray and plan how to cultivate parish nursing in the Athens, Georgia, area. Over the next few months, we wrote a comprehensive business plan that we shared with Athens Regional and St. Mary's hospitals. The VP for Human Resources at ARMC, took the plan with a promise to consider it, but ten years later I learned he never shared it with the CEO or the administrative team. Sister Patricia , VP for Community at STMH, was interested in the parish nursing and shared with me her experiences as a nurse and missionary in Africa. Sister Patricia read the plan and seriously considered how parish nursing could be added to her division, but their budget would not allow it.

Without the support of the hospitals, Carol and I decided to go it alone. After months of research, consultations, and much prayer, we formed a non-profit organization called the Parish Nurse Resource Center. We shared our vision with colleagues and acquaintances and recruited a board of directors, who crafted a mission, vision, and articles of incorporation. I was president, Carol was vice-president, Martha Kimbrell was Treasurer, and Kathy Parish was secretary. Attorney Alec Hodson filed the paperwork and the Parish Nurse Resource Center (PNRC) became a legal entity.

The PNRC was committed to whole person health, serving God by helping people live physically, mentally, and spiritually healthy lives. PNRC sought to heighten awareness and understanding of the role of the spirit in health and healing, foster collaboration within the faith and healthcare communities, improve access to appropriate resources, decrease fragmentation in the healthcare system, and reduce incidence of preventable diseases and injuries. This was accomplished through the recruitment and development of parish nurses and through the formation and support of health and wellness ministries.

That spring while Carol and I were working on PNRC, I was invited to attend a Walk to Emmaus. The retreat was memorable to say the least. The first speaker was a preacher speaking on prevenient grace and, even though I knew him and the subject matter well, I will never forget my response. As I listened, I sensed my heart growing inside my chest, so large that I thought it would explode. It seemed to leap out of me towards him as I sensed a deep, deep longing and ache to be where he was. Not to be who he was, but, somehow, it was as if I knew I was supposed to do what he was doing. I almost cried aloud the ache was so strong, and I became frustrated, simultaneously recognizing an unborn desire and hopelessly rejecting it at the same time. How will I ever do what he was doing? Why have such a deep desire and yet not be able to satisfy it? I was reeling with conflicting thoughts and stole glances at my tablemates to see if I was being obvious. Thankfully not.

The next afternoon, during chapel, I prayed and then sat quietly to hear what the Lord might say. "Lord, what do you want me to know? What is your heart's desire for me about that strange reaction to the speaker," I asked?

The Lord said, "It is a God-given desire, Debbie, you cannot control it. Receive it. Allow it to flow. Cry out for it, it is your place." God spoke of repositioning me and invited me to consummate our relationship, which I understood to mean trusting myself to Him by laying down my protection of myself. I prayed for God's help. I prayed about my willingness to do that. My desire was that there be nothing between us, but love—absolutely no protection or guarding of myself from Him.

I said, "I trust You, Lord, with school, with nursing, with Gary and Andy and Gary. I trust you Lord with our relationship, but what does that look like, Lord? What do I need to know?" Then I watched as God took my heart out of me and put it in His heart and then put it back in me. It was strangely warm and radiating. His heart was so much bigger than mine, it completely absorbed my heart. No more barriers between us. Our hearts had become one flesh.

"You know I love you," the Lord said, "I can see your heart and feel your love. There is no deceit in our love. You hear me and I lead you. Walk quietly beside me through the life I've called you to lead."

That night, at the altar I shared with a pastor this burning desire to speak and God's leading to stop trying to protect myself from Him. The pastor laid a hand on my head and prayed and then said, "Debbie, it sounds to me like you need to preach," and with a passion that surprised myself, I replied, "I will die trying to speak God's Word." Upon returning to my cabin, I found a card on my pillow, which read, "For the preaching of the cross is to them that perish foolishness, but unto us which are saved it is the power of God (1 Cor. 1:18).

Soon I went to bed, but, alas, NOT to sleep. Instead, I swam all night long, restlessly tossing and turning, trying to get comfortable and be quiet, because my every move was announced by the plastic mattress cover on my bunk bed so loudly that I knew I was disturbing my cabin mates. I prayed and tried every sleep-inducing tip I knew, but alarming thoughts kept popping into my mind. Preaching—me? More school, surely not! An MDiv would be ridiculous. I'd never heard of anyone having three master's. I prayed and commanded myself to relax and go to sleep and forget all that stuff, but then I'd have another thought that would send shock waves of tension throughout my body.

Through the wee hours of the morning, I struggled with myself, or at least that is what I thought until finally it dawned on me that God was keeping me awake to listen to Him. So, I decided to listen. "Lord," I said, "are YOU telling me you want me to get a M.Div.?" Well, amazingly, something like relief seemed to be the answer. I stopped struggling and got still. Intently I considered the price of an M.Div., not in money, for I knew God would provide the dollars, but of the time, the study, and the delay again in taking my place in God's plan. Then, I counted the cost of disobedience, rebellion, and separation from God. "Lord, I'll get an M.Div. if that is what You want"—and then, I slept!

Almost immediately it seemed, I woke with a start and sat bolt upright in the bed. There were ladies and coffee and laughter and joy in our little room. Ohhhhh, what a short night, I moaned to myself as I struggled to shake myself awake. "Good morning! How did you sleep?" they chirped. "Well, I slept pretty good," bemoaned one woman, "that is, until Debbie woke me up," OH NO, my heart sank. "I'm so, so sorry," I said, "I tried to be quiet."

"Oh, I did not hear you," she said. "I was dreaming. I dreamed that I walked into a church and there you were—standing behind the pulpit, in a blue dress—preaching!"

"Yes Lord," I literally cried in the shower, "Yes, Lord, I'll go!"

Okay, so now it was not just 10 courses I needed, I was to get another master's degree, but I still needed money and it was too late to apply for a scholarship for fall semester. I needed to change my status at Candler from part time to degree seeking and then apply for a scholarship, but I had until January to get it all done. In the next few months, I told my prayer partners and friends the amazing story, but I did not do any of the things I needed to do to make it happen. Over time, the clarity of God's direction blurred, and I began to believe and even say that as soon as God confirmed his directions to me, I would apply. Before long, I had forgotten about them altogether.

In early January, Jean Holley, Director of Parish Nursing at Gwinnett Medical Center, invited me to go to a Southeastern Parish Nurse Coordinators' meeting in Orlando, Florida. We talked non-stop during the eight-hour drive and long into the night, but it was not until the next morning at breakfast that I told her about my experience on the Walk to Emmaus. I ended it with the same caveat that I had said so many times over the past few months, "Just as soon as God confirms that to me, I will apply."

"He already did," Jean said, looking sternly into my eyes. "Debbie, He confirmed it in the dream about you preaching in a blue dress." Somehow when Jean said that all the memories of that night came rushing back, crystal clear. God had confirmed his word. I knew beyond the shadow of a doubt that I was to get a Master of Divinity, but I had spent the last six or seven months doing nothing. Now it was January.

Oswald Chambers writes, "I know when the instructions have come from God because of their quiet persistence. But when I begin to weigh the pros and cons, and doubt and debate enter into my mind, I am bringing in an element that is not of God." Oh Lord, please forgive me, I cried. Am I too late? Well, almost!

As soon as I got home, I emailed Candler admissions and requested a change in my status. Then I called and emailed their financial aid department and quickly completed the paperwork they sent. It was Wednesday and—somehow, someway—on

Friday I received acceptance into the Master of Divinity program, a small scholarship, and a federal loan.

Now I did not want to go back to school. I did not want another master's degree and I was probably still frustrated that my Wheaton degree was not enough for the ministry, but God had given me an indisputable, undeniable direction and I had not obeyed. I was shocked and heartbroken at what I had done. Please forgive me, Lord, for I have clearly sinned. I told you that I would go, but I did not, and I can now see how my delay in obeying you separated me farther and farther from you and your will. Thank you, Lord for sending Jean to help me get back to you. Thank you for forgiving me and for helping me get accepted and get a scholarship.

FCN Graduation

Debbie Huckaby

Preacher in a Blue Dress

FCN Graduation Class 2007

Leading 3 day retreat

I Can Rest, Lord, Because of You!

In June 2009, Jean Holley asked me to consider applying for the position of Education Coordinator in the Parish Nurse Department of Gwinnett Medical Center. I prayed and sensed this would be a good way to learn more about parish nursing, and, since it was part time, I could still do it along with taking classes at Candler. I applied and was offered the job, but another even more amazing opportunity occurred before my first day there.

During the Parish Nurse (now Faith Community Nurse) course, I was introduced to the work of Dr. Harold G. Koenig, a psychiatrist, professor, author, and the Director of Spirituality and Health at Duke University in Chapel Hill, North Carolina. Dr. Koenig had begun offering a five-day research intensive course each August on spirituality and health, which was very interesting. The cost was $1500, which fortunately I had available. I also had that week free, so I applied late in July and got the last seat. Part of the intensive included an hour interview with one of the instructors and because I was the last to be admitted, Dr. Koenig said all the other professor's appointments were filled so I would be "stuck with him." That was definitely not a problem to me. I was elated and could not imagine getting an hour interview with someone who had written more than 260 scientific peer-reviewed articles, 60 chapters in professional books, and authored more than 35 books on spirituality and health.

The Spirituality and Health Research course exceeded my expectations. I learned about 30 years of studies that show, in summary, that people who maintain spiritual practices stay healthier, have fewer hospitalizations and surgeries, and recover more quickly after hospitalizations. To my surprise, however, the research course was designed to help the participants with their own research, but I was not doing any research and had no plans to do so. Five years later I found out that God did, and this intensive was just the beginning.

As so often happens in my life events, orientation at Gwinnett Medical Center (GMC) coincided with orientation to Candler School of Theology. To help with school and travel, I purchased a new laptop and a new iPhone. So, all in the same week, I was learning to drive a new car, use a new phone and computer, navigate Atlanta rush hour traffic, orient to graduate school, and understand the policies and procedures of a new employer. What was I thinking? By the end of the week, my life was moving at such a pace that I was making lists of lists just to keep up.

What I remember most about that week, however, was a "God moment" that happened my first day at Candler. During orientation to Emory and the School of Theology, the speaker asked us to introduce ourselves to the others at our tables of 10. Each person gave their name, hometown and one thing about themselves. The lady directly across the table from me gave her name and laughed and looked right at me and said, "I know you are going to think I am nuts, but this will be my third master's degree." I could not help but laugh aloud. Sixteen months had passed since the night I wrestled with God about a Master of Divinity. "I've never even heard of anyone with three masters," I had said that night. Well, now I had and, thankfully, by God's grace and patience with me, I was where He had wanted me to be all along.

That fall, along with starting a new job and pursuing another degree, I was preparing to lead a three-day St. James UMC women's ministry retreat. I had worked with the seminar coordinators for months to envision and plan, but time to work on my own messages was often usurped by school and work. I had never led a retreat before, so I was creating the messages, slides, exercises, and prayers from scratch. Abundant life was the topic and I had plenty of material to draw from, but a couple of weeks before the seminar, I was near panic. In tears, I cried out to God, "Help, Lord Jesus, please help." When the tears subsided and I sat in exhausted silence, I felt God drawing me closer and closer into His incredible presence. Peace enveloped me like a blanket and these words began pouring into my head and heart.

I Can Rest, Lord, Because You Are Elohim

You created the world and You created me. You hold me in the palm of Your hand. I will never be somewhere that you can't find me because Your eye is now and has and always will be upon me. You created me for a purpose, to prosper me and not to harm me. I can rest because You created me to enjoy life…life in You and life with You.

I Can Rest, Lord, Because You Are Jehovah Jireh

You are my Provider. You guide me and provide for all my needs.

Like the birds, Lord, you provide my food and water and clothes. You give me the desires of my heart. You make a way in the desert and a path through the seas. When I walk through the waters, they will not overflow me and when I walk through the fires, I will not be scorched. You are omniscient. You know what I need, and You are good, so I can rest knowing that what You provide will be good for me always and forever.

I Can Rest, Lord, Because You Are Jehovah Raah

You are my Shepherd. You bring me to the green grass to nourish and comfort my body. You give me quiet waters to soothe my fears and replenish my soul. You protect me with your rod and keep me close with your staff. You take responsibility for me. You are the good Shepherd. I can rest because You are always looking out for me.

I Can Rest, Lord, Because You Are Jehovah Rapha

You are my Healer. I am healed by You and You only. You know me completely…not one cell is hidden from You. You created each one. You know my needs. You see what is hidden from human eyes and understanding and what you once created you can always repair or replace. You give me life and life abundantly.

I Can Rest, Lord, Because You Are Jehovah Sabaaoth

You are the Lord of Hosts. You are mighty and victorious. You are omnipotent. No one or nothing can command You. There is nothing that can move Your hand. Your will, will be done. Who can be against me if You are for me, and I know You are for me. You have the power to make me poof and be gone forever, yet You fight for me...You even died for me. I can rest because with You on my side I know that I will never be forsaken.

I Can Rest, Lord, Because You Are Jehovah Shalom

You are my peace. Your peace, not like the world's kind of peace, is beyond all my understanding. You are perfect peace, and You keep me in perfect peace with Yourself because my eyes, my heart, and my mind are fixed on You. In You, I walk upon the waters in a storm. I soar on eagles' wings far above the strife of the world. I am at peace with You and within myself. I am at peace with others. I can rest because I am cradled in Your arms in sweet peace.

I Can Rest, Lord, Because of You! You are MY God. I am YOUR child. We are ONE. I Can Rest in You.

Somehow the lecture notes, slides, exercises, and prayers came together, and I successfully facilitated the retreat with a peace and presence only possible through the Lord Jesus Christ. Through that experience I found I thoroughly enjoyed teaching and I am forever humbled and grateful for the beautiful prayer that calmed and centered me in his strength. I also embarrassed myself and learned a hard lesson in the way the seminar ended.

It was Sunday morning, and after having breakfast and checking out of our rooms, we assembled for a morning worship service. I had planned to end the seminar and service with communion. Rev. Dr. Jerry Meredith had consecrated the elements, and the table was prepared before the service began. I conducted the service and preached the sermon and brought the seminar and service to an end with my prayer. Then, a couple of minutes later, I realized with a shock that I had forgotten communion. I was so embarrassed! Some participants had already left and everyone else was gathering their belongings and sharing goodbyes, but I regathered them together and we shared communion. Then we said our goodbyes. Fighting tears of exhaustion and humiliation, I returned the elements to nature and made my way to the lake. Sitting alone in the quiet, staring at the water, breathing deeply of the cool breeze, I placed the seminar, the participants, and the fumbled communion service in Jesus' hands and found peace.

It Helps to Have a Personal Mission Statement

One speaker at the parish nurse meeting Jean and I attended impacted my life significantly. J. Keith Miller, counselor, and author of more than 20 books including the bestselling book The Taste of New Wine, spoke about his latest book What to Do with the Rest of Your Life: Awakening and Achieving Your Unspoken Dreams. It was not so much Miller's presentation as the book itself that changed my life. I bought it and read it cover to cover. Then I read it again, taking copious notes, and one more time through it as I developed a curriculum to teach the book. Why? I did not know. I just knew that I was passionately driven to learn and apply that book, and as I began implementing the steps Miller recommended, I was even more driven to share what I had learned with others.

A seminar, that is what I could do. So, I crafted the material into a one-day seminar, reserved a room at Jennings Mill Country Club on April 9, 2009, acquired additional copies of the book, created an announcement flyer, and sent it to friends and acquaintances. Twelve attendees came to answer the questions: Why are you here? What plans has God written in your DNA?

Two of the attendees applied the principles to their lives and started ministries of their own.

While I was studying and teaching the techniques in Miller's book, I acquired a practical tool that helps me keep my life in focus. One that I am still using today. It is a personal mission statement, a statement of who I am and how I am to use the gifts and graces God created in me. It has given me a richer, more content perspective on my past experiences and, along with prayer, helps me determine which opportunities, now and in the future, are right for me and which ones are not.

Personal Mission Statement

Spiritual gifts: Leadership, Prophecy, Teaching

A. I minister whole person health by speaking and writing God's word and by facilitating individual and group new beginnings.

Speaking and Writing God's Word
1. Preach and teach
2. Write and administer courses
3. Write books and commentaries
   a. The Bible and Healing
   b. Praying for Whole Person Health
   c. Memoirs

Facilitating Individual and Corporate New Beginnings
1. Prayer ministry
2. Personal consultation
3. Resource liaison
4. Facilitate individual and corporate new beginnings
   a. Develop and implement personal mission statement
   b. Develop and implement group endeavors

B. I exemplify whole person health
   1. Relationship with God

2. Conduit of God's love to family
3. Physical size and strength
4. Eating nutritious food
5. Stimulating mental faculties
6. Striving for financial freedom
7. Simplifying personal possessions

C. Build a City of Refuge

D. See statues in Texas

In March 2009, WINGS, the Christian women's group that God formed through me, asked me to lead them through Miller's principles on What to Do with the Rest of Your Life. I revised the seminar curriculum by expanding it to include individual and small group exercises, and prayer and devotion time, and we spent three days working through it in the beautiful mountains of Highlands, N.C.

Candler: The Bride, The King, AND The Lion of Judah

Almost every day that year, I would get up very early, drive to Atlanta ahead of the traffic, attend classes; stop at GMC for a few hours of work, and then head home to study. It was a hectic pace, but I believed that I was where God wanted me. Still, I was overwhelmed with it all, and one day, the traffic was even worse than usual! As I inched along the five miles from the school to the I-285 loop, I prayed. What am I doing here, Lord? I am so tired. I don't know how I can keep up this pace. You know how old I am! Tears filled my eyes as I pleaded. Please, Lord, give me peace and help me know that I am where I should be.

After thirty minutes of this, I finally made it to the 285 by-pass and took the merge lane but looking back over my shoulder and in the mirrors, I was literally stunned by what I saw or did not see. Wowwww!! I blinked and my mouth fell wide open. It was 5:00 in the afternoon, one of the busiest hours of the day in Atlanta, and the six-lane Atlanta autobahn was EMPTY!! NOT A CAR IN SIGHT! Not a car behind me or in front of me as far as I could see. I was alone in Atlanta on 285 during rush hour. Now, that was a sheer impossibility! Was there a rapture and I was left?

As I moved along the empty highway and looked around me in wide-eyed wonder, a thought made me laugh and cry at the same time! Well, Lord, You parted the waters so the children of Israel could pass through on dry land so I guess You can part the Atlanta traffic too. Tears of joy ran down my face. "Thank you, Lord, for loving me so much!"

About a mile or two later, cars began to appear behind and ahead of me and come alongside but the parting of the traffic that day on 285 stays with me as a sweet but powerful reminder that our Lord hears us when we cry and is always able to do exceedingly abundantly above all we can think or ask.

My year at Candler was hard, and not just physically. I was stretched in all aspects. I only survived through constant prayer. While the academic learning was stimulating and the new culture was interesting, the spiritual climate was cold. I truly believe that if I had not known Jesus Christ as Lord before, I certainly would not have found Him there. Through the Candler population of students and professors, and more specifically through my weekly reflection group, I became acquainted with fellow students from a wide variety of backgrounds, beliefs, and practices. Each week we met with a professor and a site supervisor to discuss the weekly readings and apply them to our lives.

Feelings and thoughts experienced during reading, reflection and discussion allowed wounds to surface so that healing could begin. The chosen method of healing, however, was somewhat synonymous with debriding a red, swollen and deeply infected wound without anesthesia. Through a bombardment of questions, accusations, insinuations, and cynical harassments, including profanity, the student (or victim) of the day was systematically stripped of all confidence in their own beliefs and personal awareness. The process was painful to watch and extremely painful to experience. Of the twelve students in my group, one attempted suicide and three soon left the college and their calling.

As the oldest student in the group, my age, white hair, and different interests were especially obvious. Yet, as a nurse, I am skilled at maintaining proper control of my demeanor until I am in private, which, of course, was not a tolerated response in the weekly healing encounters. This was the reality of my life in late spring of 2010 as I neared the end of my Con-Ed course at Candler. Wednesday, April 14, 2010, was the last day of Con-Ed and, more ominously, it was the day I was scheduled for the surgical table under the professor's scalpel. I knew that prayer was the only way I would make it through the inquisition.

The day before, I had left GMC about 5:00 in the afternoon and checked into a small hotel a few miles from Candler and spent the evening studying. I was reading an article for my preaching class on imagination when I came to a sudden convicting realization that I had kept my imagination from God's use, so in repentance I prayed for forgiveness and gave my imagination to God again. I prayed again for peace and protection in the class and then tried to sleep.

I began the next morning, with the usual coffee and prayer time and then set about getting dressed. I was tired and stressed, but somehow at peace. I knew that I was not alone and that, somehow, I would get through it. As I was putting on my makeup, the mirror changed and suddenly there before me was the Con-Ed classroom and the professor. I blinked and stared when into that room walked the Bride adorned in the most amazingly beautiful gown of lights in all different colors. I thanked God for what He was allowing me to see and asked what else He wanted me to see. Then, the King entered the room, and the aura, brilliance and authority of His majesty was almost more than I could bear. The joy that bubbled up in me was overwhelming and I giggled and laughed out loud. So, I asked again. "Lord, is there anything else you want me to see?" And then I heard…I literally heard birds singing and saw a HUGE lion walk into the room and just stand there in quiet authority. The Lion of Judah, HUGE and powerful, yet elegant, and gentle with the most beautiful eyes.

WOW!!! I was overwhelmed, speechless and so excited. The Bride, The King AND The Lion of Judah all came to show me the support and protection I would have in that classroom that day. Thank you, Lord! Thank you! I was ready! I knew God would protect me and I could not wait to see what God would do or say to the professor when he got his scalpel after me.

But he didn't. He did not get his scalpel after me; in fact, he did not even see me. He did not mention me. He did not call on me. He did not say my name. Somehow, I was invisible. He never fired one question, accusation, insinuation, or cynical remark at me or anyone. He didn't even remember that I was to give my "victim of the day" presentation. The others watched and grinned. I even responded to something he said, and he didn't even acknowledge that I had spoken. I was invisible, miraculously hidden by The Bride, The King, and The Lion of Judah.

Finding Home at Asbury Theological Seminary

One weekend that spring semester I attended a True Identity conference at Strong Rock Camp with friends Debbie Jones and Pam Brown. Debbie wanted me to meet Marilyn Goss. When I met Marilyn, she immediately said, "Debbie, you've got to meet my husband, Bill." He was on the board of Asbury Theological Seminary and wanted to talk with me about Asbury. I had been through so much getting everything settled at Candler that I really did not want to think about another school. Besides, it was a women's conference, so I did not think too much about talking with Bill until I found out that he and several men were there at the conference preparing and serving the meals. Soon, Bill stopped by and introduced himself to me. We talked briefly and I agreed to a telephone appointment the next week.

Bill and Marilyn called that next Thursday and talked for about an hour while Bill regaled the attributes of Asbury Theological Seminary (ATS). He insisted that I check out ATS. I typically regarded such situations as doors that God had placed in my path. I have always believed that I should try to turn the knob. It might open and it might not. If it opened, I believed that

I should attempt to enter and walk the proverbial hallway as far as possible, believing that God's grace would lead the way or stop me according to His will. So, I agreed as Bill requested and set out to find out more about Asbury.

I explored the ATS website and read the mission statement: Asbury Seminary is a community called to prepare theologically educated, sanctified, Spirit-filled men and women to evangelize and to spread scriptural holiness throughout the world through the love of Jesus Christ, in the power of the Holy Spirit and to the glory of God the Father. My heart leapt at the very thought. Now I sincerely wanted to know more.

A friend, Phyllis Kiser, was attending Asbury, so I asked if she would talk with me about her experience at ATS and when we talked, she convinced me to come to Wilmore, Kentucky, and let her show me around the campus. My friend Pam agreed to go with me and that May 2010, during finals week, Phyllis spent the better part of two days introducing us to her beloved school. We took pictures of the statute of John Wesley in the quadrangle and ate at the local landmark restaurant, The Porch. My breath caught in my throat when we visited Estes Chapel, the beautiful historic sanctuary where so many sermons, prayers, graduations, ordinations, and weddings had taken place, and I pondered the many ways that lives had been changed in that very room. Then, as if that thought was a prophecy over my own life, the Holy Spirit engulfed me from head to toe and I knew that Asbury was where I should be.

In the fall of 2010, I returned to Asbury as a full-time Master of Divinity student. It was a seven-hour trip from my house to campus, two hours just to get to the other side of Atlanta. Being in the correct lane and taking the correct exits were significant matters of prayer for me each trip. I always prayed,

Lord, please send your mighty warrior angels to keep the cars and animals and debris on the road away from me. Help me be in the correct lane at the correct time and help me see the signs and roads I need to take. Well, I hadn't made too many trips before I recognized His amazing answer. I traveled from Athens, Georgia, halfway was Athens, Tennessee, and my exit was Athens, Kentucky. Most importantly, walking the campus in the cool Kentucky breeze, I sensed the presence of the Prince of Peace Himself and a peace that only He gives permeated my being, settled all my uncertainties, and affirmed that all my directions were correct. In an unexplainable way, Asbury felt like home.

While attending classes at Asbury, both online and on-campus, I continued to work at GMC where it was my responsibility as Education Coordinator to provide monthly educational opportunities for the 10-15 Faith Community Nurses affiliated with GMC and to coordinate an annual basic preparation course for new FCNs. I had attained FCN faculty status through the International Parish Nurse Resource Center in August of 2010 and thereafter rewrote the GMC prep course curriculum. Our course capacity was 16 and soon we were offering it twice a year and maintaining a waiting list a year in advance.

I was also completing UMC ordination paperwork. I had become a candidate for ordination in 2010 and had spent a year under the mentorship of Rev. Allen Smith, pastor of the Young Harris UMC here in Athens and Rev. Dr. Jerry Meredith at St. James UMC. I completed the ten required courses at Asbury and was recommended by my district to the North Georgia Conference Board of Ministry. On an appointed day, I would be interviewed by three groups, Theology and Doctrine, Practice of Ministry and Called and Disciplined Life at Simpsonwood, the conference headquarters. In preparation for those interviews, I submitted 114 pages in answer to 33 questions, a Bible study, and a video of a sermon I had prepared and preached.

I had reviewed my paperwork and felt well prepared for my interview on March 15, 2011, and I felt good with my answers once the interview was over. I waited with the whole group of candidates in a room, sitting and staring, pacing and praying, until one by one we were escorted to a private room and given the verdict. I was tense, but not overly anxious because I believed I was where I was supposed to be and I knew that my preparation had been immersed in prayer.

To my utter shock, I was informed that the UMC Board of Ministry did not think I was Wesleyan enough. I was deferred with conditions that I take a leadership position in a church for a year, work with five mentors over the next year and rewrite the answers to some of the questions. I thanked those who delivered the message and somehow made it to my car, struggling to make sense of it all. Deferred, what did that mean? Why? What could I have done wrong or said wrong? What would happen next? I called Gary and Pam with the sad news and drove the 30 miles home in stunned silence. Not Wesleyan enough was their assessment of me and yet ironically that very night, while I was participating in the UMC Board of Ministry interviews, I was missing my initiation ceremony into the International Theological Honor Society, Theta Phi at Asbury, a Wesleyan Seminary in Wilmore, Kentucky.

An Asbury Doctorate and the UMC

So now, I was working at GMC, going to school full time at Asbury in Kentucky, leading the Georgia Parish Nurse Resource Center, and meeting monthly with five UMC mentors on different days in separate locations. I was also looking for a leadership position in a church. Dr. Steve Bingham, the pastor of Mars Hill Baptist Church and a director on the GPNRC board, was aware of my dilemma and unbeknownst to me asked the D.S. to recommend me to Rev. Parker Benson at Bethlehem First United Methodist Church. Bethlehem was approximately half the distance between my house and GMC yet I had never been to the little town of Bethlehem, Georgia, and had never seen the beautiful white church on the hill. Just a year earlier, Jean Holley had a sudden inspiration during a meeting one day that I should start a Faith Community Nurse Ministry there. The D.S. called me with the suggestion, and I promptly made an appointment with Rev. Parker Benson.

On April 26, 2011, I pulled into the parking lot of Bethlehem First United Methodist Church and knew by an immediate overwhelming sense of God's peace that I was to be there. Rev.

Benson was tall and slim. His voice, smile, and mannerisms were gentle and kind. We talked for more than an hour and I asked him to be my mentor for the UMC and for a mentored membership class I was taking at Asbury. He agreed and welcomed me to his staff, beginning with a staff meeting the next Monday. So, adding BFUMC to my schedule meant I was working simultaneously at GMC, BFUMC, GPNRC, taking classes and complying with the gyrations of the UMC, and by the grace of God, I survived it all.

At GMC, Jean Holley had retired at the end of 2011, and I had become the full-time manager of the Faith Community Nurses. In early 2012, Bob Duvall, Director of Chaplaincy, gave me an article about a remarkable model in Memphis, Tennessee, at Methodist Le Bonheur Hospital called the Congregational Health Network. That network was a collaboration between the hospital and the pastors in more than 500 churches in the Memphis area designed to promote the health of the community. The Network was under the auspices of Rev. Gary Gunderson, a former Baptist pastor and current VP at the hospital. In June of 2012, I was scheduled to attend a Health Ministries Association Conference in Nashville, Tennessee, so I contacted Rev. Gunderson and scheduled a site visit with him to learn more about the network.

Jean Holley and I attended the conference in Nashville together and then drove over to Memphis, met Madeline Van Dyck, GPNRC Vice President, and attended the site visit at Methodist Le Bonheur Hospital. After the hospital presentations, their Chaplaincy staff took us over to the Church Health Center, where we were given an overview of their services and a tour of their building. Both the Congregational Health Network and the Church Health Center were extraordinary concepts. All the way home, Jean and I discussed the possibility of having such entities in Georgia.

Back at GMC the concepts monopolized my thinking, and I shared the innovative ideas with everyone around me. I told the FCN staff and nurses and then Bob Duvall and his Assistant, Chuck Christie, and Steve Nadeau, the VP for our department. Each person I told suggested others for me to tell. So I did, and the numbers grew and grew. By August, someone had recommended me to the leadership team. My presentation came in late September and was unanimously received. I had presented the Congregational Health Network concepts and made a proposal to form a team to study the feasibility of such a network at GMC. The leadership team eagerly listened, asked questions, and shared potential benefits. With their vote of confidence, I began.

The Network feasibility team met every week from October to June and determined that a collaborative agreement between the medical center and the churches in Gwinnett County would positively impact community health and far outweigh the medical center's cost. The proposal was approved by the leadership team and a fall 2013 kickoff was planned. When Rev. Gary Gunderson agreed to be our keynote speaker, the response was overwhelming. With more than 145 people attending and three churches signing up, we all agreed the day was a success.

Most of the medical center's expense was the salary and operational support of a Faith Community nurse navigator, the key difference between GMC's network and the Memphis model. Mary Cooper, an experienced FCN in a Presbyterian church in Snellville and one of the first FCNs at GMC, had sensed God's leading to the position and was the first to apply. Interviewing Mary was a joy. She said she watched the evolution of the FC Network and admired my leadership and even though she loved her position at church, she had not been able to get the idea of the FC Network Navigator position out of her head. Mary soon became the GMC's FC network navigator and the only FCN navigator in the nation. With Mary, the FC Network grew to eight churches and 16,000 members over the next year.

My work at BFUMC had started out in 2011 on a volunteer basis when Parker was my UMC and ATS mentor. I attended staff meetings, Wednesday night teaching, and Sunday services. I especially liked the 8:30 Holy Communion service in the little chapel and the 11:00 traditional service in the big, beautiful sanctuary. Soon, Parker added to my duties. First, he asked me to preach during the summer at Fort Yargo State Park. I quickly accepted and preached there every Sunday morning between the two BFUMC services. One Sunday morning, I was shocked to find a six-foot grey colored snake waiting for me when I arrived, but thankfully it didn't stay for the service.

Then Rev. Harold Corbin, the pastor for the Holy Communion service, retired and Parker asked if I would like to take that position. I could not believe it. I was a few months away from graduating with my Master Divinity degree and had not yet been approved by the UMC BOM, but Parker and the SPPRC (Staff Pastor Parish Relations Committee) wanted me to be the Congregational Care pastor. That meant working 15 hours a week, officiating at the 8:30 Holy Communion Service, and providing pastoral support for the entire congregation. I knew God had called me to preach and finally having a pulpit to preach every Sunday was an indescribable blessing.

Each Sunday I assisted Parker during the 11:00 traditional service by reading Scripture, bringing the invocation, praying at the altar with people, and assisting with Holy Communion and baptisms. That service was the most impressive to me, not only because of the beautiful setting but also because of the liturgy Parker conducted during that service. He and I and the music minister wore robes and often led a procession of the choir, also in robes, into the sanctuary. The services considered "high church" liturgy, including recitation of the Apostle's Creed and the Lord's Prayer along with singing of the Doxology and the Gloria Patri. Communion was according to the UMC Great Thanksgiving liturgy. Parker served me and I served him and then we served eight pairs of servers who spread out across the front of the sanctuary. Baptisms, especially infant baptisms, included the whole family and followed the UMC Worship liturgy. Usually, every Sunday Parker highlighted a ministry or activity and those who participated in it. I loved the ancient declarations of our faith in word and song and the worship traditions that cultivated a reverent and worshipful atmosphere from the beginning processional to ending recessional.

I remember my first Christmas Eve service there. The beautiful sanctuary lit with twinkling candles, the smell of decorative greenery, the familiar carols led by a full choir and Minister of Music, Karen Smith, the crowd of worshippers attentively listening to the story of Christ's birth. From my place on the chancel, I prayed. Thank you, heavenly Father, for this amazing blessing. Here I am in Bethlehem on Christmas Eve. It was more than I could have ever imagined.

I had so many wonderful ministry experiences with Parker and the other pastors, Matt and Michele, and staff Karen W., Karen S. and Lizzy; like assisting Parker with the Great Thanksgiving (Holy Communion) in the sanctuary for the first time, and being overcome with emotion during the Ash Wednesday service when Michele and I made the sign of the cross with palm ashes on the foreheads of hundreds of our members, preaching in Bethlehem at Christmas and Easter, the Sunrise services on the front steps of the church and the Maundy Thursday service in the graveyard of the old church building. Parker even gave me the opportunity to conduct funerals and officiate weddings. I remember the Wednesday night classes I taught, the small group ministry called Grow Groups that I tried to initiate, not too successfully, and the systems I was responsible for administering (keys, vehicles). Of those systems, the Emergency Preparedness Plan was perhaps my best legacy.

We had heard that church services across north Georgia were being interrupted by masked men, yelling threatening Muslim phrases, and the government had published an Emergency Plan for religious organizations. When the UMC District appointed an Emergency Preparedness initiative, BFUMC trustees decided the church needed a plan. A committee was formed, and I was the facilitator. Members of the committee included law enforcement, firefighters, paramedics, retired military, and even a woman who worked writing such plans for insurance companies. Additionally, multiple other law enforcement officers and firefighters were usually in attendance in all four worship services. While we had a plan and believed it would work well, we did not really want to test it, but before long we did.

For about six months an unusual man had attended our 11 AM traditional service. I say unusual because he always came in just as the service was starting, wore the same brown pants and brown casual jacket, and sat in the same seat on the second row from the front on the right side of the sanctuary. That is, until one Sunday in April when Mr. Beckett wore a heavy green wool military coat, green fatigue pants, and a hat. Wool in Georgia in the spring was quickly noticed by many, especially the Emergency Preparedness team members who cautiously seated themselves nearby. The service went as expected until the end. Parker was preaching on death. "Why are we shocked when the doctor says you are gonna die," Parker preached. "You are gonna die. We are ALL going to die."

Then, as if on cue, Mr. Beckett muttered quite loudly, "Yeah and you're gonna die sooner than later." With that he jumped up and headed towards the back of the sanctuary followed by several emergency preparedness members. While he was being pursued out of the building, Parker and I were quickly ushered out of the sanctuary and the people were directed to other doors. The police were called, and the two GBI agents who had been sitting in front of Mr. Beckett recounted the story. Somehow Mr. Beckett slipped away, so the church was quickly put on lockdown and searched. After a while, Mr. Beckett was located at his home where he barricaded the doors and resisted police for more than 24 hours. Eventually he was apprehended and put in prison. Our plan had worked, and lives were saved. That is what church is for, right?

Parker was not only my mentor and boss at the church, but he was also my pastor and friend. In March 2012, I was again interviewed by the Board of Ministry of the UMC North Georgia Conference and again I was deferred. The issue arose in the Theology and Doctrine interview again led by Rev. Brent Hayes. He had asked, "What do you think Wesley thought was the difference between depraved and deprived?" My answer was I do not know what Wesley thought the difference was and with a condescending sneer, Rev. Hayes then replied, "Well I suggest you find out and if you can't then call me, and I'll tell you what he thought." This time I was shocked and dismayed. I had kept all my appointments every month with all five mentors. I had rewritten the questions and I had read the Wesleyan theology books they had assigned. I knew that I had done everything that was asked of me and had done my best with every single assignment.

Unless God insists, I am done with this "going into ministry." The incongruency in my life was unbearable. For decades I had been married, but I did not really have a husband—only a facsimile, not a warm, loving, husband who really wanted to share life with me, but somehow, I had managed to stay in the marriage for the children and then out of habit. Now I was seeing a similar dichotomy in God's calling.

Ministry was God's idea. I had been at it for nine years and had had some wonderful experiences and I had grown a lot. I knew God had called me and had given me gifts and graces, especially to preach, but I was not accepted as a called and capable pastor by the UMC. I had a 3.9 GPA, had made an A in two different Wesleyan Theology courses, was in the Theta Phi Theology honor society and had a master's in theology from Wheaton, but the UMC thought I wasn't Wesleyan enough and would not accept my theology. I was done!

Friends, family, and coworkers were kind and encouraging, but Parker was incredible. He emailed saying that he "had not changed his feelings toward me one bit…the BOM yes, you no! I think you got shafted and the Staff Pastor Parish Relations Committee (SPPRC) and I still want you."

On the way to GMC the next morning, God gave me a vision of a mass of people, and I felt their immense joy. They were all beautiful, smiling, happy, peaceful, joyful, and carrying flowers and walking with me, but I am stopped by a toothpick stuck in the ground. I soon came to understand that the mass of people were the great cloud of witnesses and God let me see and feel them. Truly, God and Parker had lifted my countenance during deep disappointment. I did not know how, but I knew it would be okay.

In the summer of 2011, I took two back-to-back course intensives, which kept me on campus at Asbury for five straight weeks. I took Hebrew for the first four weeks during the month of July and then a church history class the first week of August. The Hebrew class was the hardest course I had ever taken in any degree. I got up every morning at 4:30 am, got a cup of coffee and studied until 6:00. Then after getting dressed, I studied until 7:45 and time to head to class. The class lasted 4-6 hours. Then I would eat a quick lunch, relisten to the day's lecture, and work on my homework until 12 midnight. This was life day in and day out for four straight weeks. I got little sleep and lost seven pounds eating only cereal, chicken salad, lettuce, and saltine crackers. I was staying at the home of Dr. Dale and Myrna Hale, just a mile from campus. Dale and Myrna told me later how they got up every morning to the sound of my footsteps and went to bed each night listening to the same and how they prayed fervently for me.

The night before my final exam in Hebrew my course average was 72 and that is not an acceptable passing grade. I was devastated. If I did not pass Hebrew, I would have to take it over before I could graduate with an M-Div., and it would likely be a couple of years before it was taught again as an intensive. I had done the best I could. I knew that I had given it my all. I studied in the afternoon, ate a good supper, then played worship music and lay in the floor worshipping my Lord. I surrender it all, Lord. I surrender it all. If I fail the course, I trust you will get me where you want me to go. One word I heard in response: "Doctorate." Really, Lord? A D-Min.? Well, I guess I will pass Hebrews, and the next morning I did. I took the exam and got the grade around noon. An A! WOW! I made an A in the course! How could that be? Only God could take me from a 72 to a 93 overnight. To God be the glory.

That afternoon Myrna and Dale invited me to dinner. They had been worried about me and had prayed for me morning and night. I confessed that Hebrews was the hardest course I had ever taken in my life and shared how I was praising God for taking me from a 72 to an A. To which Dale replied, "Well, you're ready for your doctorate now aren't you?" How did he know? I had not mentioned God's word "Doctorate." A wide-eyed tear-filled stare was my only response.

While working at GMC and at BFUMC, going to Asbury and dealing with the UMC, I was also leading a non-profit organization, the Georgia Parish Nurse Resource Center. Carol Jelke was vice president, followed by Madeline Van Dyck. Martha Kimbrell was the first treasurer, followed by Jean Holley. Sister Patricia Loome, Rev. Dr. Jerry Meredith, Alec Hodson, Cheryl Wunsch, and Lex Bowen were directors on the board who worked together to promote parish nursing and to support the training of new parish nurses. Cheryl took a grant writing course and researched potential grants. Through her work, GPNRC secured a grant which provided tuition for a registered nurse to attend the GMC course. I gave a presentation at ARMC during nurses' week promoting parish nursing and we provided a small gathering of guests from healthcare and ministry to share the benefits of parish nursing to both disciplines.

While we were forming the Faith Community Network at Gwinnett Medical Center, a representative of the Georgia State government contacted me with an offer to support the initiative. Through several discussions our common interests were identified, and a cooperative working agreement was made. That state department had been promoting and supporting health ministries across Georgia for several years and agreed to endorse parish nursing as an adjunct to the formation of church health ministries. Their efforts contributed to the increased demand for the GMC FCN Faith Community Nursing preparation course. Since GMC was training 32 new Faith Community Nurses a year, Georgia Parish Nurse Resource Center concluded that its mission had been met and that it should now direct its support to the nurses in their practice of Faith Community Nursing across Georgia.

Then, while we were revising the GPNRC mission, we realized that our non-profit organization was no longer adequate and that it needed to be an association. Along with a new mission statement came a new name, Georgia Faith Community Nurses Association, and new bylaws. The association held its first annual meeting and seminar in October 2013 at Bethlehem First UMC. According to the bylaws, I would serve as president and chairman of the board of directors for three years and would thereafter remain chairman emeritus of the board while the rotation of officers and committee leaders would proceed as specified in the bylaws.

I finished my M-Div. degree and participated in the graduation ceremony on December 7th in Asbury's Estes Chapel, which was decorated for Christmas and even more beautiful than usual. Gary did not attend as he had not attended my graduation at Wheaton in 2007. Dale and Myrna took me to dinner to celebrate and I drove home the next morning. As the Lord had directed, I applied to ATS Beeson Doctor of Ministry degree and was accepted to the program but did not get a scholarship. The first on-campus session would not be until fall of 2013, but paperwork, assignments, and books began to arrive in March so my break from schoolwork was short lived. ATS provided a Kindle pre-loaded with textbooks for our reading enjoyment and along with my weekly sermons, I had a lot of reading enjoyment.

I was also trying to decide what to do about the UMC. I knew God had called me and yet the UMC did not support me in that calling. Rev. Hayes had asked me what I believed Wesley thought was the difference between depraved and deprived and said that if I could not find out I should contact him. I first went back through all my Wesleyan theology books and my general theology books but could not find any reference to Wesley's discussion of depraved and deprived. Then I wrote to my Wesleyan Theology professor at Candler, Dr. Rex Matthews, explained the situation and question and asked if he could help me answer it. I also wrote Asbury Wesleyan theologian Dr. Lawrence Wood and asked for his consideration of the question. Both Dr. Matthews and Dr. Wood replied that they were not aware of Wesley ever discussing the difference between depraved and deprived. In fact, Dr. Matthews said that it was impossible to give a concise, definitive answer to the question in the form in which it was asked.

The BOM also rejected the answers to two questions that they had approved in 2011. I was not told why they were rejected, so I wrote to Dr. John Simmons, Director of Ministerial Services and Spiritual Formation for the North Georgia Conference of the United Methodist Church. Dr. Simmons was essentially in charge of the interview process at the Conference level. I explained both issues, made suggestions to help candidates more successfully comply with the interview expectations and asked permission to contact Rev. Hayes. Dr. Simmons replied with appreciation for my recommendations, which he forwarded to the new chairman of the interview process and encouraged me to contact Rev. Hayes. Additionally, Dr. Simmons said I was an accomplished professional and that, in his opinion, was a deterrent to me in building relationships with the board members.

I made an appointment with Rev. Hayes for June 21st and prayed constantly as I drove the 1 ½ hours to Northbrook UMC in North Atlanta. Standing immediately and shaking my hand across his desk, Rev. Hayes seemed surprised to see me. I introduced myself and reminded him of the question he had asked during my BOM interview. Then I told him of the places I had looked and people I had consulted to find the answer. "So, what did Wesley think was the difference between deprived and depraved," I asked. Sitting back in his chair and shaking his head, Rev. Hayes gave a low chuckle and said, "I don't really know what Wesley thought. It was just a question to see what you would do." He admitted that he was surprised to see me and respected my courage in coming to talk. I told him that I always tried to do my best…doing everything as unto the Lord Jesus. He ended with encouraging words for my next BOM interview and even asked to read my paperwork before I submitted it in September.

On July 2, I met again with the District Committee on Ministry. After a brief interview, they shared their decision not to recommend me to the BOM in November. They wanted me to wait at least another year (November 2013) before I went back to the BOM, and with that I knew I was done with the UMC. I thanked them and left, but I knew before I reached my car that I would rescind my candidacy. God had assured me that I was called to preach His word, shepherd His people, and tend His flock, and I knew God had not changed His mind. The UMC was apparently not the way, so I was relieved. Thank you,

Lord, for making it clear. I waited a couple of days and notified the D.S., Dr. John Simmons, all my mentors, and Rev. Hayes. I sighed with relief. My steps were lighter and my countenance brighter and my sleep so much sweeter.

My Sons and the Daughters They Gave Me

Underlying all these other aspects of my life is my family, especially my sons who are and have always been the apple of my eye. People have often told me that Gary and Andy are "such good boys," and they are –good sons, men, husbands, and fathers. To this day both sons call me almost every day, sometimes twice, just to check in. It means the world to me that my sons care how I am doing and want to share their day with me.

They were the most precious little boys I think I have ever seen in my life, rivaled only by their own precious sons today. Gary II had beautiful white-blonde hair and the sweetest disposition. He was happy and content in whatever we were doing or wherever we were going. Andy's brown hair and brown eyes with a mischievous glint have always reminded me of my own father and brother Mike.

I loved being Momma to my boys and took the responsibility seriously. I read as much as I could and tried to be sensitive to how things were impacting their mind, body, and spirit. For instance, I changed their bedtime prayers because I didn't want to plant seeds of fear. Many people pray: Now I lay me down to sleep. I pray the Lord my soul to keep. If I should die before I wake, I pray the Lord my soul to take. I changed it to a kinder, gentler version and taught them to pray: Now I lay me down to sleep. I pray the Lord my soul to keep. Make me safe throughout the night and wake me in the morning light.

Just 19 months apart in age, they were the best of friends and the worst of enemies. While they shared a bedroom, they played together well with countless Matchbox cars, Legos, and Lincoln logs, but when we moved to Oconee County and they had their own bedrooms, turf battles began. Gary kept his room neat and organized. Andy not so much. Andy would borrow something from Gary's room without permission because something of his was misplaced or broken and often it was never returned. Both preferred to play outside, which was great, but I usually kept a watchful eye from the porch or deck.

When they were older, they would slip out of the yard and into the creek behind at the edge of our backyard and follow it into the river. That was off limits and if I found out, restrictions ensued. In that, Andy excelled. He was never mean, belligerent, or malicious, he just went about life, doing his own thing without regard for rules or boundaries. From pre-k to 12th grade, Andy's teachers said the same thing: Andy talks too much, Andy does not pay attention. And most relegated him to the corner or back of the room. I vacillated between being mad and being sad, mad at his willful distraction and sad at what could be detrimental to his self-esteem and emotional health. This continued until Andy was 17 years old. I remember the day it stopped.

I was standing in the middle of my living room, crying out to God in exasperation, "I have done everything I know to do. You made him — here, take him back," as I threw my invisible burden into God's arms and, while I did not see it, I believe God smiled.

You see, by trying to make Andy be someone I wanted him to be, I had inserted myself in between God and Andy. When I gave up, God worked a miracle and from that day forward Andy has been a joy. Ironically, he has spent his adult life adhering to and enforcing rules and regulations.

While finishing his senior year in high school, he completed a grueling six-month firefighter training course and went on to serve Athens Clarke County for 15 years as a firefighter and trainer and continues to serve voluntarily in Oconee County. During his years at ACC, he completed nine FEMA certifications and now works in disaster preparedness. Whether it is a fire, a shooting, a vehicle accident, or disasters such as hurricanes, tornadoes, and fires, Andy runs into it to save the victims. His safety is my daily prayer.

Andy found the love of his life in 2007 and married Kimberly Diane Huff in 2009. They bought a house in Oconee County and brought Kylie Brooke Huckaby into the world in June of 2010. Andrew Garrett came two years later in May of 2012.

My son Gary took an opposite course. Quiet and contemplative, Gary has always wanted to please others. He loves to hunt and fish and work with his hands, preferably outside. From his teens he asked for building equipment like electric saws, drills, and sanders for every birthday or Christmas gift and our storage room soon became his shop. At sixteen-years-old, he got his first job at Magnolia Estates where he moved furniture, made all kinds of repairs, completed all kinds of facility projects. Since then, he has worked building houses, furniture, tree houses, trains and so much more. Gary's faith kept him balanced, polite and kind, sometimes to his own hurt.

Gary II fell in love with Angela in high school and they dated for a year or so afterwards. When Angela suddenly broke off their relationship Gary went into a downward spiral. He was living with Corey and Ryan, two long-term friends, just a few miles from home, but I would not hear from him for days and even weeks. Finally, I figured out that he was partying a lot and not eating well. He was obviously depressed and needed help, which I got for him as soon as I found out. I am so thankful that scary situation was resolved quickly and my son was restored to his happy and industrious self.

Gary worked for several companies whose owners/bosses mentored him, not only in building procedures but in life. One such mentor is Angela's dad, who continues to be a positive influence in Gary's life. During those years, many of his friends were getting married and having children, which only fueled his own longing to have a wife and children of his own. Instead, he was in eight weddings and built tree houses and doll houses for his friends' children. Gary II moved back home and dated several girls, but one named Ashley, who had a toddler son, he dated more than others. Alas, that relationship ended too. Then in February 2010, Gary II moved out again into a three-bedroom house in Bogart and in March 2010 met April, a divorcee with two children, 5-year-old Dylan and 3-year-old Avery. April was a beautiful blue-eyed blonde and her children were precious. Dylan was quiet and reserved, but Avery was a vivacious blonde, who quickly charmed everyone she met.

Gary II and April seemed to get along well and enjoyed being together and whatever problem April had, Gary II was willing to do all he could to fix it. Not long after they met, April had car problems and Gary II worked on her car. Then, for some reason, she had to move out of her apartment and Gary II welcomed her and the children to live with him. In July 2010, Gary and April became engaged and since she loved to cook and loved a production, April decided that she and Gary would host Thanksgiving dinner for both of their families. Just two weeks before the holiday, however, the family gathering became a wedding and reception. Since all the family would be together, they, or more likely April, decided that would be a perfect time to surprise the family with a ceremony so, in a maddening rush, April planned and organized all the necessary wedding accessories, her gown, flowers, photographer, etc., and all the dinner/reception food, while Gary II carried out her plan and paid for it all. The relationship that began in March had culminated in a whirlwind wedding in November.

On November 27, 2010, Gary II and April were married on a dock on the lake behind their house. Avery and Dylan were in the wedding party and Pastor Mike Ricks officiated the ceremony. After the vows were spoken, Gary knelt down, took Dylan and Avery in his arms, and promised them that he loved their mother and that he loved them and would be good to them.

Just three months later, in February, Gary II confided in me that April was lying to others, and he suspected she was lying to him, too. Gary also noted that April had not changed her name on Facebook to Huckaby and had not changed her status to married. When he asked her about it, she said she had forgotten or had just not taken time to do it. April claimed that she had graduated from UGA with a bachelor's in marketing, but we never saw a diploma or other evidence. When asked, she couldn't remember the year she graduated. She also told us that she had had ovarian cancer while living in Cumming and had had chemotherapy but did not remember the name of her physician.

Later Gary II learned that April was paying child support to Dylan's dad, Jesse, because she did not have custody of Dylan, only visitation on the weekends, and that Avery and Dylan did not have the same dad. Even more surprising was that the man April identified as Avery's dad and who Avery thought was her dad, West, was in fact not her biological father. Oh, what a mess!

From the beginning, Gary II and April had money problems. Even though Gary II frequently worked seven days a week and long hours each day, they often could not cover their essential bills, like the power, water, or cable. Checks were always bouncing because April would write a check and forget to tell Gary about it or would spend the money he had given her on something else instead of making a payment. Gary had business expenses that he was trying to keep separate from home finances, but he always seemed to be borrowing from one to pay the other, and many times Gary I and I provided the money when there was no other way. April lost her driver's license because she was behind in child support payments and Gary II paid thousands to get her caught up.

Three months after their wedding, April became pregnant. I was shocked at the speed at which they had started dating, moved in together, got married, and were now having a baby, but I was overjoyed at the thought of another grandchild. Walter Gunner Huckaby, a beautiful little blonde replica of his daddy, was born on October 15, 2011, but his entry and first two weeks of life were difficult. April's labor stalled, so they gave her Pitocin, which caused her to push Gunner out rapidly. His little body was bruised so his PKU elevated and when his bilirubin stayed above normal, the doctor put him under a bilirubin light at home for about two weeks. Finally, when she and Gunner were doing well, April began looking for work. After several short-term jobs, she went to work for Haley Jane Catering in Monroe and loved it.

She drove the sixty miles round trip several days a week while Gunner stayed with me or April's sister or mother.

On Saturday, April 21, 2012, while we were conducting the FCN preparation course, Gary II called with heartbreaking and life-changing news. April had been arrested. Arrested? I was shocked! I could hardly speak! No one in my family had ever been arrested in my lifetime. I did not know what to think. Never would I have dreamed of such a thing happening in our family. At the time of the call, I was conducting a healing service at GMC, teaching about healing, and praying with the nurses for their specific needs. Now I was fighting back tears for myself and my family.

We finished the course the next afternoon and I fled home as fast as I could. Gary II and Gunner and Gary met me at the house and explained the situation. April was arrested and charged with embezzlement, having used the Haley Jane credit cards for her own personal use. Then we all went to the jail in Morgan County to visit her. It broke my heart to see my son crying while holding his baby boy and talking to his wife by telephone on the other side of the glass. Such a pitiful sight. We all cried, especially watching Gunner looking at his mother.

The next day after church, I went to Gary's and washed clothes all day long. On Monday I enrolled Gunner and Avery in Kid-R-Kids Day care and paid the fees, and that Friday, Gary I, April, and Gary II had an appointment with an attorney. Gary I paid the retainer of $5,000. April denied the charges, saying that Haley had given her the card and told her to make purchases and to use the credit card in lieu of her paycheck. Seemed a far stretch to me, but some businesses have poor practices.

That next week both Gunner and Avery were sick and since April no longer had a driver's license, I took them all to the pediatrician, paid the bill, and bought the medicine. The week after that Gary II's landlord told him they had to be out of their house in three weeks, which meant he had to find another house fast. It seemed the blows just kept coming at Gary.

We waited and worried week after week for the trial to be set. Gary II and April lived each day with the possibility that the sheriff could take her to jail. Each moment as a family was precious. Slowly as the weeks turned to months, life began to return to a new normal. April got her license back and found a job in Atlanta with a construction firm. Gary gave Gary II his three-year-old Ford Flex for April to drive kids to and from day care and herself to work.

In February 2013, during a snowstorm, April sat Gunner on the counter beside the cook top and, of course, the toddler leaned over and put the palm of his little hand on a still hot burner, suffering first and second-degree burns. Gary called me to tell me what happened and that they were taking him to Athens Regional. I could hear little Gunner screaming in the background. Because of the snowstorm, I could not go and be with them and see about my precious Gunner. Anguish at his pain, anger at her stupidity, and the helplessness made me almost hysterical. I sobbed, paced, and ranted as I waited for news. Finally, Gary II called to tell me that he was going to be okay and that he was sleeping on their way home, but they would also have to take him to the Burn Center in Augusta on Friday. I prayed and prayed and thanked the Lord. Gunner's hand healed without any scarring and no more pain.

While all this was happening to Gunner, April learned she was pregnant with her fourth child, and on October 21, 2013, just two years and one week after Gunner was born, she delivered another precious little blonde-haired boy. They named him Phillip Gray Huckaby—Phillip after April's daddy and Gray after his daddy Gary II. Again, her labor was difficult, and she was given Pitocin, but this time the delivery was controlled, and baby Gray did not suffer. Thankfully, April had her tubes tied as she nor Gary wanted to have any more children.

Gary had gotten upset with April several times during her pregnancy for drinking too much wine. Then, when Gray was barely three months old and still breastfeeding, April went to a friend's wedding in Atlanta and didn't get home until 5 am. She had an excuse, of course. She said that she was the designated driver and was taking friends home, but that was hard to believe considering Atlanta is only an hour away. A couple of months later, Gary discovered that April had been telephoning and texting another man and that it had been going on for at least three months. Gary talked with her, but she did not quit or see a need to quit, so I talked with her privately, then Gary and I met with her and her dad, Phillip. I explained to April that texting and talking to another man was, in a sense, infidelity. I did not think, at that time, that she was mean spirited, but her reasoning was faulty and sometimes she lied and pushed the envelope to have her way.

Her house was always a mess, in fact it was just dirty, and it upset me for my son and his children to live in such an environment. Clothes were literally piled three feet high in the laundry room and down the hall and yet she sat talking on her phone or was out with friends. Gary worked all day and then she left him to take care of two babies at night.

Gary and April and the kids started attending Bethlehem First UMC, so I was encouraged that April wanted to make the marriage work. Dylan asked some good questions regarding Jesus and asked for a cross for his birthday. I took him to the

Carpenter's shop and let him pick out the one he wanted. Then April, Gunner, Gray, and Avery were all baptized by Rev. Parker Benson, which was such a blessing, but Gary confided in me that he was not convinced April was sincere.

In July, April went to the beach with her friends and left Gary to care for the four children. Then she went to a Tim McGraw concert and started staying in Atlanta after work until late, sometimes 2, 3 or 5 am. Gary II would call and text her, but she would not answer. Making excuses that she did not have cell service, did not see the text, or forgot to answer, while Gary II was home cleaning house, washing clothes, and taking care of babies.

Gary absolutely adored the boys and would do anything for them, yet he could see that they, too, were suffering from April's absence and negligence. The kitchen was filthy with caked food lining the inside of the microwave, dirty dishes in the sink, and mold in the refrigerator. Dirty clothes were piled doorknob high in the laundry room and strewn the full length of their hallway. The kid's bathroom was beyond words. It broke my heart to see how my son and his precious boys were living. When your child is sad or hurt, you hurt. How could a mother callously leave her own children in such a nasty place?

Poppa Huck even noticed that April was posting a lot of partying pictures on Facebook without Gary II and wondered what was going on. I lost it when she posted a picture of herself in what looked like her bra and panties to show how much weight she had lost. I had her remove it immediately. That was going way too far!

April's trial finally came up on June 11, 2015, during which she was charged with a felony for embezzlement. Because it was her first offense, she was given ten years' probation and restitution and fees of $25,000, which I paid by cashing in a year of my retirement. We were so thankful for her light sentence that we took them out for steak, but April barely said thank you. I wish I knew then what I know now. Our lives could have been a lot better.

April started her own wedding coordinator business with another girl named Ashley. Since weddings are mostly on the weekend, she was often gone Friday afternoon and night and all day and evening Saturday. Then sometimes on Sunday "to clean up." We had reasoned that her time away from Gary and the children was due to work or stress of the upcoming trial, but after her release, she seemed to be away for home even more. We encouraged them to get counseling, which they did, but as Gary II said, the counselor heard only April's complaint that he worked too much and never discussed her neglect of her home and family.

Gary II and April had always had financial problems, but after the trial, the debt, overdue bills, and need for rescue loans were constant. Even though Gary worked many 12-14-hour days at whatever chore, task, or job he could get, he was always behind in his bills. I frequently let him "borrow" hundreds and even thousands to pay the utilities, the rent, and car payments, not to mention food and diapers. He would tell April she could spend only a certain amount, and inevitably she would spend more, causing checks to bounce and fees to mount.

"Gary, you've got a hole in your bucket," I said, "and I think April is the hole," because no matter how much he made, he never had any money, and he didn't know and couldn't find out where or what she was spending it on. Was it drugs? Was she gambling? It definitely wasn't on the boys, him, or the house. Occasionally she bought expensive formal dresses for dinners with her boss and their clients, she said, but shopping didn't seem to be the outlet either.

As if the money Gary made and that I provided them wasn't enough, one day Gary got a call from a loan company in Lawrenceville about a missed payment. What loan? He knew nothing about a loan, but he soon learned that April had taken out a personal loan for $1,000, using Gary I's car as collateral. That is illegal, right? Well, later we found out that the transaction was made possible by a friend of April's, who worked for the loan company and, somehow, April had coerced, or blackmailed her into approving the loan. Gary, of course, assured them that the car was not hers and that he would pay nothing on such a loan. That company hounded April for years since she didn't repay it either.

Working long hours each day, taking care of his children each evening, and then staying up half the night waiting for April had worn Gary into exhaustion. "I don't think I can go on, Momma. I don't think we're gonna make it," Gary said and yet he kept trying because of his boys. He would do anything to be with his boys and see that they were cared for properly.

Then Tuesday, November 10, Gary's world literally imploded. He called me about 1:00 pm saying he and April would be getting a divorce as soon as possible. He had just gotten a call from her boss informing him that April would be getting fired the next day for embezzlement. Ironically, Gary had also gotten other calls that morning telling him that April had had an affair with three men in the last six months. Her boss informed Gary that April had told everyone at work that her husband was a drunk and would not work and that she was divorcing him, but he had found out differently and wanted Gary to know what was going on. According to her boss, April had been using his credit card on non-work purchases and when confronted had blamed it on Gary.

Friday, November 14, 2015, April was fired after she was confronted and admitted embezzlement and tampering with the company's financial records. Apparently, she was running her own construction company underneath her boss' company, using all his licenses, permits, credit cards, workers, materials, and even insurance. All of it, embezzlement and fraud, she admitted in writing.

While all of this was going on at her work, April mentioned none of it to Gary. Each morning she left home supposedly to work and didn't come home until after midnight each night, never saying anything. Gary knew of course that she wasn't going to work. He had even seen her copy of the confession on the front seat of her car, but he didn't confront her. He just waited to see if she would tell him, and while he waited, he had made an appointment with Harry Gordon, the attorney who represented April in her June embezzlement trial.

Finally, on Thursday, November 19, 2015, while Gunner and Gray stayed with Kimberly and Andy at our house, Gary I and I went to Gary's to be there while he confronted April with what he knew. Waiting outside on the porch, Gary and I paced back and forth while Gary and April sat and talked. In an amazingly gentle and quiet way Gary told her he would no longer live with her, that they were getting a divorce, and that she needed to get some stuff and leave. She tried to deny the accusations but to no avail. Their marriage was over, so she called Melissa, her sister, to come and get her.

November was Gary II's busiest month of the year building the specialty trains that transport people through malls and parks. That was when Ernest, his boss, participated in an international exhibition and commissioned 5-6 trains to be built and shipped in a short amount of time. Every year Gary complained about Ernest's unrealistic deadlines, which inevitably pushed Gary to work 12-16 hours a day to get the work done. This year was no different. He had to work, and now that April was gone, he desperately needed to be with the boys. So, for at least two weeks, I picked up the boys from day care and took care of them each night. Gary came as soon as he could, and all three slept together on the sofa bed in our living room. During the day, I cleaned Gary's house, vacuuming, mopping, changing linens, washing, and putting away mounds of clothes, and studied and worked on lessons for church at night. We were all physically and emotionally exhausted but doing all we could to help the little boys whose world had turned upside down.

Gary began divorce proceedings with Kim Michael, who according to Harry Gordon, was the best in the area. She was good to Gary. Attorneys are expensive so Gary I paid the retainer and Gary II sold his red truck to begin paying the balance. Somehow, we will get through this I kept praying. Mary Cooper said that April was an assignment of the Devil to infiltrate our family. Elizabeth prayed warfare prayers and sent me Scripture and prayers to pray. Gary told Poppa Huck and they both cried. I talked with my brother Allen and my sister-in-law Robbi. Both were shocked, to say the least. Worst of all was having to allow Gray and Gunner to go home with April for a day or overnight. I was afraid she would steal the children and we would never find them again. I constantly prayed for the Feds and DA in Forsyth County to arrest her, because I believed that her being in prison would make all of our lives so much better.

January 2, 2016 was a freezing cold day. The boys had spent the night before with their mother, as required by the judge, and she brought them home that morning wearing only a diaper and tee shirt. No shoes, socks, pants, or coats. Her sister and brother-in-law told Gary that she had already begun dating and had had men, several different men, spend the night with her at her parents' house, even while the boys were there, sleeping in the same room with her and her latest man. I prayed earnestly day and night and I cried almost constantly. She never willfully hurt the boys but her care of them was certainly not in their best interest. Never in my wildest dreams could I have imagined my son and grandsons in such a precarious situation.

Then on January 13, 2015, after five hours of court proceedings, the judge awarded Gary II physical and legal custody of his precious boys. Words cannot express the relief and gratitude to God I felt, and I praised God for his answer to the deepest prayers I had ever prayed. God had truly given Gray and Gunner their lives back—lives which would have been subject to all manner of evil had their mother gotten authority over them. I praise God every day for this blessing.

Although the worst was over, the next few months continued to be stressful as Gary waited for the divorce to be final and April disrupted and delayed the divorce proceedings in every way she could. Both Gary and April were required to take a parenting class, and while Gary complied as soon as possible, three times April forgot her appointment and had to reschedule. She was required to pay child support of $500 per month, but she has never paid it on time or the amount she owes.

Her disregard for the custody decree was even more stressful because of the potential harm to the boys. She was not allowed to have men around the boys, but Gary II found out that April was spending several nights a week with her ex-husband, Jesse, and taking the boys with her to Jesse's house. She bought Dylan, her

9-year-old son, a machete and allowed him to play with it unsupervised near Gray and Gunner. I prayed constantly about the things they saw and heard in her presence and gave God many, many thanks for bringing the boys safely home each time they had to be with her, and I still do.

Waiting Is the Hardest Part

I always thought of my mother as the quintessential hostess and she loved to have people come to visit, but she also said that guests are like fish, they begin to stink after three days. I remember her cautioning me "not to overstay my welcome" so I am always watching to be sure I am not smelling like a fish. Over time I developed a keen sensitivity to people and circumstances in my surroundings. From a sense of being welcomed, received, valued or useful, to being superfluous, rejected, and irrelevant, this sensitivity has occasionally prompted me to make an honest assessment of where I am, what I am doing, and how God is leading me to move or wait. Waiting has been the hardest.

At the end of 2013, I knew that the GMC Faith Community Nurses (FCN) and the Faith Community Network were thriving. The FCN prep course was taught twice a year with a waiting list for both sessions. The FCN nurse group was growing with four new nurses in four new churches. The Faith Community Network was established with properly functioning systems and growing into its second iteration of church partnerships. But I was beginning to feel like the man on the Ed Sullivan Show who spun plates on top of sticks. Once the plates were spinning, he'd just tap them to keep them going.

For months, I had prayed for enthusiasm and resolved to occupy my mind and hands with valuable, if not urgent, tasks. To this end, I cleaned out the files. I streamlined the policies and procedures, and I coordinated a retreat to assess the strategic vision and goals of the groups. I studied the changing healthcare and ministry environment and through this seemingly quiet contemplative season, I came to realize that I was not the person to take the department to the next level and, honestly, I was bored.

By March 2014, I had exhausted all the busy work that I could invent and my discontentment with GMC and all things of the Faith Community Nursing/Network had reached epic proportions. Additionally, I felt trapped between my need to convey the vision of the department to my successor and GMC's archaic policy against hiring a replacement before a position was vacant. All this I lamented on March 6, 2014, to my prayer partner, Beth, who thoughtfully replied, "Did you ask God if you could leave GMC?"

"Well, no, I guess I haven't actually asked," I said. The next morning, in my quiet time with God, I thanked Him for the work that I had been able to do at GMC and professed my trust in His care of the nurses, the network, and the churches, but that honestly, I had come to despise my work and if it was okay with Him, could I leave GMC and how?

A little while later, in the shower in fact, as God often speaks to me in the shower, washing dishes, folding clothes, or other mundane tasks I do by rote, God said, "You could take Joan's position."

"WOW, Lord," I said, "that is brilliant!" Joan Pardon was the Education Coordinator who was retiring in May. I could take her position at 20 hours a week and be instrumental in hiring the next manager. I would be able to impart the vision and then assist the new manager in hiring the next Education Coordinator. What a brilliant plan and it addressed all my concerns. God is SO good, all the time, and I could not wait to implement His plan.

On March 28, 2014, I shared the flawless plan with my Vice President and, to my shock, he refused to accept it. I knew God had said I could take Joan's position, so I thanked him and waited and waited and waited. I felt like my body was at GMC and my heart was not, but what else could I do except wait? I trusted God and His word, and I truly believed that God would work out the way. Finally, on April 21, 2014, deep into the budgeting process, the director asked, "So when are you going to move to Joan's position?"

"I haven't gotten Steve's approval," I said, to which he replied, "Go ahead. He just told me to tell you it is approved." I smiled and thanked God, who is always faithful.

And that is what I did. I moved to the 20-hour-a-week position at the 20-hour-a-week salary but continued to perform the responsibilities for both positions (essentially working 60 hours a week on a 20-hour-a-week salary). I hoped the process would move rapidly, which, of course, it did not. The new manager was not in place until December and the new Education Coordinator not until January 2015.

Along with the regular workload of the two positions, I also coordinated a 20-year anniversary celebration of the Faith Community Nursing (Parish Nursing) department at GMC. The evening included a $16,000 dinner at Stone Mountain Park, a published review of those 20 years, and speakers, including the current and past CEOs, directors of nursing, and directors of the department, and all but three of the many Faith Community nurses. It was a storybook evening. The setting and decorations and food, the speakers and attendance were just perfect. My support staff worked so effectively that I literally sailed through the evening, checking in with them now and then, keeping an observant eye on the progress, but free to talk with the guests and enjoy my meal. Amazingly, Gary attended the dinner with me as well.

Only by God's grace during those six months, I worked at GMC, covering two positions, and at BFUMC, preaching each Sunday, while also taking D-Min classes and writing my dissertation. In both the waiting and the work, God's grace was sufficient for me. 2 Corinthians 12:9 says it best. My grace is sufficient for you, for my power is made perfect in weakness.

Someone You Need to Meet

I have had an office, somewhere, for almost 50 years, which has given me a lot of time to reflect on their use and meaning. As a nursing supervisor in 1979, I shared an office with the supervisors who covered the other shifts, so it was technically only mine for eight hours. From 1982-1985 I had my first private office, but it was in a patient room across from the nursing station on the fourth floor. For a few months, I shared a tiny space accommodating three people at three desks and for ten years, Joyce McCrudden and I shared an extra-large office, which was the former CEO's office with its own bathroom. When I worked in IS, I had an office in a renovated apartment building and then when I became the Director of Quality Support Services, I had a beautiful new office in the new Medical Services Building (MSB). The most prestigious office I ever had was on the administrative wing near the boardroom and the worst was a desk in a large room with nine other people in a trailer across the parking lot from the loading docks behind the hospital. My desk faced the dumpsters.

According to business etiquette, decorating an office with homey knick-knacks and memorabilia projects the message that you are satisfied with your rung on the corporate ladder and plan to be in your position a long time. Ironically, all my offices were bereft of personal items and elaborate décor. That is until my office in QSS.

It was a new office in a new building with large windows and a great view, so it definitely needed décor, which I bought and Beth arranged. I loved my position and having an esthetically pleasing office was a joy, but that didn't last long. Less than six months later, I took the CIS position and left my beautiful abode. Little did I know then, but that was the first of several such scenarios.

At Gwinnett Medical Center, when I took the position of manager for the Faith Community Nurses and Network, I had an office with an exterior door on the second floor of a medical office building adjacent to the hospital, which was convenient considering most of my appointments were with people from the community. I decided it needed to be tastefully decorated so I placed beautiful pictures on the walls and meaningful objects on the bookshelves. I enjoyed it for less than a year. At Bethlehem First UMC, I loved the church, my position, and my office, which was transformed by an interior decorator. I enjoyed it for less than a year. I don't know what it was about decorating my offices, but contrary to business decorum, decorating my offices did not ensure longevity.

Three months after taking the manager position at Gwinnett Medical Center, my boss, Bob Duvall, sent me an article about Methodist LeBonheur Hospital's Congregational Health Network in Memphis, Tennessee. I was already planning to attend a Faith Community Nursing Conference in Nashville, Tennessee, in June, so I arranged to extend my trip and visit Methodist LeBonheur Hospital and the Church Health Center in Memphis. Jean Holley and Madeline Van Dyck made the trip with me.

Under the direction of Dr. Gary Gundersen, Methodist LeBonheur Hospital had partnered with pastors and their congregations in the Memphis area to create a Congregational Health Network. When a member of a participating congregation was admitted to one of Methodist LeBonheur's seven hospitals and identified themselves as a member of the network, their faith community was notified of their admission. Then a designated hospital network navigator contacted the church's health liaison and through them the two organizations worked together to support the acute and long-term care of the patient. Since its inception, the network had grown to include more than 600 churches in the Memphis area. A study of 473 participants revealed a 50 percent decrease in mortality, lower healthcare cost and charges, reduced readmission rates, increased referrals to hospice and home health care, and increased patient satisfaction. What an incredible model!

Only one thing would I change. Methodist LeBonheur hospital navigators were social workers instead of Faith Community nurses, which would be ideal since the nurse navigator would be better able to communicate with doctors, nurses, and hospital professionals on a clinical level and a Faith Community nurse would also be better able to understand and communicate with ministry professionals, church staff, and congregations. That was the model I presented to GMC.

From June 2012 to August 2013, I led a team of hospital leaders in completing a feasibility study on the implementation of such a network in Gwinnett County. The study was approved and in October 2013, GMC launched a national precedent setting Faith Community Network with a Faith Community nurse as the hospital navigator. Mary Cooper, RN, BSN, was hired to be the first and only FCN navigator in the nation and Dr. Gary Gundersen came to the kick-off ceremony for the eight congregational charter members.

In June 2014 at a Faith Community Network pastor's meeting, an assistant pastor attending the meeting for his senior pastor said, "Debbie, I would like to connect you with someone. Could I share your email and introduce you to a friend, someone you need to meet?" Sure, I said, and went on with my day without giving it much thought, but later that afternoon I got an email introducing me to Dr. Joanne Lyon and her to me. A few days later, I wrote a short introductory email to Dr. Lyon, but weeks went by without a reply. Finally, out of curiosity I googled her name and found out that she was a superintendent in The Wesleyan Church, which district I didn't know, but that explained why she didn't have time to answer emails from strangers.

In August, while attending a class at Asbury, I spoke with another student, Clint Usher, who I remembered was a pastor in The Wesleyan Church, and told him the story. I ended by saying, "I found out that she was a district superintendent, so no wonder she hasn't answered me." Clint just laughed and said, "Debbie, she is not just a district superintendent. She is The Superintendent, The General Superintendent for the whole denomination."

"Oh wow! No wonder she didn't answerer me," I said. "I must be number 500 in her email." But to my great surprise, she did answer.

While leading the GMC Faith Community Network development and implementation, significant changes were also happening in ministry. After another deferral by the UMC Board of Ministry in March of 2012 and a disheartening meeting with the Athens Elberton District Board of Ministry in June 2012, I rescinded my candidacy in the UMC in July 2012. The BOM thought that I wasn't Wesleyan enough and the District BOM wondered if I was even saved. I was upset to say the least and determined that God had not called me to be a candidate for

12 years, which is what the BOM projected it would take before they would approve me as a minister. I also decided that if someone recognized the Holy Spirit in me that told me a lot about them and if they didn't recognize the Holy Spirit in me that told me a lot about them too. Apparently, the conference and district boards did not sense the Holy Spirit in me and sadly that told me a lot about them. So, in July, with a deep sense of relief, I left the UMC candidacy process.

At BFUMC I was serving as the congregational care pastor, providing pastoral care to the congregation of more than a thousand people and every Sunday conducting the 8:30 Holy Communion Service. When I told Rev. Parker Benson what I had done, he was distressed, as was the Staff Pastor Parish Relations Committee. The committee met and discussed my decision and decided to support me and continue my employment. In fact, they offered me a full-time position instead.

Parker always called me Reverend, and I was always touched each and every time I heard him say it. I had a master's in theology and a master's in divinity and God had called me to ministry more than ten years before so it was good to be recognized with a title that I believed fit, but when the district superintendent saw Reverend in front of my name on a church conference report he told Parker he could not call me a Reverend anymore. He said it was not fair to the other candidates, but it felt like a kick in the stomach to me. I was so disappointed, and it made Parker angry. He continued to address me as Reverend, just not in writing.

In 2013, while on a mission trip to Jamacia, Parker talked with Rev. Mark Danzey from Mount Pisgah UMC church in Atlanta, who had also rescinded his candidacy in the UMC and was then ordained through the International Ministerial Association. Parker shared the information with me, and I contacted

Reverend Jim Gable, the Mid-South District Chairman of the International Ministerial Association.

In a matter of weeks, I was licensed by the IMA as a minister in November 2013 and began the application for ordination, again answering questions, but unlike before, my answers were graciously received and approved. Now where and how to be ordained, I didn't have a clue. In the UMC, ordination is conducted each year during an annual conference held at the Athens Classic Center. Each ordinand is allowed only a few guests to witness all being ordained together. I would be ordained by myself, but as plans were initiated, people joined the process.

Parker offered to hold the ceremony at Bethlehem First UMC. Rev. Jim Gable would officiate, and Parker asked to preach the message. I asked Rev. Michele May, Rev. Matt Parker, and Rev. Dr. Jerry Meredith if they would participate in the service also. Rev. Rich Tuttle, a BFUMC member, and Rev. Harold Corbin would be present also. Rev. Meredith wanted to present me with a new Bible and Ron Agnew agreed to sing The Lord's Prayer for us. A reception was needed, and I calculated the cost and estimated how many I could afford to invite, but again Parker stepped in to make my day an amazing event. He wanted the whole BFUMC congregation, along with my friends and family, to be invited and approved the church to cover the expense.

So, on January 19, 2014, at 4:00 PM in the beautiful sanctuary of Bethlehem United Methodist Church I was ordained, and the ceremony was witnessed by approximately 250 people, including Gary, Gary II, and Andy and their families, Poppa and Granny Vicky, Allen, Denise, and Heather, WINGS, nurses from GMC and ARMC, friends from SJUMC and members and staff from BFUMC. Rev. Gable officiated and Rev. Parker Benson preached a sermon based on II Timothy 4:2, which says, Preach the Word; be prepared in season and out of season; correct, rebuke, and encourage—with great patience and careful instruction. Rev. Jerry Meredith presented me with a new Bible, and seven pastors—four UMC, two Baptist, and one Church of Christ—prayed over me the prayers of ordination.

Ephesians 3:20, which says, Now to Him who is able to do exceedingly abundantly above all that we ask or think is the only way to describe that perfect day. After two degrees, six years as a candidate in the UMC, hundreds of pages of ordination paperwork, and numerous grueling interviews, I was ordained when and where and how God had planned it. I will never forget the sense of God's presence and His joy that permeated my whole being when I was anointed, and those seven pastors laid hands on my shoulders and prayed. I was incredibly blessed with acceptance and affirmation and, other than the birth of my sons, that was the happiest day of my life, yet that very afternoon, while I soaked in the blessings of my ordination, Parker was receiving news that would again rock my world.

That very day, the UMC North Georgia Conference Bishop called Parker with the news he had longed for years to receive. His request to transfer his appointment to Maryville, Tennessee, his hometown, had been granted. Parker would be leaving BFUMC in June and while I was so happy for him and Carol, his wife, I was so sad for myself and BFUMC. He told the staff on Monday and the congregation the next Sunday and over the next five months, as Parker prepared himself and his family for their departure and prepared the staff and people for a new shepherd, he did his best in everything. I continued to be a recipient of his undaunting support.

I had conducted the 8:30 Holy Communion Service for almost three years, but an ordained elder, either Parker or Matt, had to be there to bless the elements. After my ordination, Parker determined that I would be able to do that myself, however, the DS, countered Parker's decision and denied me the privilege.

The choir and ministers wore robes during services in the sanctuary. After my ordination, Parker indicated that I could now wear a stole over my robe, signifying my ordination. I was happy for the affirmation, so I purchased four. A green, red, white, and purple stole for services according to the liturgical calendar, and while I wore them with the grace and authority of my calling, the joy was short lived.

One Sunday, about five weeks after my ordination, the D.S. came to BFUMC for the 11:00 service, and seeing me on the chancel in my robe and stole was a definite problem for him. Again, he intervened and told Parker that I could not wear a stole because, according to him, it signified an ordained elder in the UMC, which would not be fair to other candidates and would mislead the people.

Again, Parker was angry, but we had to comply. The SPPRC, however, was unwilling to accept the injunction and went over his head and made an appointment with the bishop. When members of the SPPRC and Parker arrived, the district superintendent was also there, at the invitation of the bishop. The complaints were presented, including the D.S's demands that I not be called Reverend, that I not be able to bless the communion elements, and that I not be allowed to wear a stole. The bishop said I could be called Reverend because of my degrees but would not rescind the D.S's injunction on the other two. Parker had done all he could. He and the SPPRC had been my advocates and had supported me in every way they could. So, with mixed emotions I ministered with Parker over the next few months and learned all I could from one of the best friends, mentors, supervisors and advocates I had ever had. This was the presentation I made at his farewell service.

> "You can tell a lot about a person from the stories that people tell about them. In these past nine years with Parker and his family, we have made a lot of memories together, so I thought it would be interesting to describe Parker through some of those "special" memories.
>
> "We always learn a lot from Parker's sermons. We know that Parker was a coach before God called him for the ministry, so his life of football and wrestling often makes it into his sermons. On my second or third Sunday here, Parker gave a football blocking demonstration in the 11:00 traditional service. He needed the assistance of someone from the audience, so he got the help of a young muscular built man at the front. In his robe, in formation, and with great energy, Parker proceeded to perform this blocking maneuver towards this unsuspecting young man. Later we decided that he was a first time visitor who learned never to sit on the front row again!
>
> "Karen Whitehead has worked with Parker since his first day here. From all the sermons she has heard, she remembers when Parker talked about our world filled with iPhones, iPads, laptops, internet, voicemail, and how, according to Parker, we are just a quivering mass of availability.
>
> "Joyce Corbin recalled Parker's compassion for her when Rev. Harold got hurt. Parker and Rev. Harold were on a pastor's conference when Rev. Harold slipped and fell. Parker took him to the hospital and the next morning he called Joyce. The first thing he said was, "Joyce, this is Parker. Harold is O.K., but he got hurt."

"I came to BFUMC as a ministry student; Parker had agreed to be my mentor. I had a lot of love for our Lord, and a lot of education, but very little ministry experience, but Parker never seemed to notice and so he gave me many opportunities for which I will always be grateful.

"One of the things I admire most about Parker is his humor and his ability to incorporate the unexpected into the moment. A couple of months ago, on an especially busy Sunday morning, Parker asked me to assist him with Holy Communion at the 9:30 service. In his sermon that morning, Parker had talked about how Peter had rebuked Jesus when Jesus told the disciples he would suffer and be killed. After the sermon, we prepared for Holy Communion. As Parker was speaking, I was pouring the juice and somehow, I clicked the pitcher and challis together and spilled some of the juice—but Parker didn't miss a beat. He said, "And Jesus took the cup and he blessed it—and he spilt it and Peter rebuked him…" I could hardly keep from laughing out loud, but thankful for the rescue!

'Lynn Smith told me she will always remember how Parker's face just beams when he talks about his wife, Carol. Parker always says, "I love my wife," and as Lynn says, it shows. From these stories and many more, we know Rev. Parker Benson to be an excellent preacher, a kind, compassionate and humble man with a quick wit and great sense of humor, a man who loves his wife, his family, God, and God's people. Parker, Carol, Gabe, Tilly: thanks for the memories. We will all be together again one day!"

Reverend Frank Bernat came in June to lead BFUMC as our new senior pastor and while my relationship with him was not as instantaneously congenial as it had been with Parker, we worked well together helping him become oriented to BFUMC and us to him. I knew that the D.S. had informed him about all the staff, and I was sure he had included his difficulties with me. Tactfully, Frank never mentioned anything, and I didn't elaborate, but I did wonder and regularly prayed about my future there at BFUMC.

After church on Sunday, September 9, 2014, as I pulled into my garage, I sensed the overwhelming peace and joy of the presence of the Lord, so I sat very still and listened. God spoke: "Take the first step toward cessation planning at BFUMC. I know you think it is June, but it's not. It is March. I know you don't understand now, but you will. Remember Elijah. You will see my glory."

The first step in cessation planning to me was to tell the senior pastor and then follow his lead. I met with him the next week and because we were in the midst of budget planning, he needed to tell the SPPRC. Telling SPPRC meant that soon he would need to tell the Finance Committee and once that many people knew, the congregation would hear. So, the first week of November 2014 I told the precious people of BFUMC that I was leaving at the end of March. Where are you going? I was asked over and over again. I don't know was all I could tell them. I only knew that I would be working on my dissertation, making a trip to China and Korea, and graduating. That was all I could see, but Saturday, November 15, I found out more.

It had been three months since I had emailed Dr. Joanne Lyon that introductory email. In fact, I had forgotten that whole episode until Monday, October 28, when I received an email from her seeking to schedule an appointment with me in November when she would be in Georgia. I looked forward to meeting such an amazing servant of God. A woman who had been a minister in a local church, a missionary, the founder of a World Hope

International, a seminary vice president, and now the General Superintendent of The Wesleyan Church.

On November 15, I met Dr. Lyon at a hotel near the John C. Maxwell Leadership Center at 12 Stone Church. I felt like I was in the presence of a larger-than-life personality, yet she was kind and congenial and always smiling. We talked for over an hour, as she shared with me how she too was a pioneer in starting new things, globally. Then she asked the question I had come to dread, "What are you going to do now?"

I answered, "I don't know. I know that I am Wesleyan, but I don't know where to be Wesleyan." Without hesitation she said, "I do" and began writing on a white card. "Here," she said, "these are numbers for Dr. Dan Berry. He is the District Superintendent for the South Coastal District. Call him. Tell him I am endorsing you for ordination."

I was elated with our meeting and with anticipation of meeting the DS, but I was also inundated with course work and a 25-page paper due in a week, so my contact with Dr. Berry was delayed. Apparently, Dr. Lyon knew because exactly a week later she took matters in her own hands and connected Dr. Berry and me by email.

My meeting with Dr. Berry the day before Thanksgiving was similar to my time with Dr. Lyon. I liked him immediately. He was a big man who perfectly fit the large desk in the middle of the office. Yet his demeanor was approachable and welcoming. Smiling and listening to my story, he said that I was a lot like Dr. Lyon, which I received as an incredible compliment. Then to my surprise, he opened a file containing several papers already labeled with my name. "Fill these out," he said, handing me the papers needed to process my ordination in The Wesleyan Church.

I promised I would, but first I needed to complete my time and responsibilities at Bethlehem First UMC, and that is what I did.

The Lord had indicated that I should end my time at BFUMC in March, but the last Sunday in March was Palm Sunday and the first Sunday in April was Easter, so the SPPR asked if I could wait. "You don't want to compete with Jesus do you?" they asked with a grin. No, definitely not, so my last day at BFUMC became April 12, 2015.

I preached my farewell sermon to my 8:30 Holy Communion Service congregation and stood with Frank during the 9:30 and 11:00 Services as they prayed for me. Following services that morning, I was given a reception with food, fellowship, gifts, and goodbyes. The church presented me with a Bible that had been passed through the congregation and favorite passages signed. I was given the reception flowers in a beautiful bowl with a glass cross holder. Pete Black made me a hand-turned wood bowl. Kathy Brown gave me handmade cards with my name on them. Lizzy Sutton gave me a bookmark and J.P and Evelyn gave me a gift certificate and a picture of the church signed by well-wishers. Much more than gifts, they loved me, and I loved them. Leaving BFUMC that day, looking back in the rearview mirror with tears streaming down my face, I knew I was leaving more than a beautiful church; I was leaving people I loved and a ministry I thoroughly enjoyed. It felt like I was leaving home and somehow, I knew I could never return.

God had blessed me so incredibly by allowing me to be loved by so many people as I grew into the preacher, pastor, shepherd, and minister that God had created me to be. I will forever be grateful to Rev. Parker Benson, Rev. Michele May, and Rev. Matt Parker, to the staff and to God's people at a beautiful white church on a little hill in Bethlehem, Georgia.

Just nine months had passed since that meeting last June when the pastor said to me, "Debbie there is someone you need to meet," and like God said a few months later, I didn't understand, but I knew the Lord who makes a path through the sea had a plan for me. I left GMC on December 31, 2014, and BFUMC on April 12, 2015. Where I would be going from there, I didn't know, but I knew the One who did and that was sufficient for me.

A Roller Coaster Named Shemitah

A pastor once asked, "What does your family think about that?" referring to an imminent transition in my life. "They have been through so much I don't think they will give it much thought. My life has always been a roller coaster and they are used to it," I answered, and while that was certainly true, every high or low and each jolt to the left or the right still took me by surprise. That was never more evident in my life than in the 2014-2015 year of Shemitah.

What is a Shemitah, you might be asking. Shemitah is the seventh year in a seven-year agricultural cycle described in the Old Testament. It is a year when debts are forgiven and set aside, and land is left fallow. In his best-selling book, The Mystery of the Shemitah, Messianic Jewish Rabbi Jonathan Cahn teaches that an understanding of Shemitah is fundamental to understanding Biblical prophecies and mysteries, as well as the consequences, that are applicable to us today. For example, in his book Cahn correlates Shemitah years with significant events pertaining to the World Trade Center: its conception in 1945, groundbreaking in 1966, opening in 1973, bombing in 1993, the 9/11 destruction in 2001, and most recently the Freedom Tower replacement, which opened in 2014. All were Shemitah years.

Long before I learned about Shemitah, I thought of my life in seven-year increments. The places I lived, the people I knew, and the events of my life when I was seven, fourteen, and twenty-one, and so on. Since 2007, I had become a Faith Community Nurse, coordinator, educator, and manager at GMC and started the Faith Community Network. I had worked at BFUMC preaching every Sunday. I had gained two daughters-in-law, four precious little grandchildren, Kylie (2010), Gunner (2011), Garrett (2012), and Gray (2013) and two step-grandchildren, Dylan, and Avery. I had graduated from Wheaton, then attended Candler School of Theology and Asbury Theological Seminary and graduated with a Master of Divinity. I was now working on a Doctor of Ministry. I had been inducted into the International Order of Theta Phi, an honor society for theological students and scholars, while being rejected by the UMC Board of Ministry. I had been licensed and ordained by the IMA, lost Parker to his home in Tennessee and got a new senior pastor, Frank Bernat. All that in seven years was overwhelming, but the events of 2014-2015 were even more surreal.

My Shemitah year began in the fall, as does the Hebraic calendar, with God's instructions to begin cessation planning at BFUMC and with the employment and orientation of Cheryl Wunsch to lead the Faith Community Nurses and Network at GMC. When my ministry at BFUMC ended on Sunday, April 12, 2015, I was grieving. I missed the people and the activities, but most of all I missed the staff, who had become family to me. Pondering my life that next week, I felt like a fish out of water. I believed I was in the center of God's will, but I felt so alone and even though I was writing a dissertation and doing course work, I felt useless.

Toward the end of that first week, I wondered, would I go to church and if so, where? I knew I could go to 12 Stone, but I had driven 316 to Lawrenceville for six years and I just didn't want to drive it anymore, so I searched and to my amazement found a Wesleyan Church, right here in Oconee County. I never knew there was such a denomination until a few months before and now to find a Wesleyan Church in my hometown was astonishing. So, Sunday, April 19, 2015, I attended Oconee River Church.

Led by Reverend Richard Hoard, Oconee River Church was 180 degrees different from BFUMC. The church was in a strip mall complex. The congregation was 30-50 instead of 300-500. There was nothing beautiful about the sanctuary. It was just a room full of chairs and a stage equipped with a pulpit, chairs, and a piano. The preacher was in a suit, instead of a robe, and the choir, attired in casual clothes, even jeans, sat in the congregation until it was time to go to the front and sing. There were no processionals, recessionals, or creeds.

As I sat among the congregation and not on the chancel while others read Scripture, prayed, and preached, I reflected on the many transitions of my life, and how I seemed to go from one extreme to another. From an office near the hospital board room to a desk facing the trash dumpster. From Wheaton to Candler to Asbury, from ARMC to GMC and from the beautiful sanctuary of BFUMC to the utilitarian Oconee River Church (ORC).

After the service I introduced myself to Rev. Richard Hoard and asked if I might schedule a time to talk with him about The Wesleyan Church. He did and we met the next day and talked for three hours. Rev. Hoard, Richard as I came to call him, was also a member of the South Coastal District Board of Ministry, which only met once per year and ironically was scheduled to meet the next week, so the next morning Richard called Dr. Dan Berry to ask if I could be added to that year's agenda. Dr. Berry agreed and said he was expecting to hear from me. To appear before the Board meant I had to be a member of The Wesleyan Church. Fortunately, there was one more Sunday before that meeting, so on April 26, my second Sunday at ORC, I joined Oconee River Church.

That next Friday, May 1, I met with the South Coastal District of the Wesleyan Church Board of Ministry. It was such a pleasant experience, so very different from the grueling UMC interviews. One man said I was the sweetest person he had ever met and wondered how I could have been a healthcare executive. We talked about taking the Myers Briggs personality test, which I had had several times. Years ago, in the eighties when I took that test at the hospital, I was a D-Dominance and S-Steadiness, but the last two times I had taken the test, the scale indicators were flat, i.e., 49, 50, or 51, which the Board members liked a lot. They also asked if I was coming to The Wesleyan Church just because I had been rejected by the UMC. I explained. I am Wesleyan and really did not find Wesleyan theology in the UMC. They especially liked my degrees and said I met all the qualifications, except for a Wesleyan polity course, which I could take online. Dr. Berry hugged me and in his infectiously jovial voice welcomed me home. It had been only two weeks since I left BFUMC and now I was a pastor in The Wesleyan Church.

I wrote Dr. Lyons an email, thanking her for help in getting me to The Wesleyan Church and the South Coastal District. She wrote me back almost immediately, saying she had heard from various persons on the District Board of Ministry Development and how impressed they were with the interview and with me as a person. She also said, "I believe God has great things ahead for you." Then, that very afternoon, Russ Gonzalus called, welcoming me to The Wesleyan Church and saying that he was looking forward to getting to know me better. He is the Director of Education and Clergy Care for the denomination and has an office in the same building with Dr. Lyons. I smiled at the thought of their welcoming affirmations. Only God's amazing grace could have connected me with them. I wondered if those connections would bear fruit in the coming years.

Richard asked me to be the Associate Pastor of ORC and to write my job description, and on Wednesday, May 6th, the ORC Local Board meeting approved my appointment, with a small salary of $100 per week. I shared the news with Parker, the one who held up my arms when things got so bad with the UMC. Always supportive and encouraging, he wrote:

Dear Rev. Huckaby,

Way to go, way to go, way to go!! This is quite an accomplishment! The Wesleyan Church is very fortunate and the one in Watkinsville is especially fortunate. Let me know where the new building will be, and I will tell my son to come visit you (Gabriel lives in Athens and attends UGA). I am so proud of you. You work so hard, and you are so determined—I would follow you into battle! I'm also sure you will do well at Ed's funeral. He loved you and loved coming to the 8:30 service. I feel for Lora and the church. God bless you and thanks for the update. I always like to hear from you. Parker.

With the title and salary came a new and different responsibility. ORC was in the process of buying a new church building and Richard asked me to lead the effort. The District and Headquarters both agreed to match the church in funds raised to purchase and renovate the building, so we held a banquet at Jennings Mill Country Club on July 1 and a barbecue with music on August 8 at Norman Grayson's Farm. In total, we raised $57,000, which was matched with a $50,000 grant from TWC and on September 1, Oconee River Church purchased its first church building in its 15 years of existence. That is when the real work began, but I had been working hard all summer.

I thought when I left BFUMC that I would spend the summer completing the D-Min course work, writing the dissertation, and preparing for the October trip to China and Korea, and I still had all that to do along with serving Oconee River Church. For the courses I had 12, yes 12 books to read and prepare notes. I was on number two. Along with getting my passport and visa and the other requisite travel documents, I still had to go to the UGA Travel Clinic and get typhoid, flu, and hepatitis A vaccines and malaria pills and I had to create 101 questions to answer while I was in China and Korea. All of the above items were in my control but getting the Asbury Institutional Review Board or IRB to review my application and approve my research plan was beyond me. The dissertation was composed of five chapters. Each had to be approved by a committee of two professors and a coach before going forward, but the IRB had not reviewed my research methodology and unfortunately it would not meet during the summer, which meant I would not graduate in 2016.

Pastor Hoard was away on vacation for two Sundays, so I conducted the services, which also meant I had two sermons to prepare and Holy Communion to administer. The South Coastal District Annual Conference was the 2nd week of July, and the Board of Ministry recommendations were voted on, which included me. I was introduced and approved as an ordained minister in transfer.

The trial for April, my daughter-in-law who was charged with embezzlement, came up on Thursday, June 11. I could not imagine how we would go forward if April was convicted of a felony and put in jail. Gray was a six-month-old baby and Gunner a two-year-old toddler. Those babies needed their mother and Gary needed his wife at home. I prayed and prayed and prayed. Asking God for mercy and protection. That there be no jail time. No residual harm to her civil rights and for God's favor through the judge and others who would make decisions over April. I believed she was just a young woman who had not been instructed well or supervised properly by a busy boss.

Court was scary. No one in my family, immediate or extended, had ever been in jail or charged with anything more than a speeding ticket and there were only a few of those, so I knew nothing about violations of the law and its consequences. After hours of waiting and listening to the lawyers and their clients talking to the judge, the judgment was handed down. April was charged with a felony, but no jail time. She was on probation for 10 years and had to perform 240 hours of community service. She also had to pay $23,000 in reparations, which I paid, and while I hated to cash in my retirement, it was worth it for my son and grandsons. We were so happy for the favorable outcome that we took Gary and April to dinner to celebrate. She was quiet that evening and never actually said thank you. I just assumed she was a little ashamed from the day's proceedings. It would be a few months before we would learn what devious crimes she was committing in plain sight.

The next day I had a chiropractor appointment just like I had had each month for the last 15 years, but that visit was anything but routine. Every few months, Jerry, the office manager, and Dr. Cook's assistant, checked my vitals, blood pressure, pulse, and weight, but today she stopped the usual chit chat and checked my blood pressure a second time. "Your blood pressure is high," she said with an unfamiliar look of concern.

"What is it?"

"140/78."

"What, my blood pressure has never in my life been high. That can't be right! My blood pressure is never above 120/80, in fact, it is always low. You probably need to have your cuff calibrated," I said and proceeded to tell her how she could take it to the hospital's biomedical engineering department, and they would calibrate it for her. She was not convinced and both she and Dr. Cook urged me to go see my primary physician. Reluctantly I agreed and called Dr. Downs for an appointment early Monday morning.

I didn't really think there was anything wrong with me, but that morning at the doctor's office, I found out that there was. The nurse checked my blood pressure and went for Dr. Downs, who came in immediately and checked it herself. It was up, way up, she said and after a few minutes she checked it again in both arms. Wow! Not only was my blood pressure high, but it was also different from my right arm to my left. 158/90 in my right arm while my left was 134/78. Well, that set the doctor in motion. She called for a stat EKG and started ordering blood work. She checked pulses in my neck, arms, and legs. What was she looking for, I asked? Could be heart, carotid, subclavian/brachial plexus blockage, or dissection of the aorta.

I felt like a time bomb on the verge of exploding. "Had I had any other symptoms?" she asked.

"Some dizziness and spontaneously resolving heartburn and,

oh yes, I had had a little pain in my left arm a few days ago," I said. All classic symptoms of heart problems, but I had not put them together. I am a nurse, and I knew better. I felt so stupid, but I had been so busy and occupied with so much going on I had not made the connections.

She made an appointment for me with a cardiologist and ordered a carotid ultrasound and a Cat Scan of my chest. Wednesday, I had the ultrasound and the CT. I saw the cardiologist and had another EKG and a stress test. I bought a digital sphygmomanometer and started tracking my blood pressure in both arms. From 158/90 to 100/60, it was bouncing up and down. I could feel it, too. When it was up, I felt a rush in my head that made it feel like it would pop, and my ears roared. When it was down, I felt light-headed and a little dizzy.

I was still busy with Gary and April, the church, and Asbury coursework and dissertation, and the upcoming trip to China and Korea, and now I was worrying about my health. I was also praying constantly, and God heard my prayers. While I was at the hospital for the tests, I met a friend from my SJUMC Sunday School class. She prayed for me while I waited for the CT scan. I saw Beth who stopped with encouraging words and even met Elizabeth in the corridor as I was walking to the cardiologist office. God is so good, and I know those precious sisters in Christ just happened to be there that day to give me a smile and a hug from Him. I was constantly praying for healing and protection, for medical excellence by my doctors, and for good results from my tests. The episodes, however, continued, more frequently and more intense.

I also began to have numbness in my hands and toes and hearing loss during the episodes, so I had an Echo and two MRIs (head/brain and cervical spine). The day after those tests I had lunch with Madeline Van Dyck, a friend and a former GFCNA Board Director who I had not seen in years. I shared my issues. Madeline is an RN, nurse practitioner, and CRNA, and while she didn't have much to add, she reminded me that her husband Phil was a neuro-radiologist and oh, by the way, he just happened to be on call tonight. So, if I would give him written permission, he could look at my record and check my films. Imagine having the number two person in the nation on neuro radiology boards on my case. God is never late and never early, and so good all the time.

A couple of days later, I got the results, some protrusions and foraminal stenosis, but not cause for my erratic and asymmetrical blood pressures, so I was referred to a vascular surgeon and a nephrologist. The vascular surgeon said my vessels were not the problem. "Your vessels are so clear; you won't ever have to come see me for the rest of your life." The nephrologist said my lab work was clean and clear. No kidney problems. Next, was a neurosurgeon. Dr. Cuff, a colleague from my earlier healthcare career, said he had never heard of such "episodes," and they didn't correspond to the symptoms of nerve problems. He just suggested that I continue with the chiropractor and keep good posture and he released me to travel overseas.

At the chiropractor's office the next day, we were all shocked to find a pressure in the 140s and 120s, simultaneously. The day after that it went to 165 with nausea and shaking and the doctor sent me to the urgent care center. Possible pheochromocytoma, the fight or flight part of the adrenal medulla. I needed rest, which meant vacation, so off to Hilton Head Island we went, but a week after our return, my blood pressure became lethal at 191/110 and I was admitted to the hospital. It was September 18th, one month before my trip.

I had learned to eat properly in nursing school and while I am always trying to lose just five more pounds, I am not really overweight, and I exercise daily. Trying to build physical stamina for the trip to China and Korea, I had increased my treadmill walking time to 60 minutes a day and was lifting weights and doing 70 sit-ups three times a week. I took my vitamins and ate spinach in salads or smoothies every day. And I slept, maybe from exhaustion, but I slept about seven hours every night. What else could I do?

I had had every blood test imaginable and tons of x-rays, EKGs, MRIs, Cat Scans, and ultrasounds. All negative. Nothing that could cause my chaotic blood pressure, but there I sat in a hospital bed. The nurse had given me an IV medication, which seemed like hours ago, but instead of dropping my blood pressure like a rock, it was merely inching down a few degrees every hour.

Why, Lord? What is wrong with me? I prayed. "It is not your neck," I heard in my heart. What is causing my blood pressure to be so high? "Fear. You are afraid. I can protect you wherever you are in the world." God speaks only truth and God's truth cannot be denied. His words rippled through me like ripples of water on still water. I didn't know I was afraid. I would have denied it had you asked, but God said it and that is truth for me, so I prayed.

Lord, I am so sorry for allowing fear to have a place in me. I am sorry that I was not trusting You to take care of me. I open my hands and release my grasp on myself. Please forgive me and heal me, and He did. In a couple more hours my blood pressure returned to normal. I was discharged from the hospital the next morning. That was seven years ago, and my blood pressure has never been high again.

The Ends of the Earth

Fifty days after His resurrection, Jesus led His disciples to the Mount of Olives. "Are you at this time going to restore the kingdom of Israel," they asked. "It is not for you to know the times or dates the Father has set by his own authority. But you will receive power when the Holy Spirit comes on you; and you will be my witnesses in Jerusalem, and in all Judea and Samaria, and to the ends of the earth." Then Jesus was taken up before their very eyes, and a cloud hid him from their sight. (Acts 1:7-8)

That phrase "ends of the earth" has held my attention for decades. I remembered a book I read by J. Oswald Sanders on Spiritual Leadership in which he says that going from New Zealand to Israel was like going from one end of the earth to the other and that was the way I felt in 1998 when I went to New Zealand, came home, and a week later went to Israel. Now, as I was leaving home for China and Korea, I was comforted by Job's words in 28:24 which says, "God looks to the ends of the earth and sees everything under the heavens."

I trusted God would see me every step of the way from here to China and Korea and back and I trusted that He would provide all I needed along the way. I would be with 49 other Asbury D-Min students and several professors, still, I was concerned that I would be in a country where I did not speak the language, couldn't read the signs, and didn't know where we would be staying. I prayed and God answered in the most amazing ways.

Our trip was designed to immerse us in Chinese and Korean culture and compliment the dual focus of our Doctor of Ministry degree program, which was Global Transformational Leadership and Preaching. We began in the homogeneous culture of Beijing, China. Our tour guides and Asbury professors highlighted the common physical features of the people, their similar attire, and mannerisms. Next on our itinerary was Xian, which was once the end of the silk road and was where we saw some evidence of western influence, such as dual signage and the western restaurant with hamburgers, fries, pizza, and coke. The last city we visited in China was Shanghai, which is the largest city in the world and the most modern and western in China.

When we landed in Beijing, China we were collected at the airport in two large buses and escorted by our professors and Chinese contacts to a three star hotel where we gathered in the lobby with all our luggage. What a scene! Smiling and laughing and greeting each other, yet tired, a little nervous, and desperately wanting a bath, food, and sleep, in that order. We were given room keys and roommate assignments and off we went, but only for an hour's reprieve before we were to return to the lobby.

This was typical as we were given only minimal information about what we were doing and where we were going. Planning ahead was almost impossible. We just showed up when and where we were told and lived through whatever happened to the best we could. Most days were non-stop, and the evenings were late, so many nights I was upright with open eyes, but not much else.

My room was nice on the surface but not really clean. The carpet had obviously not been vacuumed. In fact, I don't remember ever hearing or seeing a vacuum cleaner in any hotel in China. Thankfully, the bed was clean as were the bathroom fixtures and there was a western toilet with a little toilet paper. Since we couldn't drink the water, we were given bottles of water and cautioned to remember to use only bottled water when brushing our teeth. The lights in the room did not work unless you put your room key in a slot beside the door. The elevators worked the same way.

When we gathered in the lobby again, we were taken to a meeting room for introductions and an initial briefing. Hello, sounds like nee how; Thank you is shi shi. We were told to assume that cameras were on us at all times. We were warned not to evangelize or give any impression of being pastors and to remember we are Christians, but we are in the country as tourists, learning about the culture and people of China. We were instructed to use the word "club" instead of church, P instead of preacher, M instead of missionary and B instead of bible. They shared a story about how a person infiltrated a house church even becoming a leader and then reported the members of that congregation. Mao Zedong said, "One more Christian, one less Chinese," so a government vacation or prison is often given to Christians deemed to be enemies of the government and we certainly didn't want to be considered an enemy of the government.

Our lunches and suppers were in restaurants selected by our Chinese contacts to provide us with diverse dining experiences. The dining tables were round and seated 10-14 people with a glass Lazy Susan in the center. We were given bottles of water on the bus to bring into the restaurant to drink, but there were also liter bottles of Coke and Sprite on the tables. The table was set with chop sticks and little plates, bowls, and cups, but no forks or spoons.

Dishes of food were brought to the tables, one at a time and in no particular order, a soup, then a dessert or a meat and then a vegetable and rice. The lazy Suzan brought the food around to you, and you used your own chop sticks to serve yourself and also to feed yourself. My nursing education and experience caused me to be concerned about how we were sharing germs with other people. Supper was interesting and I recognized rice and some vegetables, but not the meats. There were a lot of noodles, which I did not recognize, but I tried most every dish. Some were very spicy, and I later had indigestion. One dish of clear noodles was particularly attractive and enjoyed by me and my colleagues. Later we learned that those delightful noodles were actually jelly fish tentacles.

The restaurant bathroom was an unusual and unwelcomed experience! Once inside the door you stepped up onto an elevated surface with two stalls. Inside my stall was a squatty potty, a porcelain toilet bowl in the floor with treads around the surface. You stood on the treads, squatted, and used the toilet. My hips ached from the position required. One ply paper was available, but you put it in the trashcan instead of flushing it. It was apparently impossible not to wet or soil the surrounding area.

Finally, we were able to go to our rooms and sleep. It had been a very long time since leaving home at 5am the day before and I was exhausted and slept even though the bed and pillow were incredibly hard. Thus, my roommate Cynthia Talley from Ohio and I ended our first day in China.

Breakfast in Beijing was usually provided in the hotel lobby or café, typically limp bacon and rice and a bottle of diluted apple juice. No coffee since we could not drink the water. We were soon back on the buses and headed out of the city for an hour and a half bus ride to the Great Wall.

The country was mountainous, but the sky was blue, the sun

was shining, and the air was clear. While traveling we were given a historic briefing about the Great Wall. Various sections were built as early as the 7th century B.C. but weren't joined together until approximately, 220–206 BCE by Qin Shi Huang, the first Emperor of China. Work was intermittent over the next millennium with the majority of the existing wall being completed during the Ming Dynasty 1368 to 1644. We visited the wall at the Juyongguan area and spent the morning exploring the wall and the shops at the base. I walked on the wall a short distance but decided not to climb the very narrow and steep steps.

It was there at Juyongguan that I first noticed raised thresholds but saw them throughout China. A threshold is that section of wood or tile or stone that lies under a door sill and denotes the separation of one space to another. Those spaces in ancient Chinese buildings were typically raised about eight inches or more. Why we wondered. Someone suggested that thresholds were there to make you bow, but our travel guide said that Chinese people believe in ghosts and the thresholds were there to keep ghosts out because the ghosts could not jump. "Practically," he said, "the thresholds were used to keep out rain and to remind you that you are entering a home."

After the great wall and lunch, we traveled back to Beijing and visited the Lama Temple. Construction on the temple began in 1694 during the Qing Dynasty. It was at one time the residence of the Prince Yong (Yin Zhen), a son of the Kangxi Emperor and himself the future Yongzheng Emperor. After Yongzheng's ascension to the throne in 1722, half of the building was converted into a monastery for monks of Tibetan Buddhism. The other half remained an imperial palace.

There I saw people of all ages, but the majority were young adults in couples or groups of three or four people, holding hands and worshipping together before the statues and architectural symbols. They bought incense stems from conveniently located vendors and lit three of them and bowed three times in all directions before the altars. In In the Hall of the Heavenly Kings was a huge statue of Maitreya Buddha, adorned with flowers and other trappings of adoration.

I also saw a prayer wheel, which is a highly ornate cylindrical object made of stone or metal situated on a vertical post, which allows it to be spun. It reminded me of a rosary, and I sat nearby and watched as the old and young came to spin the wheel and offer their prayers.

The racial homogeneity of the people was strikingly evident. The people were primarily Chinese with maybe one or two Australians or Western tourists and us. If we weren't conspicuous already, my white hair glowed like a beacon of light in the dark. In fact, I may have been the only person with white hair that some had ever seen because occasionally people would point to my hair and their camera asking to take a picture of me or a selfie with me.

What I noticed mostly was the absence of joy. I don't think I ever saw a Chinese person smile or heard someone laugh. Instead, I saw longing, hunger, or searching in the eyes of the worshippers that day at the temple and thought of them as starving people yet, I was not allowed to give them food. Our visit to the Lama Temple made me sad.

The despair I saw in the people was but a reflection of their destitute environment. The city air was so polluted, you could only see a few lower floors of the enormously tall buildings. The smog was so deep and dense that it literally blotted out the sun and sky every day we were in Beijing. Many people wore scarves over their face to filter the smog and the smell. The streets reeked of sewage, especially near the manholes, presumably from raw sewage under the streets and above. Toddlers and young children typically were not wearing diapers or pants and were permitted to void and defecate near the manholes. Dogs' waste was not removed because of the Chinese belief that stepping in it brings good luck.

Amid the putrid smell of waste was an occasional whiff of spices from the food vendors who lined the streets in some sections, which we did not eat. Carts with souvenirs congregated near the tourist attractions and we were warned that some vendors might become aggressive and that we should not look at them but keep walking. One vendor actually pulled a pastor by his arm trying to get him to buy something. The wide streets were jammed with vehicles such as motorcycles, bicycles, tri-wheel and four wheels of various shapes and sizes sometimes carrying enormous bundles of goods. Then, of course, there were many BMWs and Mercedes and even the occasional Ford. Even though their driving was fast and seemingly reckless, I never saw an accident.

China has many Christian churches. Some churches, like Three-Self Church are registered government churches and can operate openly, but under the watchful eye or ear of the government while most are not registered and operate underground. We were told that some of the unregistered churches are quite large and meet after hours in businesses, such as salons or in apartment complexes.

We visited Three-Self Church just a couple of blocks from our hotel. We were met by the senior pastor who invited us in and shared her testimony of how God had impressed upon her to attend Bible School and provided her way when she had no money. She conducts services every day of the week and three services on Sunday with approximately 2,000 attendees total each week. We had been briefed to expect that government was both listening to us and looking at us, so the obvious cameras in the sanctuary and foyer were not unexpected, but still uncomfortable.

A few blocks from the church was Tiananmen Square. We entered through a gate and a guard with an automatic weapon. Tiananmen Square, named for the gate that leads to the Forbidden City to the north is a 109 acre plot of land covered completely in concrete. On the west side of the Square is the Great Hall of the People and along the east side is the National Museum of China. A Mausoleum of Mao Zedong is found in the center.

The Square is perpetually guarded by Chinese military with automatic weapons, and since we were a large group and easily visible, we were instructed to walk alone or in small groups of two or three and silently pray as we walked from one corner of the square to the corner diagonally across the walled enclosure. In that corner was a huge flowerpot structure with flowers and a flagpole flying a red flag guarded by even more troops. There we assembled for a group picture, which seemed counterproductive to try to remain incognito and then gather as a group, but picture taking is what tourists normally do. Finally, we walked out of the square under the highway and into the Forbidden City.

The Forbidden City was the Chinese imperial palace of 24 emperors from the Ming dynasty to the end of the Qing dynasty (1420 to 1912). It is a walled rectangular enclosure around 8,707 rooms where approximately 20,000 people lived who cared for the emperor and his family.

Imagery and symbolism are everywhere. Replicas of animals and birds adorned the roofs of many of the larger buildings to invoke wellbeing and protection. Outside of the Palace of Tranquil Longevity, one of twelve palaces, is a pair of lions. The female lion, on the left, has a cub underfoot and the male lion, on the right, has a globe or world underfoot symbolizing the family roles.

After supper we boarded a train for a 1,000 mile overnight train ride to Xi'an. Our accommodations were high scale comparatively speaking. Our compartment had a small aisle and a very small table between two bunk berths—two lower and two upper. I had an upper so I had to hoist myself up to the top bunk. It was incredibly uncomfortable. Sleeping in the clothes I had worn all day was cumbersome and the roof was only about a foot above my body so turning over was somewhat claustrophobic. The mattress and pillow, if you can call them that, were hard as a rock—so hard that I could not sleep from the pain in my hips, neck, and head. I finally put the covers underneath me and put my jacket under my head and finally got a little sleep.

In China, Buddhism is the nationally accepted religion and Christianity is not, so a group of fifty Asbury Seminary students, twenty five Americans and twenty five from European, African, and Asian countries, and their professors were conspicuous, which meant we were under surveillance the entire time we were in China. We were reminded almost every day that there were microphones in our buses and meeting rooms, and that we were being videoed wherever we went. Our Chinese contacts frequently cautioned us about saying words like pastor, church, or missionary because it was commonly known that Christians were sometimes apprehended and never seen again.

One particularly scary event happened that night on the train from Beijing to Xian. Compartment assignments are made on a first come, first serve basis, which results in separation of families and groups and that is exactly what happened to me. When I got to my compartment, I found that I was rooming with three males, none of whom I knew. Thankfully, some of my colleagues saw what was happening and came to my rescue. They shifted me to an all-female compartment with two women I knew. The fourth woman was a tiny Chinese woman, who avoided eye contact and sat huddled in the corner of her bunk.

Fortunately, we were too tired to talk and pray. We just crawled into our narrow coffin like bunks and tried to sleep. The next morning, one of our colleagues, who lives in Korea, was able to converse with the Chinese woman and to our shock learned that she was a Chinese Communist Government employee. Thank you, Lord for Your constant protection!

My roommate in Xian was Joyce and although we had been in class together for three years, I didn't know her very well. What a blessing to learn that she is Chinese. She had been in the USA for most of her life, but her family still lived in Taiwan, so she spoke, read, and wrote Mandarin Chinese fluently. My greatest concern was being in a country where I didn't speak the language and couldn't read the signage, so Joyce was a gift to me from God. We prayed together each morning and sought the Lord's protection for ourselves and our families and as we toured together and ate in various restaurants, Joyce talked with me about the sites from her native perspective.

Breakfasts were better in Xian with real eggs and French toast with honey along with the usual apple juice and rice. The city was cleaner, and the smog was much lighter and almost nil in the countryside and there were more houses than apartment complexes.

During our stay in Xi'an, we visited the Terra Cotta warriors. The place was much like an American historic museum. There were several buildings with unearthed terra cotta warriors constructed by emperors over the centuries. Each warrior was constructed as an exact replica of a real human being. The facial details were amazing. The warriors were generally life sized, but some were decidedly larger than normal. There were horses and weapons as well.

Afterwards we stopped with great enthusiasm at a local Kentucky Fried Chicken fast food restaurant to have a supper that was not Chinese. We were, however, disappointed. I ate the bread of a chicken sandwich because I was afraid to eat the lettuce and I didn't think the meat was really chicken. I ordered a coke and forgot to tell them no ice so after a few sips; I quickly resorted to bottled water, so my much anticipated western meal turned out to be only bread and water.

We also visited the Daquin Pagoda located on a steep hill about two hours from Xi'an. It is the remnant of the oldest surviving Christian church in China. Daquin is the name of the Roman Empire in Chinese. The church and monastery were built by early Nestorian missionaries in 640. In 845, the persecution of Christians in China led to its abandonment. A Buddhist temple was later installed in the pagoda approximately 1300. In 1556, the pagoda was severely damaged due to an earthquake and was finally abandoned. Daqin was "rediscovered" in 1998 and now it is recognized as a significant part of the history of early Christianity in China. Currently it is a Buddhist temple.

We climbed the hill using a steep foot path of rocky crevices and slippery soil. The pagoda has an octagonal shape made of bricks with seven stories. There were four doors on the first story and two doors on the others. Near the pagoda were two altars to burn incense to Buddha. We were told not to go inside the Pagoda, so I just looked in and saw a picture draped in cloths near an altar where incense had been offered.

A replica of the Nestorian Stele supported on a stone tortoise was located to the left of the pagoda. The Nestorian Stele is a Tang Chinese stele erected in 781 that documented 150 years of early Christianity in China. It is a tall limestone block with text in both Chinese and Syriac describing the existence of Christian communities in several cities in northern China. It reveals that the Nestorian Christian church was recognized by the Tang Emperor Taizong, through the work of the Christian missionary Alopen in 635. According to the Stele, Alopen came to China from the Roman Empire bringing sacred books and images. Buried in 845, probably during religious suppression in conjunction with Buddhists, the stele was rediscovered in 1625.

In the village at the foot of the Pagoda hill was an orphanage with approximately 100 children who had been abandoned by their parents because they were deaf or had other special needs. Our Chinese contacts led us through the village and to the orphanage. There were approximately 30 little boys who sat on a porch step, uncharacteristically still, because as I was told they were not allowed to get up and run and play. Young girls performed a choreographed dance to a song for us — much like the worship dancers in our American churches. My friend and roommate Joyce said that she saw lice crawling in the girl's hair, which was a concern since several hugged me after a picture together. I bought a small handmade ornament for five Yuan, and we took up a collection and donated it to the orphanage, which is privately supported.

The orphanage was surrounded by kiwi, orange, and pomegranate fields. It had been a long time since we had had the opportunity to use the restroom, so the orphanage leader took the female students to the restroom. How relieved and happy we were until she led us to a kiwi field behind a house and motioned for us to go there in the open air, which we did out of desperation. This was definitely a "bring your own paper" occasion.

The next day we worshipped in a Xi'an church that seated at least 500 with overflow seating outside. The congregation was approximately thirty percent male and seventy percent female. Some smiled at us as we were led to the seats reserved for us, but most looked forward without eye contact. The service followed a typical order and when I sensed the Lord's presence, He spoke to me saying, "I am everywhere, and I am drawing all people to myself." After church we ate at my favorite restaurant in China. At TENG SHI NONG JIA DA YUAN or Big Court the food was fresh with many different kinds of vegetables and the spices were not so hot.

That afternoon we traveled to the airport to fly from Xian to Shanghai. Some luggage had to be shifted from checked to carry-on, including one of my bags, which had my toiletries in it. At the security check they confiscated my saline because it was too large and also saw scissors in my attaché case. Oops!! I had meant all that to be checked. Fortunately, Joyce was with me and interpreted so that they let me go through.

We landed and took the bus trip to our hotel. Joyce and I continued to be roommates, which was a joy. We were most compatible and enjoyed the same things. We often prayed and shared prayer requests. Our room had a fantastic view. We looked out over three streets that seemed to converge at our hotel. The buildings in Shanghai were enormous, maybe 50-75 stories. There was a river that ran in front of the hotel, and we learned that we were only a few blocks from the ocean. We arrived about 8:00 pm and were allowed time to get to bed earlier than usual. Joyce tried her computer before bedtime and burned out the battery with a converter and adapter that obviously didn't work right, so I didn't even try.

Our Shanghai hotel was the most elegant of all and the breakfast food was excellent. Eggs and bacon prepared according to Asian taste. The bacon was actually cooked well done and somewhat crispy. We had rice and some mousse type desserts and pastries that were mildly sweet. For lunch we went to a buffet style Western food restaurant. I had Asian American pizza, French fries, chicken strips, Pepsi without ice and soft serve chocolate ice cream. My being was SO happy. I felt nourished for the first time in a long while.

After lunch, we went to the Transformation Academy. It is a private school in Shanghai administered by Christian teachers. The school curriculum does not include any Christian material, but the after school activities do. English as well as Chinese is taught. Grades begin in K5 or first grade through ninth. Thereafter college prep is provided by families and tutors. College acceptance is a reflection on the whole family and each student tries earnestly to pass the entrance exams for the best schools. A volunteer parent named Sophie gave us an overview of the school and took us on a tour.

After the school we were taken to the Bund or the glitzy shopping district, which is blocks and blocks of LED lit shopping buildings. The bus left us to stay as long as we wanted and return by taxi. We walked and looked but didn't find anything we wanted to buy. We paid 80 RMB or about 25 dollars each for a taxi ride, a mere four blocks. Again, I was thankful that Joyce understood the language and knew the culture well enough to hail a taxi and haggle the fare. It was 10:45 and we had to be in the lobby with our luggage at 4:30 am to fly to Seoul, Korea.

Korea was much more harmonious, with many Western and

Christian sensibilities, yet there I found myself stretched in another direction. My heretofore familiarity with the casual and increasingly cynical climate of the USA was jolted by the more formal and wonderfully respectful culture of the Korean people. I sensed joy and life beginning with the Korean flight crew and thereafter in every introduction and setting, such as bowing and shaking hands with two hands, the generous outpouring of food—meals, snacks, coffee, etc., and their willingness to include us in the National Wish for Unification Prayer Day trip and house church prayer service. The practice of removing shoes before entering a room was the most uncomfortable Korean cultural difference that I experienced, but it is a custom that I would like to retain.

I also observed that the standard of living in Korea seemed to be higher than China and perhaps even the USA. I did not see homeless people, beggars, or persons selling food or souvenir quality goods on street carts. I saw evidence of concern for the comfort, wellbeing, and health of the people, including the disabled, which was totally absent in China. There were many people in the parks with babies in carriages and dogs on leashes. There were joggers, walkers, and families with tents having picnics beside the river. The people were always respectful, bowing to each other and smiling. In Korea, there were spoons to serve the food and the water quality was generally acceptable and the cities were generally clean. A drastic change from China.

Airport check-in went much smoother, and the Korean crew was so nice, always bowing and smiling. We were given hot cloths to bath our hands and face before a meal of sashimi salad. When we landed at Incenon Airport in Seoul, we were greeted by our host, a Kwanglim Church Pastor.

With 85,000 members, Kwanglim is the largest Methodist

church in the world. We were staying at Seminar House, Kwanglim's retreat center located about an hour from Seoul. When we were in China, I had a Chinese roommate, Joyce, and when we got to Korea, I got a new roommate—a Korean pastor named Yong-Hui McDonald. Thank you, Lord!

Our room at the Kwanglim Seminar House had a foyer area where you took off your shoes and put on slippers. The floor was heated, and the room was hot, so with some help from our colleagues, we got the air conditioner switched on and the windows opened. My pillow was too big and caused my neck to be bent at such an angle that I experienced numbness in my left hand and fingers, so I stuffed the pillowcase with dirty clothes and slept on that.

Our bathroom was clean and there was a western toilet and there was also a roll of toilet paper, which is considered a luxury in S. Korea. In fact, Yong Hui told me that toilet paper is so scarce that people steal a roll whenever they can. Seminar House had an elevator and a unique winding walkway adjacent to all floors, which was the quickest way to the dining hall and all our meals. Supper was kimchi, spaghetti, and seaweed soup with tofu. I enjoyed the soup and spaghetti but was disappointed in the kimchi. I had often heard of kimchi and looked forward to trying it, but it was far too hot for me to eat.

After supper we were briefed on proper etiquette and learned a few new words. Hello in Korean is phonetically spelled anu ha say yo and Thank you is calm sa ha me da. Pastor is mok sa nim and Deacon is gip sa nim. We were reminded to bow and were shown how to shake hands properly—with two hands.

The next morning, we traveled an hour and a half to Kwanglim Church in Seoul where they assigned us to groups of four and paired us with a Kwanglim pastor and a lay person to attend a house church prayer meeting. The meeting I attended was held in the home of a deaconess in a high rise apartment complex. We were given access through an elevator with a monitor and communication system on the wall that allowed the resident to see and converse with the person ringing their doorbell downstairs. Entering the home, we were reminded to take off shoes and I was embarrassed because I didn't have on socks or hose, but thankfully, we soon sat on the floor at a table with our feet under the table.

There were approximately thirty women in attendance, along with the host, Pastor Kim, a lay person named Joe, and the four of us. The worship service included hymns and a message and prayers. We sang two familiar hymns, Blessed Assurance and When the Roll is Called up Yonder, according to words provided in Korean and English. Then we prayed.

The Korean way of prayer is a cacophony of voices praying out loud simultaneously. The leader prayed the loudest, but I could hear some voices praying in tongues and even though I had no idea of what was being said, I sensed the presence of the Holy Spirit. I observed the passion and earnestness of the leader and the members. During one of the prayers when all of us were praying fervently together, I sensed openness above us as if the very ceiling had become open to heaven itself. Then quite suddenly and unexpectedly, the prayers ceased in unison in a quiet and gentle way as if led by the Spirit. A confidence rested in my spirit that the petition had been heard and the Lord had answered our cries. Then the pastor gave the message.

After the service, we were served an amazing meal—probably 15-20 dishes, prepared by a Korean chef, the sister of the host. Then gifts were exchanged. The Pastor gave the deaconess a statute of Jesus and the hostess gave each of us a gift bag. I received a fan and scarf.

After two such services we gathered again at Kwanglim Church coffee shop and toured Kwanglim Church, which included a high rise cultural and educational center, a social welfare center, and a Wesley Chapel. In the Wesley Chapel was a death mask of Wesley—one of only three in the world. The other two are in England and at the World Methodist Museum in North Carolina, USA. I saw many beautiful paintings including "Prodigal Son" and "Laughing Jesus," both painted by a quadriplegic using his mouth. On the eighth floor was a 1,000 seat theater that was used for concerts by local popular artists. A line of book bags held someone's place in line to purchase tickets, which spoke volumes to me of the respectful Christian Korean culture. Most impressive was a cross with the statute of a kneeling worshipper made of wood from North Korea, Antioch, and China for unity for the church's 40th anniversary.

The next day was one of the most exciting days of my life. We were up at 3am and rode the bus back to Seoul, an hour and a half ride. When we got there, we were told that we were going to one of eight military bases to participate in the National Wish for Unification Day of Prayer. We were told there we would leave in approximately an hour, so I walked with a small group of pastors to a nearby 7-11 to get coffee, but suddenly I heard my name being called out through the store. David, our Chinese host, was calling me to run and board a bus of Kwanglim Church members bound for the military base on the Demilitarized Zone (DMZ). So, I literally ran to the Kwanglim Church bus, and I was late! They had been waiting on me for about 30 minutes, but I had no idea and, of course, I was embarrassed to have delayed a bus full of Korean clergy and church members. There were two other Asbury pastors and me and one of the other pastors shared an official apology for the delay.

My seat was directly behind the church clergy who gave me a smiling welcome and a goody bag for the three hour drive from Seoul towards North Korea. The temperature dropped significantly as we rose in elevation, and I only had on a three quarter inch sleeve shirt. No jacket as there had been no words about preparation. An elegant older couple behind me spoke English. The lady's name was Tre, and she shared her scarf with me so that I could be warmer. The husband had graduated from Georgia Tech, so we had a time of sharing, and the gentleman gave me a high five.

We were greeted at the DMZ by a military band dressed in red uniforms and playing a salute to us. We bowed and shook hands with the officers and a group of soldiers. We had our picture taken with the clergy and the military officials and we attended a service held in an observation gallery with a 180 degree view of the DMZ. There were speeches and hymns and prayers. I was reminded of Beth's vision regarding my "lighted" footsteps in Asia. From our position we could see North Korean fences, a village, gardens, and a military base and Star Mountain, a North Korean stronghold. At precisely 11:00 am, we joined eight military bases and churches across South Korea praying simultaneously for unification.

After the service, my ATS colleagues and I were guests of the clergy on our bus at a restaurant near the base. We ate from a hot pot placed in the middle of the table. I was able to eat short spareribs with chop sticks and white kimchi, which I thoroughly enjoyed. There was also a bean based chocolate tasting milk shake in a bag, which was very good.

On the way back to the church we stopped at a government park to climb a mountain side with a spectacular view, but I was cold and tired and needed to get some rest, so I stayed at the bottom and talked to others. The leaves were changing, and it reminded me of fall in North Georgia. Soon we were back in the bus for the three hour ride back to Seoul and then another hour and a half ride to our Seminar House home away from home.

Unfortunately, my Korean roommate, Yong Hui and I were not compatible. She got up at 3:00 in the morning and answered emails and worked on a book she was writing. The beeping of her emails and texts woke me and when I turned on my back, I woke here with my snoring. I suggested that maybe she could find a place outside our room to work during the middle of the night, which thankfully she did, and I asked her to please wake me if I disturbed her. She was staying in Korea to visit her family after our class trip and brought them rolls of toilet paper she had stashed in her luggage. I had only one roll of paper left to last through the rest of our week in Korea and I put in our bathroom to use. The next day it was gone. I was furious and confronted Young He about the missing roll of toilet paper. She, of course, denied knowing anything about it, but the next day, it reappeared in the bathroom, so I got it and locked it in my luggage for safe keeping.

The next morning after a breakfast of warmed, not toasted, bread and Korean style coffee, we loaded our luggage onto the busses for a move to Prayer Mountain, but on the way there we visited Visionland, Kwanglim Church's youth retreat center. At Visionland, we saw a beautiful church and swimming pools, several courts and fields for sports, and a large dining facility being enjoyed by a multitude of smiling elementary age students. We ate lunch in the cafeteria and had some quiet time on the grounds.

Then back to Kwanglim South Church where we met with Bishop Sun Do Kim who spoke with us about the birth and mission of the church. Ten beautiful steps led to the altar, which according to Dr. Kim symbolize the 10 commandments and a pulpit made of alabaster stone from his homeland in North Korea. Dr. Kim had been a medical doctor in the North Korean army and escaped. Within five minutes of his escape, he met the South Korean Army and was welcomed into it as a soldier-medical doctor. Eventually, he became a South Korean four star Colonel. Dr. Kim started Kwanglim church with 115 members and a vision to grow the largest church in the world. That evening we were his dinner guests and received a gift of his book, which he signed individually for each of us.

After dinner that evening, we went to Prayer Mountain, the retreat center for Yaido Church. It was late and there were no elevators, so the men formed a line and hoisted the luggage up the stairs. My roommate was still Yong-Hui, and our room was more distressing than anywhere we had stayed before. The pillow was acceptable and there was adequate bottled water, but the bathroom was full of mold and mildew. We kept the bathroom door closed to diminish the mold spores and tried to hold our breath when we were in there. Fortunately, Yong-Hui went to another room to do her three am work.

My time on Prayer Mountain was the best experience of the whole trip. We were given a few hours of free time to walk Prayer Mountain with its more than 200 grottos with statues of Jesus and stories in the Bible. I walked slowly, savoring every moment of the peace and quiet and beauty. I stopped by each grotto and contemplated the scene and the Biblical story it portrayed, and I prayed and listened for His quiet voice in my heart. Sometimes I stood briefly giving thanks before the replicas of characters like Mary and Joseph. Other times I lingered with tears running down my face.

I was physically tired and mentally saturated from the sights and sounds and experiences of the last two weeks. I longed for my Lord—to hear His voice, feel His presence, and learn what He had to say to me. Why am I here Lord, at the ends of the earth? What do you want me to know, Lord?

Soon I sensed His presence. I held my breath in anticipation, and I was blessed beyond belief. Jesus began to speak and talked to me constantly as we walked the winding path all the way to the top of the mountain. I had no way to write His words, so I prayed, "Please, Lord, help me remember all that you are saying to me."

He talked about me speaking His words and feeding His sheep and how that gives Him joy. He talked of living waters, His cross, and reaching the lost and spoke about me traveling and speaking to multitudes. His words sunk deep in my heart, and I received their meaning, but it was all too wonderful to put into words. As the bottom of the hill, I was led to a chapel where I sat for a long time savoring the echo of His message. "Yes, Lord," I prayed, "Thy will be done."

The next day we attended services in the two largest churches in the world. The morning services were at Kwanglim Church, the largest Methodist Church in the world. The first service, for approximately thirty ten to twelve year old children, included worship, a choir, two pastors who used PowerPoint during their message, and ended with an offering. After the message the children went into classrooms where they cooked an entrée. One class cooked a Korean pizza dish made of fish and sprouts and mushrooms. The other group made a sandwich, which looked like chicken salad on whole wheat bread with lettuce. The dishes were submitted to judges and the best dish, the sandwich, was announced.

We then attended the 11:00 am worship service in the beautiful sanctuary and used a translation device to understand the Korean singers and speakers. The service included hymns sung by a 120 member choir with a huge orchestra. Lunch was with Senior Pastor Kim in the church's large dining hall. The food was excellent and included steak and chicken.

That afternoon we attended services at Yoido Full Gospel Church, the largest church in the world with 880,000 members. The church services, which are offered night and day every day of the week are projected on five huge screens in a huge auditorium with several balconies and broadcast live on television. There is even a bus route throughout the city, specifically transporting people to and from Yoido Church and Prayer Mountain. Again, we used a translation device to understand the service which included singing led by a large worship team, choir, and orchestra and worship dancers followed by a message. As we were leaving, we gathered for a picture on the front steps of the church and there we said our goodbyes and headed to the airport for our journey home.

Doctor Professor

I have often said that my life is either feast or famine because it seems to go from one extreme to the other, sometimes by way of sharp rights or lefts. That was my life in the fall of 2015 as I was preparing to go to China and Korea.

I was leading the renovation of the new Oconee River Church on Research Drive. The church had been repainted inside and outside and the lights replaced in the sanctuary and fellowship hall. The altar or stage, as the pastor and congregation called it, was widened. Gary II had built and installed an altar rail and privacy wall for the choir, who later refused to sit on the stage, but there had been issues with the choir for years. We had deliberated about the pews for weeks during which I produced countless drawings of the pews and spaces between them and the aisles beside them. Finally, the Pastor agreed reluctantly with the board's preferences.

I was working with Gary and Chuck to track, purchase, and install the items identified by the congregation and approved by the board. Everything was on time and on target (another one of my favorite sayings) for the move and our first Sunday in the new building on November 1. For fourteen years, Oconee River Church (ORC) worshipped in temporary locations, such as a school cafeteria, the community civic center, a funeral home, and most recently a renovated storefront. We believed that God had given us the building in a new location and now we were all excited to see what God would do through us in our new church home. I left for my trip with the confidence that everything would be ready for that momentous day.

Another significant event that happened during those days of preparation was the receipt of an email from Athens College of Ministry announcing the position of Chair of the Christian Ministry Program and giving the requisite position qualifications and a description of the responsibilities. I read and reread the details. It got my attention, and I thought, "I could do that. I have those qualifications." I put the email away, but those thoughts stayed at the back of my mind for the next few days. I also remembered Hezekiah. 2 Kings 19 which tells how Hezekiah received a letter from the messengers and read it. Then he went up to the temple of the LORD and spread it out before the LORD.

So, that is what I did. I printed the email and laid it on the table before the Lord and prayed, "Lord, I seem to be interested in this position and I believe I have the qualifications. I don't know if this is Your will for me or not, but I lay this out before You and pray Your will be done. If this is for me, would You have them contact me as you usually do." I was not laying out a fleece because I had had so many positions and titles and not one of them had I sought, so if God wanted me to take that position, He would move ACM to contact me. Then, I folded up the letter and focused on my trip.

This was also when Gary and April were having the worst of times. Gary called me one night. It was late and April was not home again. Gray was sick and Gary had worked all day, came home to wash clothes, and take care of babies, feeding, diapering, bathing, and getting them to bed. He sat in the recliner holding Gray and poured out his heart to me. He couldn't go on, he said. He was tired physically, but worst of all he was tired of April's lies and late nights, avoiding his calls, making excuses, and ignoring his pleas to come home and be the wife and mother she had vowed to be. My heart ached for my child and his children.

Along with Oconee River Church, the Athens College of Ministry position, and Gary's marriage, I also received approval to begin my research from the Asbury IRB—another thing swirling in my mind. Then it was time to go. For two weeks, I left all that behind.

I arrived home from Korea on Tuesday, October 26, and slept the majority of the next two days. Jet lag was rough going over there, but it was so much worse coming home. Friday, I went to the church. Everything looked great and seemed to be ready for Sunday, the first service in our new building. I did notice a different kind of lighting in the sanctuary than what had originally been ordered, but those were very nice, so I was happy that whatever happened had worked out.

The Nov. 1st service was the culmination of five months of coordinated work by multiple ministry teams and an ad hoc renovation and decoration team. Although it was not flawless, the congregation overwhelmingly rejoiced in praise and worship to God for the bountiful blessing of such a beautiful traditional church home. While the first service in our new church building went relatively smoothly, the second Sunday service did not. It was clear that the building was ready for the people, but the people were not ready for it.

That afternoon was the monthly board meeting and the atmosphere was cool, to say the least. I reported that yes, there had been glitches and snafus during the service, but the issues were related to practice changes necessitated by the new facility and were being addressed. For example, the new facility warranted four ushers instead of two and their lack of coordination and communication were obvious to the whole congregation during offertory. Additionally, a second station for Holy Communion was added and even with relevant instructions, the members were unsure of when and where to move.

Directing his comments at the pastor, Gary complained that the services in the new facility were an "appalling embarrassment" and that the ushers looked like "Keystone cops running around in circles" and that the service was "being micromanaged by that woman (a relatively new member named Suzanne) who directed the rows of people during Holy Communion." Chuck entered the diatribe by reiterating Gary's complaints, again directed pointedly at the Senior Pastor, and adding his concerns that "people will not stay if they are not happy with the church."

Both Gary and Chuck stated that although Oconee River Church was in a new facility, that it was not a new church and that "we don't need any big church ways." All of that was directed at Pastor Hoard, but it sure felt like it was meant for me. I listened and looked Gary and Chuck in the eye as they spoke, rarely would they even look at me.

When Gary ended his harangue, the Sr. Pastor didn't speak, so I spoke. I said I was sorry that he was so upset and would be happy to talk with him about it. I reminded them that change is not easy to some people and not everyone's expectations could be met. I noted that the ministry teams had worked together very well and had made a lot of progress since their beginning in August, but acknowledged that there was certainly room for improvement.

The Senior Pastor, who was laughing and obviously uncomfortable, nervously said it was his fault because he had worn a suit, which he never did, and thus his "putting on airs" had made everyone uncomfortable. Then, as if to fix the problem, he professed never to wear a suit again. Gary apologized for taking so much time and the meeting was adjourned.

At first, I was stunned by the emotional passive-aggressive behavior of two adult businessmen with whom I had worked so closely and amicably all summer. Since returning from my trip, I had sensed an aloofness about them and a few of my emails had not been acknowledged. But with so many tasks associated with moving into the church, I did not think much about it. That Sunday morning, I had also noticed a few small clusters of women in hushed conversations, and I had also heard a grumbling comment from long time member, that we (ORC) are not a "big" church.

I had come to ORC from a very big church and assumed the derogatory remark was aimed at me, but I had expected some resistance to change, and the general uncomfortableness people experience in a new environment, so I did not become overly concerned. Most people were happy and very thankful for the traditional church facility, so the vehemently emotional comments were unexpected.

At home after the meeting, I prayed. Lord, what is going on? Did I say something or do something wrong? Please convict me if there is something. "It will be ok," I understood the Lord to say. "You are right where you are supposed to be, doing what you are supposed to be doing." So, I prayed for the pastor and the board and the church as usual and left it with the Lord. A day or so later, Chuck called and apologized for his behavior during the meeting. I told him that I had prayed about the situation, that God had not convicted me of any wrongdoing on my part, and that I had left the situation to Him. I also told Chuck that I had no ill feelings toward him or Gary.

Later that week I had a meeting with the pastor and found out more about what had happened while I was gone. Apparently, a women's decorating team had met over the need for a last minute decision pertaining to the light fixtures. While there, a few remaining renovations were discussed and unequivocally dismissed by the group. Those renovations included two flat screen TVs above the stage and risers for a seated choir, which were, coincidentally, the only requests the Senior Pastor made during the whole renovation process. The women, who summarily rejected those renovations, included Chuck and Gary's wives and coincidentally, a few days later, a called board meeting was held during which Chuck and Gary stated that those specific renovations were technically impossible to accomplish.

The Senior Pastor's response was avoidance and depression to the point that observant members called his demeanor to my attention in great concern. To me he complained saying, "I didn't get a thing I wanted" and surmised the incident to be a power struggle—"a hill he was unwilling to die on." He had asked the choir to be seated and they had refused. He didn't want pews, but the congregation did, so he was overruled. He wanted a screen, but two board members had resisted him. All those issues had caused him to have a meltdown at home and at church.

The next morning, I was asking God for help with a case that I needed to write for my last paper at Asbury, a Critical Review Essay. Suddenly, I had the answer. The board meeting was the case study for my paper. How amazing! The issues and the board's response totally exemplified the principles of two of the books, *A Failure of Nerve: Leadership in the Age of the Quick Fix* and *Immunity to Change*, I had had to read and reference.

Now I know God did not cause the board meeting to happen as it did so that I could have a case study, but God does work all things together for good for those who love Him and are called according to His purposes. It was a lesson I will never forget. Most of all, I am thankful God was present with me through it all.

When life comes at you that fast, you just live through it and process it later. The week after the ORC board meeting experience was when April was fired from her job for embezzlement and Gary found out about her many adulterous affairs. They separated, and he began divorce proceedings. That is also when I started taking care of Gary, Gunner, and Gray, cleaning his house, while continuing to teach and preach at the church, finish the papers for my ATS courses, and prepare to conduct the research seminar in January. Life since my return had been nonstop, in the secular and in the spiritual.

On October 31, a few days after returning home from overseas, I got a call from Annunciata, a Haitian woman who had attended ORC only a couple of Sundays last May, but the connection we made in that short time was significant. I met Annunciata literally in the door to the church. I opened the door to go out and there she stood, and my spirit was immediately drawn to her so I welcomed her with a hug. She had a beautiful radiant smile, and I could just feel the love surrounding her. She said that God had nudged her to come to our church. I was so affected by her presence that I cried all the way home. The Holy Spirit in Annunciata and in me rejoiced at our meeting and the tears were tears of joy. I wondered what God had planned for us, but she attended only one other Sunday that summer. In fact, I am not even sure how she got my telephone number.

She left a message asking if I was okay and said, "You are

a woman with a beautiful spirit, and I want to tap into it." Wednesday morning November 3, I was awakened at 5:00 am. I sensed that God wanted me to get up and pray so I did and had a couple of hours of quiet time reading and praying and writing in my journal. Then I was reminded to return Annunciata's call. WOW!

She said that she was an apostle and that God had brought her to ORC specifically to see me. She said that she had had a vision of a gray haired lady who opened the door and hugged her. Then she came to ORC, and I opened the door and I hugged her and told her how beautiful she is. She said that she had been praying for me all summer and knew I had been through a lot. She spoke of my calling and said I had an anointing and that others were drawn to me because of the Spirit of God in me. Then she began to speak things no one else in the world knew. Things only God could have told her. Things I had not even put in words, spoken or written. She spoke the things Jesus had put in my heart on Prayer Mountain.

Annunciata said that I needed to speak extemporaneously instead of using a manuscript and that I was being kept back or hindered in flowing with the Holy Spirit and all God had for me and to not be surprised if God moved me. She said I needed to be at ORC to get the credentials of pastor, which God had already given me. Annunciata said that I had come out of Egypt (which I understood as the UMC) and that some people were missing me while I was gone saying, "I want my Debbie back." She quoted Jeremiah 1: 9-10 (the Scripture God had spoken over me when he called me into ministry). She spoke of a healing anointing that was powerful and said to take the authority that God had given me or was about to give me.

Annunciata also spoke of ORC. She said that I was carrying

ORC on my shoulders and that God had told her about the fear and harassment I had had during the summer. She ended our conversation by saying that God had instructed her to call me and tell me all this so that I would be affirmed in all that God had spoken to me in Korea. "Thank You, Lord," I prayed, "How very precious to bring an international apostle to speak Your words to me." That was seven years ago, and I have not heard or seen Annunciata since.

A few days later, on November 7, as I lingered in my quiet time I sensed His sweet presence, so I sat very still, and without speaking, I waited and listened. I was led to open my mouth and Jesus fed me something like sugar and kissed my forehead. Then He said that He had given me a coat of many colors anointing and that I was to come out of the world (family, church and ???) and move into the place He had prepared for me. Like Joseph, a coat of many colors anointing is a nation's anointing. He said and then promised that my family would be taken care of, and it would not hurt to move. God would take care of it all. He called me a general and said that I was born for such a time as this and that now is the time to put my hand into Jesus' hand and walk with Him.

When He finished speaking and I felt His presence lift, I thanked the Lord and prayed to be open and trusting and to obey God's will. Then I googled a 'coat of many colors anointing.' The Hebrew word for 'coat of many colors' means a long robe of distinction and refers to the robe of the priest. The anointing represents the call of a priestly ministry unto God—separated, consecrated. The article said that an anointing is not for after we die but for the body of Christ now. It also mentioned that in the natural after we have received a prophetic word from God, our lives will often take a downward position—to humble and prove what is in the heart and overcome self.

Like Joseph, every trial brought him to a lower place in the world with more confinement for a few years, but then the dreams or prophecies over his life came true. In just four days I had gone from one of the happiest times of my life in receiving the amazing confirmation through Annunciata and the coat of many colors anointing, to one of the worst experiences of my life with Gary and April and Oconee River Church.

Through it all, the letter from Athens College of Ministry lay on the table essentially forgotten until December 27 when I received an email from Dr. Marcia Wilbur, President of Athens College of Ministry asking me to consider "joining our leadership team" as the Chair of the Christian Ministry Program. I just smiled. Thank you, Lord, of course, I would be happy to do that, Lord.

I reviewed the position description and agreed to meet with Dr. Wilbur on January 5, 2016, to discuss the responsibilities. The salary was low as compared to my RN salaries, but not as low as the ministry salaries. The position was 24 hours a week but was considered a full time position and could be worked in a 12 month or nine month period. It also required a two-year commitment. I believed that this was brought to me by God and that this was where God would like to use me, his vessel. It would be a new and different opportunity for me that I thought would be personally rewarding, so I submitted my application on January 5 and was offered the position on the 23rd. The position didn't actually start until June when the funding would be made available.

From January to June 2016, I conducted a research seminar, and the post seminar interviews. The data was analyzed by the UGA Statistics department, and I finished writing the last two chapters of the dissertation. Gary and April's divorce papers were finalized through mediation in February, but April refused to sign the papers, making one excuse after another until the attorneys and judge got upset. I was beyond upset. She finally signed them in July.

I also went to ACM each week for a staff prayer meeting and met with Dr. Wilbur occasionally to become oriented and acclimated to college life. As I got to know more about ACM, I learned that many of my WINGS sisters were already involved there. Peggy, Cindy, Martha, and Pam were serving in the Prayer Ministry and had shared our earlier vision of Betheland with Marcia. She asked me to prepare a syllabus for Systematic Theology and Preaching by June. I gave the keynote address called Journeying to Your Destiny in a Women's Ministry Seminar there at the college. This is what I said...

"It is an honor to be with you. I have known and loved some of you for decades, but others I am just meeting today. Cindy gave you the facts about me; RN, Pastor, but maybe you are still wondering why God gave me the opportunity to speak with you today. Well, let me introduce myself to you as one on a perpetual journey.

"My name, Deborah means bee in Hebrew. It comes from the root word dabar, which means "to arrange"; When used of words, it means "to speak". Both of these derivations describe my life. First like a bee, I am a social creature. In fact, I married a bee. My husband is Gary Huckaby, a pharmacist and avid golfer. His friends call him "Bee" and of course that makes me "Mrs. Bee". We have two sons, who are known as "Little Bees" and our grandchildren call me "Mommie Bee."

"Have you ever heard of the cliché busy as a bee? Well, I think that I can claim that description as well. I have moved 22 times in my life. I have attended 17 different schools, which include eight colleges, and I am completing my seventh and final—I pray—degree for a total of 39 years of education.

"Beekeepers say that the social organization of a beehive rivals even the best run corporation. I, too, have the gift of organization or arranging, as my name means. I once dreamed that I would be the person responsible for organizing the Macy's Thanksgiving Day parade. Although I have never had that employment opportunity, like a bee moving from one flower to another, I have held 23 different positions and titles. Now I didn't set out to be a professional student, and I wouldn't recommend it. I don't mean to be boastful by sharing all this—it's just as Parker Palmer said, 'My journey is no more or less important than anyone else's, it is simply the best information I have on the subject.'

"Through all of this, God has taught me a whole lot about this journey called life, so today I'd like to share with you some observations, and stories that hopefully will be useful to you on your journey. So let us begin with prayer:

"Ephesians 2:10 says, we are His workmanship, created in Christ Jesus for good works, which God prepared beforehand so that we would walk in them. That says to me that we were created and called for a purpose. God calls us to Himself to do all things and to live all our lives as unto the Lord Jesus Christ. We are called into HIS ministry, into Jesus' ministry to God the Father, through God the Holy Spirit for the sake of the church and the world. To be a disciple of Jesus Christ is to be a follower of the Way, His Way. And we remember that Jesus walks in some interesting places. Like walking on mountains and on water, through doors, and even in the air. So, we must realize and accept that as we follow Jesus, our journey can get exciting.

"In 1997, God called me to feed His sheep and tend His lambs, but I didn't know what that meant, so I just kept doing what I was doing. Then in 2002, at the height of a successful healthcare career, God said, 'It is time!' Now, I didn't know how to go from being a nurse and healthcare director at Athens Regional Medical Center to being a pastor, preacher, or whatever God was calling me to do, but God did, so I just said, 'Lord, I don't know how to do that, but you do, so go ahead.' And He did! Well, that was 14 years ago and if God had told me then what was ahead of me, I would probably still be running.

"Calling in the Bible is a theme that becomes a metaphor for life. Some people say that life is a journey, a battle, a roller coaster ride, a river or maybe a box of chocolates and you never know what you'll get. Eugene Peterson defines metaphor as language that in a single word conveys the indivisibility of the visible and invisible, of the seen and unseen, of heaven and earth, so a good metaphor moves us to see our ordinary world in extraordinary ways.

"People of faith sometimes see their lives like the stages of a butterfly. We say we have 'mountain top experiences' and we go through the valley of the shadow of death. We follow the path, the road, and the way. We ask God to open and shut doors and we see ourselves as children of God and we long to be held in our Father's arms. Our personal metaphors have the ability not only to reflect, but to shape our understanding of who or where we are.

"For years I struggled with God's call. I knew God's hand was on me and life was amazing at times, but I seemed to move from place to place and position to position and I didn't understand why. God called me 'Deborah Shepherd' but where were the sheep and lambs. I began to receive sermon outlines and whole sermons and one of you sweet sisters said I looked like a fish with my mouth full of words, but I didn't have a pulpit. People would ask me what I was going to do, and I didn't know what to say. Some people thought I was a professional student and that I just liked graduate school. My family wondered if maybe I was nuts!

"For years I had dreams of losing my pocketbook. In each dream, in different settings, I would be searching frantically for my lost pocketbook. Did I need to be more careful with my pocketbook? Was someone trying to steal it? Finally, one night I dreamed I was sitting at a kitchen table and Jesus was teaching us a Bible Study. He was sitting across from me, and the Bible was open on the table in front of Him and while He was teaching, while Jesus is in front of me speaking, I get up and go around behind Him and start looking in the cabinets and drawers for my lost pocketbook. Jesus said, 'Debbie do I need to get up from here?' 'OH! NO!!! NO, Lord. I will come right back over here and sit down!!' Well, that got my attention and soon the Lord gave me understanding. 'Debbie, what is in your pocketbook that is so important to you?' Well, it wasn't money! It was my driver's license, my nursing license, and a credit card. They all represented my identity. I was frantically searching for my identity.

"It's like a parable I once heard about a beautiful tree. In the beginning the tree was skinny and frail but it grew and grew and before long it had a luscious mantle of green leaves. The tree saw how the people and the animals came to rest under its branches, so the tree decided it was a big green shade tree and spread its branches out far and wide. But one bright spring morning the tree was covered with little buds, which soon burst open with flowers. Oh, thought the tree, I am a flowering tree, and it was sure it would spend the rest of its days as a sweet smell and a pleasing sight to everyone who came near. But as a spring progressed. the flowers dropped off and little hard balls began to form where the flowers had once given the tree such beauty. This was most confusing to the tree which no longer knew what it was. Time passed and the little hard balls turned green and then they grew bigger and bigger and eventually, they ripened into delicious red apples. Only then did the tree realize what it was created to be all along.

"Like the apple tree, I was searching for my purpose in life. What I would be when I grew up and that was part of my problem. I still saw 'my calling' as what I was to do, instead of who I am to be. I thought God was calling me to a particular title, a job description, another position. Something that I could well, something Debbie could do. But God is calling us to 'be' instead of 'do.' And the One who created us to be who we are and calls us to be who He alone knows we can be wrote the blueprint in our hearts.

"Eccl. 3:11 says, 'He (God) has set eternity in our hearts. So where is eternity written in your heart? The answer is in your desires. John Eldredge agrees! In his excellent little book, Dare to Desire, he says that the secret of our life's existence is written in our heart's desires. Unfortunately, most of our lives are lived according to a script that someone else has written because if we are not in touch with our specific purpose, we will become attached to or co-opted by someone else's. So, if we are ever to find ourselves, we must find what God has set in our hearts. Eldredge says, 'Instead of asking what you ought to do or what the world needs. Ask yourself what makes you come alive, what stirs your heart and go do that because what the world needs is people, who have come alive!'

"Os Guinness writes that God calls us to Himself so decisively that everything we are, everything we do, and everything we have is invested with a special devotion and a driving force to be lived out in response to God's summons. In other words, God has created us and our gifts for a place of His choosing and we will only be ourselves when we are finally there so do what you are!

"Well, I didn't know how to do that either! I had had many positions and honestly, I enjoyed each one, but I had always been what I did. That's the way of the world, isn't it? You assume an identity, you learn the language, you buy the proper clothes, and you climb the appropriate ladder, but with the help of J. Keith Miller and his book called, What to Do With the Rest of Your Life, I found out. I studied every position and role I had ever had; Wife, Mother, Nurse, Director, Ministry Leader, and I identified the desires and motivations that gave me such joy in each one. What activities seemed to best fit my gifts and abilities? What gave me a sense of satisfaction? Where was my greatest passion or sharpest pain? It was then that I learned who I am and who God had created me to be and now, I know what I am called to do.

"To help me stay the course and be true to my calling, I wrote a personal mission statement. It goes something like this; I minister whole person health by speaking and writing God's word and by facilitating individual and group new beginnings. To me, speaking and writing God's Word meant preaching, teaching, writing, and administering courses, and writing books and facilitating individual and corporate new beginnings could be done through prayer ministry, personal consultation, resource liaison, and developing and implementing small and large group endeavors. That resonated with my soul! A preacher, A teacher, A writer. Helping people and groups discover new things and experience new beginnings. That is what I love to do! This was the blueprint written into my heart!

"These were the things I do or should do because of who I am, who God had created and called me to be. When I looked back on my unusual journey, it made sense! Through many people and places and experiences I could see how God had shaped and transformed me, I could see God's plan! Well, this has been the story of my calling, but it is just one story.

"Mother Teresa was once asked if she found her work futile and hopeless given the immense task of caring for so many helpless children. In her typically humble fashion, she replied, "I was not called to be successful, but faithful."

"Each one of us has something beautiful to do for God. An ancient Christian tradition states that God sends every person into the world with a special message to deliver, with a special song to sing, and with a special act of love to bestow. No one else, please hear me, no one else can speak your unique message, sing your song, or offer your act of love.

"We are all created in Christ Jesus for good works and called into His ministry, but how do we do that? A few weeks ago, while praying I heard our Lord say, 'You are in the way!' Well, my eyes flew open, and I sat there stunned. I knew it was the Lord's voice, but it didn't sound like a conviction.

"As I continued to listen and pray, I realized He had said, 'You are in the way—not, My way!' Then I understood I was in, The Jesus Way! Jesus says, 'I am the Way. Follow Me!'

"Eugene Peterson discusses The Jesus Way, saying way is a metaphor designating a road that leads to a destination and also the way we go on the way. It is both the root or route we take and how we make the journey. The way of Jesus is not only the road that Jesus walked in Galilee and to Jerusalem. It is also the way Jesus walked on those roads, how he acted and talked and prayed. It is how He healed and also how He died. Peterson also reminds us that Jesus is both the way we come to God and the way God comes to us. God comes to us in Jesus speaking the words of salvation, healing our infirmities, promising the Holy Spirit, and teaching us to live in God's

Kingdom. Through Jesus, we pray to God and believe. We hear and obey. We love God and praise God. Jesus is our way to God, at the same time Jesus is God's way to us.

"As I said earlier, the Jesus Way leads us in some strange and unfamiliar places, so you can be sure that following Jesus means change. If my life testifies to anything, it is that how we are called to achieve our purpose can be done in many different and creative ways, but change is not fun, is it? If we are in a great place, we may not want to leave. If it is a hard place, we may move too soon. Between one place and another is transition. People say when God closes one door, He will open another, but what happens in the hallway? On my journey, in the many different places and through the transitions between, I've adopted these five precepts that guide me in my journey.

"First, I have learned that God usually takes a place or something out of me before God takes me out of it. Before God told me I was to be a pastor and a preacher, I was in a Baptist Church where I was very involved in ministry. I taught Sunday School, sang in the choir, served on the Constitution Committee, and was the Director of Discipleship Training. One Sunday sitting in the choir, looking at the people I loved, I felt an overwhelming sorrow. It was as if I was gone. I sat there in stunned grief wondering if I was about to die.

"Before long, things began to happen. The Constitution committee finished its work, my term as the Director of Discipleship training came to an end, and one by one all my assignments ended. It was that August that God moved me out of that church and when I looked back, I could see clearly how God had taken everything out of me and then moved me out of it.

"So, when things begin to happen, when you see patterns, especially things in threes—open your hands and release every weight, every care and concern to the Lord. God will not remove what is still pertinent for your time and place but clinging to things or even people will only cause pain when Jesus says, 'It's time. Follow me.'

"I've learned how God gently nudges me to do His will. In 2003, God made it very clear to me that I was to go to Wheaton College in Chicago and get a master's in theology, so I went willingly, but I thought that was all the higher education I needed. So, when I graduated, I thought I was ready for ministry. I soon learned that the ordination track required three more courses, so I said, oh well, what is three more courses after all I had been through.

"I enrolled at Emory in the Candler School of Theology. In the middle of my first semester there, I learned that because of some transfer rules, it was not three courses I needed but ten. Well for about a month I whined and complained, finally I agreed. So, I enrolled in next semester but then my money source dried up and I had to drop out. Now what?

"That spring I was on a Walk to Emmaus when God spoke very clearly and very persistently for hours in the night, that it was not a few courses I needed, I was to get another Master's. Three Masters...that was ridiculous!! I had never heard of anyone who had three Masters, but when I showed up for orientation the first day of my M-Div. degree, sitting across from me was a woman who said, 'She knew it was crazy, but this would be her third masters.'

"Two years later at Asbury Theological Seminary, I was taking Hebrew, the hardest course I have ever taken in my life. For four straight weeks I studied from four A.M. until midnight. The night before the final exam I was barely holding onto a C, which is not acceptable. It was that very night when my physical strength and mental abilities were totally exhausted that God broke the news to me of a Doctorate. Really God? Really? Well, I guess that means I'm going to pass Hebrew, which I did, and I made an A.

"A wonderful song by Babbie Mason goes like this:

God is too wise to be mistaken. God is too good to be unkind. So, when you don't understand When you don't see His plan When you can't trace His hand. Trust His heart.

"I also learned—the hard way, that unless Jesus says move, don't! 2008 was one of the worst years of my life, not because I was busy, but because I was supposed to be resting. You see, I'm the kind of person that coasts at 55 miles an hour. So when God sat me down to rest, I was not a happy camper. For months I fretted. When I finally got still and was content to sit quietly, I received the rest I needed and was prepared for the next part of my journey, which turned out to be the busiest seven years of my entire life. Now, I'm convinced that if I had cooperated in the beginning, my preparation might not have lasted a whole year.

Debbie Huckaby

"Our Scripture is filled with stories of preparation: God prepared Joseph through dreams, family betrayal, and imprisonment. David was prepared through the ordinary task of tending sheep. With Daniel, God used formal education and relationships. To Mary, God sent an angel to sit down and talk with her and answer her questions. To each of us, our God, Jehovah Jireh, the Lord Who Provides, will supply all our needs according to His riches in glory!

"I have learned, at a heart level that the call of Jesus is a corporate calling. The church is an assembly of God's called out people, each one summoned individually and uniquely, but not summoned to be just a bunch of individuals but to be a community of faith. Jesus calls disciples to live and work together. As disciples and followers of our Lord Jesus, we can't be who God intends us to be in isolation. We are to share life together.

"On Sept. 24, 1999, at 12:15 pm, God said He was forming an Oconee Christian Women's Group. That very night a lady came up to me and said, 'Debbie, I think we need to get a group of women together and study the Bible.' That kind of thing happened more than 20 times over the next two months, so on Dec. 6 at the Oconee County Library, 23 women gathered with me to see what God had for us to do. That night was the beginning of a women's ministry group, eventually called WINGS that met every Monday night for more than eight years. As we shared our journey, God knit our hearts together and transformed us into the ministry leaders we are today. These women are truly my sisters, who I will always love.

"If you are in a small group, cherish those whom God has brought into your life. If not, ask our Father for journey partners, sisters in Christ, to help you be who only God knows you can be! For as Margaret Mead said, 'Never doubt that a small group of thoughtful, committed citizens can change the world; indeed, it's the only thing that ever has.'

"And the most important precept I hold is to live for an Audience of One. Col. 3:17 is my life verse; it says, 'Whatever you do in word or deed, do all as unto the Lord Jesus.' Os Guinness calls this an audience of one. Living, before an audience of one, transforms everything, every thought, word, and deed before God. I have nothing to prove, nothing to gain, and nothing to lose. No one or nothing is important enough to come between me and God. After all, it is only the audience of the One True and Living Holy God that really matters.

"As we end our time together today, I'd like to leave you with these last thoughts: Have you ever wondered why God created you to live in this day and age? Why, in all the years, across all the centuries, and in all the countries, you are here today, called by the Lord Jesus Christ for such a time as this. What do you sense God asking you to do? What makes you come alive? I pray you will dare to dream God size dreams, things only God can accomplish because God is able to do exceedingly abundantly above all we can think or ask. Today, I believe our God is calling all of us to 'come up higher.' To be willing to make the necessary changes in our life in order to embrace the blueprint already written in our hearts.

"Rev. 2:17 says, to him who overcomes, I will give

some of the hidden manna and I will give him a white stone and a new name written on the stone which no one knows, but he who receives it. Rev. George MacDonald says the new name written on the white stone is a person's true name. A name which expresses the character, the nature, the meaning of the one who bears it. It is an expression of God's creative thoughts when He first began to make the child and of God's nurturing thoughts throughout her life. It is a woman's own symbol, a picture of her soul in a word, and it is only when she has become her name that God gives her the stone and says, 'Well done, good and faithful servant, in thee, I am well pleased!' Now may God bless you and keep you and make His face to shine upon you. AMEN!"

* * *

Soon after the seminar, I had an experience that has resonated with me many times over these past few years. Pam, Debbie, Kay, and I went to a church in Jefferson that had a fruitful prophetic ministry. God had brought together several people with prophetic giftings and one Friday a month they held a prophetic service. I sat with Denise, Danny, Karen, and Robert. The session was recorded, and these are some of the things they believe God said to them about me,

"You are going to see multidimensionally—that means you are going to see past the bottle and past the water and you are going to see the molecules—the deep stuff and you are going to point out things. You are going to spot disease and different things that people don't know at the molecule lever. You are going to be confident in what you see. There is great wisdom.

You are able to take it and cycle through it and cause it to make sense. Wisdom that you will actually make sense for someone to take it and eat it. I see you writing a book, like a women's study because of the words that go deeper, dissecting, and being able to write a study. Your friends will be able to help in writing that by bouncing ideas off of them and getting wisdom from them." Finally, they emphatically said, "Don't put a period at the end of a sentence. Don't put things in a box. Let them grow because you've got great expansion in you. You like to hide behind the leader, but you can't be afraid of being seen. You are a way maker! It is for the kingdom. You have been prepared to carry the weight of glory. You are prepared."

In June, I began to work with Athens College of Ministry. I learned that there is only one department, the Christian Ministry department or program and I am the Chair of it, so that put me in charge of all curricula. I would help faculty create the curriculum, syllabi, evaluate their teaching, determine whether we are teaching what we need to teach, oversee the degrees for bachelors and masters, associate and certificate, and teach my own courses. Along with the position came a new title. Marcia started addressing me as Dr. Huckaby or Dr. Debbie, which made me feel very uncomfortable at first since I had not graduated, and my dissertation had not received the final approval, but I was excited and humbled to be given the position and prayed for the wisdom and strength to do so as unto you, Lord Jesus.

Since 2003, the sighting of a Wheaton truck was a significant event, so when I saw a triple-trailer Wheaton truck on August 12, I was excited to see what God would do. I was on my way to a virtual global leadership conference being broadcast at Living Hope Church and Marcia met me at the door, smiling and crying at the same time. God has shared with her the connection of faith and health and how it is connected with the college. She believed that the college was to be a global hub for training healthcare and ministry professionals in the integration of faith and health. I was excited and apprehensive at the same time. I was excited with the possibility that my research and study would bear fruit, but I was apprehensive about the way that might be done.

Marcia was eager for the college to implement her vision. She asked for a digital copy of my dissertation. I loaned her a copy of the unfinished manuscript instead. Two days later, she sent me a proposal for a grant to teach physicians and assess their patients' response. I didn't see the need for further research. Dr. Harold Koenig, who mentored me at his Research Institute in the fall of 2009, had conducted 30 years of research and written eight books documenting the benefit of faith on health conditions.

I prayed to shepherd the dissertation well and to hold it lightly and follow God's lead. I assumed that God would continue to bring the vision and promises to fruition and keep me involved and informed. I confessed, "Lord, I am leery of giving away five years of work for someone else to implement. I prayed against being selfish, prideful, and protective, but to be obedient and work well with others." After praying I still had a sense that things were not right, so I shared my concerns with Marcia, and we worked to develop an implementation.

That day, Wednesday August 18, 2016, I taught my first class as a college professor and left for vacation immediately afterwards. While traveling that afternoon, I was blessed to see another Wheaton truck, the fifth such trucks in the past fifteen years and it had been, yet again, a significant day.

An Honorary Master in the Art of Nursing

In February 2017, I was honored with a Master in the Art of Nursing by Brenau University's School of Nursing. Lori Floyd, Cheryl Wunsch, and Mary Cooper came to the ceremony where I was presented with several gifts and gave the following address...

"It is an honor to receive this award and a blessing to me to be able to address this gathering. I have had many opportunities in life. I have moved 22 times and I have attended 17 different schools, which includes eight colleges. I have just recently completed a Doctor of Ministry degree, which was my sixth and final degree, I pray, for a total of 39 years of education. Over these past 44 years of nursing and 20 years of ministry, I have held 23 different positions and titles and even as I say all that, it is hard for me to believe because occasionally, I still feel 20 years old.

"Seriously, I shared that because when I look back over my life, I attribute success in every field, every position, and every challenge to the skills I learned in nursing school. In fact, I believe that everyone should attend nursing school. Not because everyone should or could be a nurse, but because everyone needs the skills and experiences that nursing provides.

"People have asked me for years, what made you decide to become a nurse and I do not really know. My father was a Hospital Administrator and Comptroller, so I think I have known about shift work, financial audits, Joint Commission, and the whole medical world my entire life. It was not until the end of my first year in college that I decided that nursing was what I wanted to do. You might say that was the dark ages because I was only 21.

"While attending nursing school I worked full time on a busy 45-bed nursing unit that included labor and delivery, medical, and postpartum patients. Yes, you heard correctly! 45 patients; medical and postpartum patients and labor and delivery together and I was the charge nurse! That was because I was the closest thing to an RN, other than the house supervisor, so I learned a lot fast and applied what I learned immediately. This is the essence I believe of why I love Nursing. For me Nursing is never boring. There is always a challenge and like Forrest Gump said, "You never know what you'll get."

"My first position, after nursing school, was in L&D, but between my interview and my first day of work, the head nurse suffered a heart attack and was put on medical leave for three months. So, on my first day of work as a Licensed Registered Nurse, I was made the interim Head Nurse of L&D, Postpartum, and Nursery. That interim position lasted for two years.

"Thereafter, I began working in different areas of nursing in the hospital Medical, Surgical, Labor & Delivery, Family Care, Nursery, ICU, NICU. Each area for one to two or three years, learning new things and working to improve my skills until I knew that I could competently provide good care in that area of nursing. Eventually, because of these experiences, I became a House Supervisor, which was my most favorite position.

"Then, for 20 years, I worked as a director during which time I had the unique opportunity of developing and implementing four new departments at Athens Regional Medical Center. They were Oncology, Nursing Finance and Information, Quality Support Services, and Clinical Informatics.

"Now I was not just trying to fill out my resume'. You see, through all these wonderful opportunities, I always felt that I was not there yet! Like I did not know what I wanted to be when I grew up. I loved nursing and I often said, 'I did not care if they paid me or not' as long as someone would feed me and pay my bills, I would work for free. Yet, I always knew that there was something more and because of that, I made commitments to myself. I made a commitment to learn whatever I could in preparation for what might be ahead, and I made a commitment to excellence! My life verse, or that verse in the Bible that guides me most often is Colossians 3:17 It says, "Whatever you do in word or deed do it all as unto the Lord Jesus Christ".

"Then whatever I did was not for myself or a grade or even for my supervisor. What I did was for the Lord. I worked hard to do everything to the very best of my ability, whether anyone saw me or not. because my best is all the Lord expects of me and knowing that gives me peace regardless of the outcome!

"At the height of my nursing career, when I was making the most money, had the best position doing what I had wanted to do for 12 years, which was leading our hospital's implementation of the Electronic Medical Record, the Lord called me to full time ministry. Now Lord? Yes, now! That is what I did. I left my director position, took a staff nurse position in the Resource Utilization department, and enrolled in graduate school to be a minister.

"From a veteran director to a staff nurse was a huge transition. Not only was there a substantial cut in my salary, but for the first time in my then 30 year nursing career I was not in charge of anything or anyone, except myself, but the worst part was the grief. Every day in RU meant one day closer to leaving nursing and while I was excited about the ministry, and I was sure that I was doing the right thing, I couldn't imagine not going to the hospital every day. I thought about how I would not know about the latest drugs or latest treatments or procedures. I would not know the latest discoveries. Eventually, I reasoned that healthcare and ministry are both healing disciplines and maybe ministry was that something more that had always eluded me.

"And then, in February 2007, three months before graduation and one month before early retirement, it happened. That is when I heard about parish nursing for the first time in all my years as a nurse. Parish Nursing, what is that? Well, Parish Nursing, now known as Faith

Community Nursing, is the specialized practice of professional nursing that combines the science and art of nursing with the care of the spirit and addresses whole person health: mind, body and spirit. That was it!! My life had been on a trajectory to bring together my passion for healing and my faith in God. Finally, my soul was content, and my life made sense!

"I graduated with a master's in theology in May and became a Faith Community Nurse in June and even though it was the answer to my decade's old quandary, it was just the beginning. Since 2007, I have completed a master's in divinity and a Doctorate in Ministry but Nursing and more specifically whole person health; mind body and spirit never left my heart.

"My doctoral research and dissertation focused on the integration of faith and health and how we are transformed to wholeness and ultimately restored to the image of God. The seed for this research began in 1999 when a member of our church asked me if I would pray for her. She had been diagnosed with a breast lump on Thursday and was scheduled to have a Stereotactic biopsy on Tuesday. So, we got together Saturday to pray. During our time together, as we prayed, I thought to ask her if there were any troubled relationships in her life. She gasped and said, 'My sister! I haven't spoken to my sister in five years.' We talked and shared Scripture about forgiveness. Then when we prayed, she asked God to forgive her and prayed to forgive her sister. That evening the sisters reconciled. Just three days later, according to medical x-rays, the lump had disappeared. That was 18 years ago, and it has never returned.

Debbie Huckaby

"I am a caregiver at heart. This experience ignited a passion in me to help people be whole and healthy in their minds, bodies, and spirits. According to Dr. Harold Koenig, of Duke University's Center for Spirituality, Theology and Health, more than 30 years of medical research has shown that people who maintain spiritual practices, pray regularly, attend worship regularly, volunteer or serve others and have a social network of friends, stay healthier, have fewer hospitalizations, fewer surgeries, and recover quicker after hospitalizations. As a nurse and a minister, I see how healthcare providers and ministers influence more people in our world than any others. It seems that whatever a healthcare provider or minister believes, it is shared with others and trusted by those who hear it!

Today I am working at Athens College of Ministry. I teach courses and serve as the Chair of the Christian ministry program and, most exciting of all, we are working on implementing my dissertation by creating wholeness care teams of healthcare providers, clergy, and prayer ministers who will work together to assess and treat the mind, body, and spirit equitably.

"I do not really know why I became a nurse so many years ago, but for all these reasons, I am proud to still be a nurse today. When I see you in the hospital or doctor's office, picking up your children at school, or running into the grocery store, I consider you my colleague. You see, I know what you know about nursing, and I respect your wisdom and understanding. I know how you manage a unit interacting with patients, physicians, nurses, ancillary staff, and visitors constantly for 12 hours and I commend your leadership skills. I know how you care for others even better than you care for yourselves and how tired you are when you agree to work a double because, well, somebody's gotta do it. I know how you suddenly sit straight up in bed in the middle of the night when you remember something you forgot to do for someone. I know how you shed a few tears in the breakroom and then sob all the way home when someone loses their fight for life.

"So, from one nurse's heart to yours, may you be blessed with a spirit of gentleness and a heart that is tender. May you be blessed with a spirit of compassion for those in your care. May you be blessed with a spirit of openness, understanding, and respect for all people. May you be blessed with a spirit of courage, to be all you were created to be!"

A Doc and a Post

Thursday, May 18, 2017, was one of the best days of my life! That was the day I uploaded for publication the final, approved, and official version of my dissertation. Done! What a joy to be able to wrap five years of work like a present and put a bow on it. While that day was special, it was typical of the whole 2017 year. What a great year! What a busy year! A year of travel, transitions, and transformations.

I ended 2016 with a lighter spirit and greater hope. I had taught the research seminar in January, collected, and processed the data, completed writing the last two chapters and obtained the necessary signatures, all by August of 2016. So, I was technically ready for a December graduation, but that year Asbury eliminated winter graduations, which meant I wouldn't graduate until May 2017. I had been received and credentialed in The Wesleyan Church as an ordained minister in July 2016 and I was serving with Rev. Richard Hoard at Oconee River Church. I finished teaching Systematic Theology, my first college course, at Athens College of Ministry and Dr. Marcia Wilbur and I were working together to grow the Wholeness Care Project through the college. Then Donald J. Trump was elected President instead of Hilary Clinton, which was a great relief.

Although I had a few months before graduation, the wait was not onerous or boring. In fact, it was exciting to be preparing for graduation and a trip to Israel, one of the highlights of 2017. I had completed all the requirements for a Doctor of Ministry degree, including the dissertation. To share the collective knowledge, we, the students in my class, were gathering before graduation to present our research to each other and our professors. It would be such a momentous occasion that I spent weeks and weeks preparing the power point presentation and the manuscript by which I would speak.

On Sunday May 15, I traveled to Asbury for possibly my last such trip and stayed again with Dale and Myrna Hale. It had been over a year since I had been to their home in Wilmore, Kentucky, and I savored every sight and sound from the exit in Athens, Kentucky, past the white fences and acres of green horse pastures, to Man-O-War Boulevard, and Jessamine Station Road and finally onto Growers Mill Road, the tiny one lane road in front of my home away from home. It felt so good to be there again, even if I had to hoist my luggage upstairs to the familiar two bedroom, two bath, and living room on the top floor. Supper that night was a sweet time of catch-up with colleagues Judy, Rod, and Ray.

Tuesday, Wednesday, and Thursday were set aside for the colloquium. My presentation was on Wednesday afternoon. The feedback was excellent, and my colleagues seemed to sincerely appreciate my research and presentation. One colleague, a pastor from Tupelo, Mississippi, said that mine was probably the best doctoral level research that was presented. That was encouraging and the professors were quite affirming as well. Dr. Marmon said that my research was very good and that I definitely needed to publish articles about it.

That night, Dale and Myrna treated me to dinner at the Shaker Village, where we spent hours catching up on families, work, and life in general. They literally prayed me through so much during my many years at ATS, including the four weeks I studied night and day taking Hebrews and the morning it was so cold that my car keyhole froze and oh yes, the flat tire. Dale and Myrna were a large part of my life at ATS, and I will always cherish their friendship.

I uploaded the final version of the dissertation on Thursday, and it was sent to the editor on Friday the 19th. Dr. Guertson met for lunch on Thursday with those of us going to Israel and briefed us on our itinerary. Gary arrived late that afternoon.

Friday morning Gary and I had breakfast at a local landmark, Solomon's Porch, and afterwards we walked around Wilmore, him seeing it all for the first time and me lingering at each spot for one last look. That afternoon was our hooding ceremony in the beautiful Estes Chapel. We rehearsed the ceremony and then, with our hoods over our arm, processed to our designated seats. When our turn came, we each ascended the stairs onto the chancel and knelt on the bench. Our degree leaders, Dr. Ellen Marmon, and Dr. C. Milton Lowe positioned the hood over our head and Dr. Timothy Tennent, President of Asbury Seminary and Dr. Jessica LaGrone, Dean of the Chapel anointed us and prayed.

The hooding procedure, somewhat similar to ordination, brought a sense of sweet affirmation and an immense relief for a job well done. Then, we joined my class at the Wilmore Senior Community Center for a banquet in our honor. My place card read Dr. Deborah Huckaby, which was such a pleasing sight. We ended the evening with Myrna and Dale enjoying ice cream desserts.

Saturday was the culmination of that week and my last five years. Arriving at the Luce Physical Activities Center at 9 am, I gathered with my class in a room near the auditorium while Gary went off to find a good seat. I was happy to see my friends, but a little disappointed to learn that not all of our colleagues had finished their research and would not be graduating with us that day. We rehearsed, then had a continental breakfast together. Soon, in cap, gown, honor tassel and hood, I processed with my class into the ceremony.

My keepsake program reminds me of the order of the ceremony. I know that Dr. Tennent presided, and I remember how wonderful the auditorium sounded when we sang Charles Wesley's famous hymn And Can It Be. I remember standing as Dr. Tennent charged the Class of 2017 and the tears filling my eyes and blurring the words of my response. We are called…to preach the gospel, serve the poor, and live in holiness. We each affirmed that we have heard God's call to a vocation of ministry and stand ready to take further steps of faithful service and mission and that we trust in God and give our lives to a life of earnest piety and community with the Holy Spirit being our helper.

The most memorable part was the walk across the stage, shaking hands, receiving the diploma, receiving a Bible, and getting my picture made. A few short seconds, but they still resonate joy in my being and bring a smile to my face. Doctor of Ministry, done! To You belongs all praise and honor and glory. It was only accomplished through Your will and presence and provision. Thank you, Lord. That afternoon Gary and I gathered our luggage, ate Kentucky barbeque, and headed home.

I was so thankful to the Lord for the work that I had accomplished, and so very grateful to friends and family who had prayed and lived through it all with me that I held a graduation celebration. That next day, Sunday May 21st, which would have been my mother's eightieth birthday, I hosted a drop-in graduation reception at Jennings Mill Country Club for my family and thirty couples. I displayed my cap, gown, tassel, and hood along with my diploma and a copy of the dissertation manuscript. We ate finger foods and delicious desserts at round tables with white cloths and beautiful flowers. I was greeted and hugged and congratulated, but best of all I enjoyed seeing and hearing people I love have a good time together. It was the best way to end a phenomenal week.

Two short weeks later, on Monday June 7th I flew to Tel Aviv, Israel by way of New York and Istanbul for a two week post-doctoral seminar. Asbury had given us the choice of locations, Israel, or Kenya, and paid all expenses for my whole class of fifty students and the D-Min program leaders. I was beyond blessed to be able to go to Israel again and to have it be the site of a post-doctoral seminar was beyond my wildest dreams.

I had prayed earnestly for comfort measures aboard our eleven hour flight. I asked that I not be seated beside my three-hundred pound colleague, and I asked for an aisle seat, but in God's great wisdom I found myself in the center seat of the center aisle, next to my over-sized colleague. It was however a blessed journey and I now have a softer spot in my heart for him because I got to know him so much better.

Asbury had engaged Ronny Simon, an Israel historian, author, professor, licensed tour guide, and former Colonel in the Israeli military as our guide. He was the perfect instructor for a capstone trip covering the geographical, topographical, historical, and political impact of Judaism, Christianity, and Islam in Israel, designed to augment our studies focused on preaching and leadership in both the local and international contexts.

When we arrived in Tel Aviv, we were greeted by our Israeli hosts, and boarded motorcoach buses for a two hour trip to Tiberias and the Degania Bet Kibbutz where we would be staying. There I met my roommates, Yong Hui, the Korean pastor, who had been my incompatible roommate while we were in Korea and Kim Pope-Seiberling, a UMC pastor from central Pennsylvania, who was born a Korean, adopted, and raised in the USA, and had a ministry for orphans. Kim had graduated two years earlier, but had had to miss her immersion trip, so she was invited to join ours.

Our days were full, from an early morning wakeup call through lecture-saturated tours and the instructional briefings each evening after supper. Each day from the Golan Heights in the north to the Dead Sea in the south, I wore so much paraphernalia around my neck that I felt like a camel.

Regardless of my attire, each day I wore a long sleeved cover-up shirt, walking shoes, hat, sunglasses, sun block, water bottle, protein bar, lip gloss, passport, name tag, and travel purse, and we wore Whispers headphones through which we could hear Ronny, our guide.

Friday June 9
- Beth Shean—east side of Jezreel valley, Roman city, all built same, streets of basalt (hardest) Roman bath was probably first church, saw where first baptisms were performed (near bath) columns were heated by furnaces outside. The huge fires from the furnaces sent warm air under the raised floor which stood on narrow pillars of solid stone, hollow cylinders, or polygonal or circular bricks. The floors were paved over with 60 cm square tiles, which were then covered in decorative mosaics.

- Magdala—1st century synagogue where guide said he was sure Jesus would have taught.
- St. Peter's Primacy—Church on shores of Sea of Galilee; rock inside Church where Jesus likely ate fish breakfast with disciples after his resurrection. Jesus told Peter to feed his lambs and tend his sheep. Dead fish floating on sea.
- Capernaum—sat under tree and listened to guide outside synagogue. Basalt rock used in 1st century church; white stones used in 4th century. Earthquake level—basalt stones all over behind city. Could see city walls of basalt rock.
- Peter's fish = went to restaurant and ate tilapia called Peter's fish
- Jesus-boat. Saw boat in museum and heard story about how this boat was dug up with great care since the air caused it to disintegrate.
- Boat ride on Sea of Galilee—45 minute ride on boat from N—S end of Sea of Galilee with worship leaders who led us in singing worship songs. In background is Mount Precipice or Mount of the Leap of our Lord, just outside the southern edge of Nazareth. Point is 1296 ft. It is believed by many to be the site of the Rejection of Jesus described in Luke 4:29-30—The people of Nazareth, not accepting Jesus as Messiah tried to push him from the mountain, but "he passed through the midst of them and went away."

Saturday June 10

- Church of the Beatitudes—listened to a sermon on the mount as we looked out over the Sea of Galilee; cool breeze, pretty flowers, walked around church a few minutes. I like what Oswald Chambers says about the Sermon on the Mount. That it is not a set of rules and regulations, it is a picture of the life we live when the Holy Spirit is having His unhindered way with us.

- Tel Dan—Northernmost city of the Kingdom of Israel and belonging to the tribe of Dan. Was originally called Laish. The city is identified with a tell located in northern Israel known as Tel Dan in Hebrew or Tell el-Qadi. Only tribe that was dissatisfied with territory they were given. Moses gave permission for them to live on eastern side of Jordan River. First tribe that led nation astray to worship idols. Northern king Jeroboan built shrine with golden calf in it. First tribe that was destroyed in exile. Not in list of 144,000 in Book of Revelation.
- Caesarea Philippi where Jesus asked, Who do you say I am? Halfway up Golan Heights: Saw headwaters of Jordan River at foot of Mt. Hermon, Banias Arabic pronunciation of Panias = Greek God Pan
- Chorazim—Lebanese border/Israel...mountains in Jordan Valley—are volcanic lava
- Lunch—falafel, got locked in bathroom; Pita Bread (pita means bread) Pocket bread
- Golan Heights overlook (Mt. Bental)—saw soldiers with weapons. From battle of 1973 Yom Kippur, Syria had 1500 tanks and 1000 artillery pieces, Israel had 160 tanks and lost use of 153 of them. Syria lost 900 tanks and turned and fled; Israel won, great view
- Peace Vista—Observation point overlooking Sea of Galilee

- Adventurous drive through Yarmouk River Reserve, steep curves over the mountains

Sunday June 11
- Cana
- Nazareth Precipe — overlooking Jezreel valley
- Meggido
- Mt. Carmel and Chapel, Lunch — Schnitzel
- Toured Caesarea
- Traveled to Jerusalem — Staying at Convent near center of city
- Center of Jerusalem at night — Walked around, watched video on wall; sang Hallelujah with 50' tall hologram.

Monday June 12 —
- Negev
- Kumaran
- En Gedi — Spring of the goat
- Masada
- Dead Sea
- Jerusalem — Western Wall tunnel tour — a night 7PM walked under Jerusalem along Western wall. Approximately 488 meters of the Western Wall. The tunnels are supported by many arches and contain stairways that connected the ancient city with the Temple Mount, over the Tyropoeon Valley that ran along the western side of the Temple Mount, separating the two. Today these passageways support streets and homes in the Muslim Quarter. One such example is the famous western stone, which is 14 meters long and weighs almost 570 tons.

Tuesday June 13—
- Mount of Olives, graves; teardrop church,
- Garden of Gethsemane
- Palm Sunday walk
- Lion's gate (ramparts walk)
- Anna's church—incredible acoustics…sang hymns
- Pool of Bethsaida
- Via Della Rosa
- Muslim Quarter
- Christian Quarter
- Church of Holy Sepulcher
- Jaffa Gate—where east meets west
- Museum of the Book
- Dead Sea scrolls
- Model of Jerusalem
- Shopping in Jerusalem bought jewelry, etc.
- Spent time in convent garden and sanctuary in peace and prayer

Wednesday June 14
- Brunch with Kim—frittata; apple ginger juice
- Arts crafts district—bought mug
- Toured Zion gate
- Armenian Quarters
- Old City
- Hasmonean wall 1st century period of city
- City of David
- Upper room
- Caves of Ghenna, where David hid from Saul & where Judas died
- St. Peter's Galicantu

- Attended Conference — Hillsong and Jim Gaylord and Alan Kurish spoke

Thursday June 15 —
- Breakfast
- Shopping in old city Jerusalem
- Toured Jebusite wall
- Pool of Siloam
- Walked Hezekiah's tunnel
- Sat for a while on the Southern steps of temple
- Shopping at night with Eliseo

Friday June 16 —
- Visited Yad Vashem, Holocaust Museum
- Ate excellent lunch at Museum
- Spent a few hours at Garden Tomb, had Holy Communion together, sang
- Convent/Hostel — packing — supper > Tel Aviv...home

I could never describe what this trip meant to me. It deeply nourished my mind, my body, and most importantly, my spirit. Ronny is truly an expert in his field and poured into us, day and night for eight days straight. I have 107 audio files of his lectures. I listened and tried to remember his every word. My body was exhausted, but happy from the 22,000 steps we averaged each day and the wonderfully fresh foods like falafel and schnitzel, and oranges, tomatoes, and lemons right out of the gardens of the kibbutz and convent. My spirit was blessed. God met me in so many places, adding His words to Ronny's, making the sights and sounds applicable to my life.

In Dan, when we were walking, the Lord pointed out the

many smooth stones and assured me that my future would be like walking on smooth stones. At the garden of Gethsemane, when I knelt and prayed at the rock, believed to be the rock upon which Jesus prayed the night of his arrest and persecution, I had such an overwhelming sense of my Lord's presence that I could hardly breath or move. His touch I will never forget.

Another focus and highlight of 2017 revolved around different aspects of The Wesleyan Church. Oconee River Church had moved into the new church building on November 1, 2015, and I continued to work with Rev. Richard Hoard as the Assistant Pastor. I preached occasionally and taught some Wednesday night Bible study classes. In early 2017, Richard asked if I would teach an adult Sunday School class, which I agreed to do.

He and I met every week or two at Barnes and Noble or Chic Filet for coffee and ministry planning. It was during those times that Richard shared his frustration with ministry and his desire for rest. He was writing another book and had taken on some local sports broadcasting jobs, which he found more engaging than the church. He talked about a sabbatical or retirement. I told him that if he felt he had to get away, to go ahead, that I would hold it together until he got back. He was concerned for the people and how they would take it if he retired and I assured him that if he was okay with leaving, the church would be okay with his decision. At least that was what I thought.

Before 2017, my involvement with Dr. Berry and the South Coastal District of The Wesleyan Church (TWC) was limited to a monthly "Leader's Lift" at the district office in Conyers. That was when Dr. Berry shared updates and led us in seminar type presentations on church growth and evangelism. In 2017, my work with the SCD changed exponentially.

In March, Dr. Berry asked me to consider taking a new position in TWC called Clergy Care Coordinators. Each of the 23 districts would have such a position to provide confidential support to clergy and their families. It reminded me of the role of the Faith Community Nurse in providing personal support, prayer, and resources. Since whole person health is my passion, I accepted the role and looked forward to working with Dr. Berry and the district pastors. I have been called a pastor's pastor and have come to think of myself in that way. Just recently, the Lord told me that the pastors and their families are my congregation.

On May 31, Dr. Berry emailed requesting a telephone appointment on Tuesday June 6, which I was happy to schedule. As I prayed about our upcoming conversation, the Lord said that he (Dr. Berry) would give me many more responsibilities, and he did. On Tuesday June 6, the day before my flight to Israel, Dr. Berry asked if I would serve as the interim pastor at New Rock Church near Conyers and also asked if I would be the Assistant District Superintendent this next year. WOW! Of course, I agreed and thanked him for his confidence in me. I left for the trip the next day!

The day after I returned from Israel, I went with Marcia Wilbur and the Athens College of Ministry staff on a planning retreat in the mountains and that next Sunday I started covering for Richard at ORC while he took a six-week sabbatical. Since our paths were not crossing again until the conference in July, I had to share my news with Richard on the telephone. "What?" he said, "So you are going to be my boss?" Well, technically I would be, but I didn't say it.

The SCD Annual Conference is typically held the 2nd Thursday and Friday of July. While I was in Israel, Dr. Berry had asked me to take on several assignments. First, he wanted me to give a Ted Talk on Friday morning. I was also included in the program for the District Board of Ministerial Development luncheon and assigned to serve Holy Communion during the Thursday evening worship service. Dr. Berry introduced me to the conference clergy and church delegates as Rev. Dr. Deborah Huckaby, who has more degrees than a thermometer, and shared with them my role as Clergy Care Coordinator and Assistant D. S.

The next Sunday, an acquaintance from St. James UMC that I had not seen in probably ten years attended ORC worship services. He wrote a note and pressed it into my hand when he greeted me at the door. The note read, "I watched a green seedling turn into a beautiful white rose." What a precious word of affirmation from God through my friend. God is never early and never late. God is always right on time and that word of affirmation was exactly what I needed for the trip to Indiana that I made two days later.

My sermon series on King David ended in July and starting August 1, I began serving at New Rock Church. They had recently lost their long term pastor, Rev. Joe Harmon, and would be getting a new permanent pastor, but until then they had me. I decided to begin my time with them with sermons on the familiar prayers and creeds. My four sermon series included a message on The Lord's Prayer, The Apostles Creed, The 23rd Psalm, and The Ten Commandments. At the end of August the new pastor arrived, which ended my time at as interim pastor at New Rock.

That September I began focusing on the duties of an Assistant D.S., which I wasn't really sure about since Dr. Berry had not yet given me a formal position description. I was to facilitate the monthly Leaders' Lift as we gathered, prayed, and studied together the book, Fresh Wind Fresh Fire by Jim Cymbala. I was also a member of the executive committee of the District Board of Administration (DBA) and the District Board of Ministerial Development, which meant more trips to the Conyers office.

In prayer on September 4, the Lord said to me, "Dan (Dr. Berry) will retire. You will be the interim. Do not fear daughter. It is well with my soul." Well, I was shocked and disappointed. I had been looking forward to working with Dr. Berry and learning all I could from him, and I was concerned that I was not ready to be the District Superintendent, but I said, "Yes, Lord. Thy will be done!"

A few weeks later, on Sunday September 24, I had a meeting in Conyers with Dr. Berry and Rev. Steve Lane, the other Assistant D.S., for supper and planning. Thankfully, there was no mention of retiring, but the next morning Dr. Wayne Schmidt, the General Superintendent of TWC was at the meeting and Dr. Berry made his announcement. He said he was retiring at the end of the 2017-18 church year. I was speechless and held my breathe. I didn't know what would happen because I remembered God's words.

Then Dr. Schmidt addressed the board and asked that we consider merging with the South Carolina District and very specifically talked about not having an interim, which I found quite interesting considering what I heard from God. So, Lord, what now, I asked, and I was reminded that God's will would be done and that my way forward would be as smooth as the stones He had shown me in Israel. So, I determined to work with Dr. Berry and learn as much as I could for as long as I could and trust God to take me where I needed to go.

The DBA soon formed a merger team, and I was asked to work with the District Treasurer and a few others to assess the feasibility of the merger from a financial perspective. I enjoyed assessing financial records again, especially with Jim R., the district treasurer. Along with the merger meetings, I facilitated the monthly gathering and visited Wesleyan churches in north Georgia, but learning from Dr. Berry did not happen. In fact, Dr. Berry became so busy with finalizing his responsibilities that we rarely talked and saw each other only in district meetings. There were times when I seemed to be invisible again, not acknowledged in meetings, not included when pastors were recognized, and omitted from important emails. My friend Beth said that when Dr. Berry laid down his mantle, it was removed from me as well. That made sense, but certainly didn't feel good.

Then in March 2018, the District Board nominated and approved Rev. Steve Lane as the interim District Superintendent. So, what was I to think? I know in my heart that I honestly never had one thought about being the DS, until I heard from God that Dr. Berry would retire and that he would ask me to be the interim. So, did I not hear correctly? Had I somehow been disobedient and disqualified myself? Could someone else thwart God's will for me? These were just a few of the many thoughts that swam in my head. I knew that I heard God and I trusted God and God's thoughts are so much higher than ours. Why? I didn't have an answer.

From March to July, I continued in the Clergy Care role while Dr. Berry was finishing his responsibilities and Steve was getting oriented. My Assistant DS role continued, but in name only. At ORC, Richard had decided to retire and had informed Dr. Berry. On April 12, he announced it to the congregation and Dr. Berry met with the Local Board about the functions of a pastor search committee. Richard's last day was officially July 31 and he had asked me to preach for him June 24 and July 1 so that he could take vacation and I had agreed. It would be good to see the sweet people at ORC again.

ORC LBA invited me to meet Paul and Phoebe Kirk, pastoral candidates on Saturday June 11 and they issued a call to them on Sunday June 12. I had a thought—what if he doesn't take it and they ask me to be interim. That thought made me cry and cry and cry. I am always the alternate or when I get the prize or first place, it is lost or taken away from me. I do the very best I can, but it doesn't seem to matter. Lord, I don't want glory, I cried, and I don't want somebody else's place. I want my place! I want to be all and only who You created me to be.

At a SCD staff meeting, Dr. Berry shared that ORC's second candidate had declined their call and that they were considering a third. I thanked God that I was not on that search team. Then, out of the blue, Chuck H. called on June 25 and offered me the interim pastor position until a permanent pastor could be found. But, appointments come through the DS, and I had heard nothing from Dr. Berry. So, I encouraged Chuck to talk with Dr. Berry, who was not pleased that the LBA had taken steps without his approval. Soon, I got a text from him saying, "Chuck called, I guess we need to talk," which we did on July 2 and with his blessing and prayer, on August 1, 2018, I assumed the role of interim pastor at Oconee River Church. So, when God said Dr. Berry would ask me to be the interim, I thought God was talking about an interim D.S., but maybe He was talking about interim pastor. I still don't know.

Throughout 2017, Athens College of Ministry was a part of my daily life. I was learning more about my responsibilities, which seemed to increase regularly. I had taught Systematic Theology in the fall and was teaching Genesis in spring semester. Both were rewarding experiences. I studied diligently to bring the best instruction, not only in material, but in technique according to the principles of formative and summative learning that Marcia had shared. Another responsibility was working with faculty and students.

It was my responsibility to know each student, their declared degree, and their progress towards that degree, so that I could coordinate the course offerings with available faculty and provide the needed courses. Thankfully, there were not that many students because that was a complicated process for which there were no established procedures.

Academic quality was also a responsibility in my job description. I interviewed and engaged faculty and then collaborated with them to develop a syllabus, and to schedule the semester, day of week, and time to teach their course. Then I posted the syllabi and enrolled the students. During the semester I had the opportunity and task of evaluating at least one class for each professor and then sharing my feedback with them.

At the end of each semester, I gathered artifacts from each professor. These artifacts were tests, papers, projects etc. that the professor deemed representative of the formative and summative learning that had taken place during the semester. These artifacts were assessed and scored against the course objectives, which provided evidence of how well the course objectives were being taught and received. Then quarterly I presented that information to the Academic Deans who evaluated the courses, syllabi, and artifact assessments against the program objectives.

As you may have noticed, I was in the midst of a lot of activities, and there were many more steps I had to complete in order to accomplish each task, which was not unlike any other position I had ever had, but there was a component to this position that I had never experienced. It involved the weekly meeting each staff member had with the President to review their progress in accomplishing those minute steps. My position description provided the goals, and the progress notes provided the president with an update on my activities. Unfortunately, our individual work was never discussed as a team, so we didn't really know who was doing what.

As noted above, another aspect of my responsibilities pertained to the Transnational Association of Christian Colleges and Schools or TRACS. I think I have known about accreditations since I was a child hearing Daddy Jay talk about Joint Commission Accreditation surveys. When I was the Director of Quality Support Services at ARMC, I had an employee, Linda Thompson who was the JCAHO coordinator, so having a survey team come in to evaluate the college's policies and procedures was very familiar to me. However, it wasn't to the rest of the college's administration so as we prepared the documents for the upcoming survey, I shared from my experiences, and I think my input was helpful. The college received candidacy in April and continued to apply those practices towards full accreditation.

The most exciting and yet heartbreaking aspect of my time at ACMIN involved my dissertation. After I had finished the chapters and had gotten my coach's approval, Marcia asked for an electronic copy of the dissertation. I loaned her a written copy instead and she soon gave it back to me marked throughout in red ink. I was appreciative of the editing help, but some of the corrections went beyond grammar and punctuation. I admit I was somewhat offended by those. A week or so later at a conference Marcia had an experience with God during which she believed God was leading ACMIN to be a global hub for training healthcare and ministry professionals in the integration of faith and health, which was my dissertation. This was such exciting news to me that I even shared the plans with my colleagues and professors during my colloquium presentation.

All my life God had led me to start new things—the Oncology unit at ARMC, and the Nursing Finance and Planning, Quality Support Services, and the Clinical Informatics departments. Then there was the Georgia Parish Nurse Resource Center, which became the Georgia Faith Community Nurse Association and the Gwinnett Medical Center Faith Community Network with a Faith Community Nurse as the Network Navigator. Most recently, God had called me to lead the purchase and renovation of the facility that became the new home of the Oconee River Church.

So, starting a new global training center for whole person health was congruent with my personal mission statement and resonated as God's path for me. I also had times when I was called to function in a support role, like working in RU with Cheryl Wunsch and with Richard Hoard at Oconee River Church. Those were both times of transition for them and for me. I was excited to be a part of a new endeavor and eager to see how God would bring it to fruition. Soon Marcia and I began to conceptualize the vision. That is when our differences surfaced.

She created a proposal for another research project to show the efficacy of whole person, mind, body, and spirit healing. I didn't agree with the need for more research considering my work and the thirty years of research executed and published by Dr. Harold Koenig. I understood the project as the creation of a vast complex beginning locally and expanding to other countries. ACMIN would work in conjunction with the complex, but the complex would not be under the ACMIN organizational umbrella. Along with these differences in our vision, we had conflicts in the execution as well.

We had a project core team, which included me and Marcia, Dr. Ron Blount, and Dr. Juliet Sekandi, but I also wanted to cultivate a larger advisory group of community experts as I had successfully done with the other innovative starts in my life. It took me months to get them to agree to host a community informational event. It was a great success, but an advisory group was not understood and endorsed.

Our vision included a local network of area physicians who would include healing prayer in their treatment plan. At that time, I was still a Registered Nurse, licensed in the state of Georgia with forty five years' experience in hospitals and a doctor's office. I called it "prayer therapy," but Marcia said that she didn't know if she would agree to that terminology or not and she would have to pray about it. I talked with the former CEO of Athens Regional Medical Center, who gave me an update on the political climate of the area medical staff and made recommendations for garnering their support.

I shared this insight with the core team, but Marcia disregarded his recommendations and began meeting with physicians in her sphere of influence. I understood the copious forms and documentation requirements of healthcare professionals and recommended that we keep the intake questions to a bare minimum, which could be added easily to physician office software documents, but instead Marcia decided that the Prayer Ministers associated with the college should develop a questionnaire that would be filled out in the MD office. The prayer ministers needed orientation to the project and training in whole person health before that could happen. Marcia decided she should be the one to orient and train them in whole person health.

Through every day, every step of the way I prayed. I believed that the dissertation belonged to God and that I was blessed to be the vessel. If God brought it to and through me to bring to Marcia and ACMIN, then so be it, but I didn't know that for sure and what was happening didn't feel good. I cried out to God to understand my part to implement, and for grace to be obedient to that calling and for help to release the rest according to His will. For two days I had had a pain in my left breast, so I prayed to forgive Marcia and prayed for my healing and the next day the pain was gone! Thank you, Lord.

On November 17, 2017, God said that it was time to leave ACMIN. That I had done good work and would be leaving behind a legacy. That I had lost nothing at ACMIN and that I had helped many. He explained that I can't hold Marcia accountable to what I know because she hasn't been where I have been. Because of my experiences, I have a broader perspective and that people can't give what they don't have. God said, "I have resolved it all. You will not leave anything of value behind. You will not lose anything. I will not allow Marcia to usurp what I have put in you, and she will not hurt what I have created you to be."

"The Wholeness Care Project," God said, "is not of me! It is not the way the WCP will go forward. It is done! It is awkward! The foundations are not in place."

On January 11, 2018, I received my evaluation from Marcia and gave her my resignation or notice that I did not intend to renew my contract when it expired in June. It had been two years since January 2016 when I made a commitment to work two years, even though the contract wasn't officially signed until June. God said it was time to leave and I stayed because of the contract, but the next six months were difficult, to say the least.

Marcia sent out an email reminder of a New Year, New Heart seminar planning meeting at 2:00 PM. I had not been included in the original email, so I didn't know the meeting was about to happen and I was not aware that she had assigned me some of the topics on the agenda. She had also decided that the NYNH seminar would be about wholeness, mind body and spirit, and that she would be teaching on physical healing. It would be an understatement to say I was not a happy camper at that meeting.

Wholeness as Holiness was the title, which is the essence of my dissertation, but I was only included on the agenda as bookends, the opener and closer for a seminar whose speakers did not understand the concepts. I decided I had better give some insight into the things I would be saying to introduce and close the seminar. The whole time I was praying, praying, praying for God to keep my mouth shut, but when I spoke, a volcano of passion and hurt erupted out of me. I explained 1 Thessalonians 5:23 and told them quite frankly that they did not understand mind, body, spirit wholeness. I continued to pray that evening and found the peace that only the Lord Jesus Christ can give.

The student body at the college had dropped out significantly and with it went my workload. I literally had nothing to do but sit, which is far more difficult for me than being extra busy. I had no classes to teach, no students to advise, and very few summer classes to schedule, so I began cleaning out my desk and cleaning out my files.

Twice Marcia questioned my accuracy in public, once in front of a student. During a couple of meetings, she drilled me for explanations of an obvious answer. During a Wholeness Care Project meeting, she took over the meeting and gave assignments and then quickly realized what she was doing and said, "If that is okay with you, Debbie." A few days later she talked with me about her thoughts and behavior and concerns for the WCP, which seemed like a sideways apology.

While praying I asked the Lord why demeaning behaviors were now beyond my ability to deal with. His answer was an analogy. Every drop of rain causes an overflow if the rain barrel is full. My rain barrel was full to the brim. My capacity had been reached. I could not receive another drop.

So, at the end of January, I facilitated a WCP meeting and shared my vision and then I transitioned the prayer ministry, education, and data clearly into Marcia's hands and backed out of that project completely. Later, when the others had gone, Marcia asked me for my dissertation. I told her it was not mine to give; it was God's and that she should take that up with Him.

As the boring weeks went by, I decided that I would be present when needed and would complete my responsibilities, but otherwise, I had too much to do to just sit. I shared that decision with Marcia and that is what I did. I walked on smooth stones for the rest of my time there.

One day at the college I spoke briefly with Janie Griffith who stopped in to see Marcia. Soon Janie came back and said, "I think I have a word for you." She recalled a story about red high heels and said, "You are moving to a higher level, and like the bright shiny shoes, it will fit you like a glove. Red indicates love—a place where you will be visible, shining and loved." Thank you Lord, I am ready.

A Scene I Have Always Feared; Alone, Lost, And Vulnerable

It was the middle of July 2017 when I flew to Indiana for a Wesleyan Church Clergy Care Coordinators meeting. To say it was a very hard trip would be a gross understatement. The flight was scheduled for 5:40 pm and since you are required to arrive two hours prior to your flight and the airport is an hour and a half from home, I was really looking forward to getting settled and resting on the plane. Well, about 5:00 they announced that the captain's chair was broken and had to be repaired, so there was a delay and then it took longer than expected, which required another delay.

Finally, we boarded and taxied out to our spot fourth in line for takeoff, but that is when the captain said that one of the engines was idling too hot, and back to the gate and off the plane we went, for a delay and then another. While the maintenance people were working on the engine, a thunderstorm rolled in, and lighting forced them to come inside. Another delay! Eventually we boarded and took off at 9:40, four hours late. As we are flying,

I was praying, of course, when I distinctly received the Lord's assurance that I was right where I was supposed to be. That was exactly what I needed to know because I still had a 45-minute drive from the airport to my hotel in Fishers.

We landed at 11:00 and I waited another 20 minutes on the deserted airport curb for a shuttle to take me to the rental car place. A sole employee curtly greeted me, gave me keys and paperwork, but no map or directions, and pointed toward the car lot, which was quite dark, and took a few scary minutes using my cell phone light to find the car. Lord, are you sure I am right where I should be?

Safe inside with doors locked and engine running, I breathed a deep sigh of relief, typed the address into my iPhone GPS and off I went, driving after midnight, to a place I had never been before, following directions from a voice on my phone. Traffic was sparse. It was only me and few other cars on the interstate highway, which was good because I had been wearing my contact lenses for 19 hours and I was having trouble seeing more than 100 feet in front of me. And when I thought I was on my last nerve, I came into a construction zone, a ten mile stretch of dark road where the pavement was uneven, the lanes shifted to the right and back again, and then narrowed to single lane lined with encroaching orange barrels. It was a scene I have always feared; being alone, lost, and vulnerable. So, why was this exactly where I needed to be? What did I need to experience? What did I need to learn? Then like a drop of rain, God's word dropped into my heart, "Fear not, for I am with you."

In the worst whirlwind night of my life, I was not alone or lost or vulnerable. I KNEW Jesus was with me and even if I did not find my hotel, I KNEW He would protect me. I did not panic, although I thought about it. I kept my hands on the wheel and my foot on the accelerator and I set my will to trust Jesus and I prayed, fervently, for His peace, His presence, and His protection. I asked Him to drive, to help me see where I was going and to guide my car, and I thanked Him for my life and my salvation.

Debbie Huckaby

His Mustache Was the Key to My Fifty-Year-Old Secret

I was reflecting with a prayer partner about times in my life when I had been sorely deceived and about the people who had perpetrated that deception. She reminded me to pray and suggested I pray with someone for healing prayer. So, I asked God to show me if there were any ways Satan had a foothold in me that had left me open to deception.

A week or so later, I was driving to work at the college and noticed the man in the car behind me. He had a mustache like a man I once knew, named David. David was an acquaintance of my stepfather's and after my divorce, I dated him a couple of times as a friend. Seeing the man in my rearview mirror reminded me of a time I had behaved particularly naïve in David's presence. That memory immediately took me to something my stepfather often said to me, "You are so gullible, Debbie. You will believe anybody."

As if a light bulb had turned on inside my head, I realized that was a word curse that my stepfather had spoken over me. Now, I know that Daddy Jay never intended it that way, but he was my parent and the authority in our home. My young mind believed what he said, and worse, the enemy used it as a weapon against me.

Following my recognition of the word curse, a succession of pictures, places, and people paraded before my eyes, like a view master slide reel, showing me where deception had impacted the trajectory of my life. So many times, I had believed key people, who had hurt me intentionally, and now I could clearly see the damage. I was stunned to say the least.

So, first I confessed in believing that lie and asked God to forgive me, and with deep, deep gratitude thanked God for protecting me in all those times and situations when I had acted in accordance with the curse and allowed myself to be harmed or endangered. Then I broke the word curse off of me and my children. Never would it manipulate me again. I prayed to forgive my stepfather for speaking those words, and I asked God to bring healing in all the places and relationships where injury had occurred as a result of that curse.

Then, I prayed to forgive those who had intentionally taken advantage of a "gullible" girl. I prayed to forgive Danny for the date that changed me forever. I prayed to forgive John for intentionally getting me drunk and attempting to wife-swap me. I prayed to forgive Gary for inconsiderately usurping so much of my life. I prayed to forgive myself for innocently allowing myself to be deceived, coerced, and manipulated. Most importantly, I thanked God for protecting me in so many more situations that could have been disastrous.

And I grieved. I grieved for the loss of innocence. I grieved for the hidden wounds that I had suffered, never realizing before how intentionally they had been done. I grieved for a love that I lost, deceptively believing it wasn't real. More deeply I grieved for a relationship I had endured for decades, deceptively believing that it was the real thing, only to realize that it was never more than smoke and mirrors. Mostly, I grieved for the many years of my life that are gone forever, which is the real loss of blindly believing.

Still, I grieved and grieved. It was the only thing I could do.

Grief is necessary!

Debbie Huckaby

My Family, My Heart

In two months, I will be seventy years old, that is seven decades, which even sounds old. Lord willing, one day my precious sons, Gary, and Andy, will be this old and those who are little now will be in their thirties, the age of their parents today. Will they have questions they wished they had asked me while I was still alive? Will they wonder about things they never heard me mention or things long forgotten.

My mother died in 1995 when she was just sixty years old. Momma Erline died in 2000. Daddy Jay in 2002 and Daddy Jerry in 2003. I have been the matriarch of the family for almost 20 years. During those years, I have often had questions I wish I had asked my family. Why did Momma and Daddy divorce when I was five? When did Aunt Josephine and Aunt Pearl die? What was my great grandfather, Daddy Jiles like? How are we related to Elvis Presley? The answers to those questions, I will never know this side of heaven. So, I write these words today about things my sons and their families may one day wonder about me and those precious family members who have gone on ahead of me.

When Momma Macel was alive, she was the cornerstone of the family. We gathered as a family for holidays and birthdays and just to be together. Mike and Robbi and their sons, Grant and Adam would come from Brunswick. Allen and Denise with their son Christopher would come from near Atlanta. Their daughter Heather was only six weeks old when she came to meet Momma Macel for the first and only time before momma died. When the family gathered, we ate and talked and talked and ate and always laughed a lot. After Momma died, we didn't gather as a family except for funerals.

In 2000, Momma Erline died, quietly one night in her sleep. She had been in a Nursing home on St. Simons Island for a few months. I had prayed and prayed that when her day came, she would just go to sleep and wake up with Jesus. That is what happened. She was buried in Newnan, beside Daddy Leon.

Mike and Allen and our families gathered at Momma Erline's house and shared her belongings. I brought home her bedroom suite and the dining room table, chairs, and hutch. I think Gary II now has the hutch. Mike and Robbi got Daddy Leon's Navy trunk. Joe and Judy got Momma Jiles' bed and the Houser cabinet from the kitchen. Then Mike sold the house, and because it was so beautiful and structurally sound, it was moved to a neighboring street.

In 2001, Daddy Jay was diagnosed with esophageal cancer. He had served in the Army, coding and decoding messages. He had been stationed in Korea as well as Arizona where they were testing atomic weapons. He told me about the mushroom clouds and how most all of his company had perished with cancer, but Daddy Jay fought it. He lost 85 pounds from bouts of C-Difficile and received food only through a feeding tube for more than six months, but he lived. He had a ruptured aortic aneurysm and was life flighted to Savannah for surgery, and survived, which was a miracle. I brought him to Athens Regional Medical Center in

December of 2001 where he stayed for six weeks. During those weeks he had a heart attack and didn't even know it until the doctor told him. The nurses loved him, and they spent lots of time in his room talking and laughing, but I am most grateful to the chaplain who led Daddy Jay in prayer to receive Lord Jesus Christ as his Lord and Savior.

Finally, Daddy was discharged to a rehab center and spent a few months at Allen's house and eventually went home. He regained his strength and even drove to his hometown of Wedowee, Alabama to attend a class reunion. Then one night in December 2002, Daddy Jay went to sleep and woke up with Jesus. We gathered again as family at his funeral, and they asked me to officiate the service, which I did. It was my first sermon, and this is what I said.

"My name is Debbie Atkins Huckaby. Jay Kirby is my Stepfather. On behalf of his family, we thank you so much for coming. You are here today because in some way Jay Kirby touched your life. You may have known him as family or friend, but your relationship with him was unique and we will miss him, each in our own special way.

"First to Lurainor Shaw and Ishmael Jasper Kirby, Jay Clennis was their first child. Born August 2, 1933, in Woodland Alabama, he had his mother's statue and his father's infectious laugh. Both Maw Maw, 92 and Paw Paw 90 will mourn the loss of their son. To Blaine, Jan, and June, Slick was a big brother—taller, older, and of course 'always right'. The brothers are together again. The sisters will keep his funny memories alive for the many nieces and nephews.

"Jay Kirby graduated from Randolph County High School, class of 1950. I am somewhat familiar with this school. Daddy told me several times while I was growing up how he walked to this school five miles in the snow and uphill both ways. This past summer there were 17 of that class who returned for their 54th class reunion. Now, 16 friends will remember Jay Clennis as another one gone home.

"Jay Kirby was a veteran. He served his country as a Cryptographer in the Korean War. Just recently he told me of being in a place in Arizona where he watched a huge mushroom cloud rise out of the desert approximately 1,000 yards away. His country will honor him as a Veteran of Foreign Wars.

"On March 5th, 1960, Jay Kirby became the husband of Macel Nevell Atkins and June 5, 1995, he became her widower. Momma and Daddy were best friends and after 35 years of marriage and nine years of separation, today they are together again.

"When Momma and Daddy married, I was eight years old, and Mike was six. Overnight Jay Kirby became a stepfather. Daddy always enjoyed telling others how I cried and got mad because they would not take me on their honeymoon. On February.4, 1963, Allen Jay Kirby was born, and Jay Kirby became a father.

"Daddy taught me to drive. He taught Mike to fish. He shared his love of computers with Allen. No matter what was going on, we could always count on Daddy to listen. Allen and Denise, Mike and Robbi, and Gary and I will miss our Daddy and Father-in-Law.

"To Grant and Adam (Adam Ant), to Gary and Andy,

to Christopher and Heather, Jay Kirby is Poppa or Daddy Jay. You each hold a very special memory of your granddaddy. You were each very special in his heart.

"As a Hospital Administrator, he was considered a 'good boss'. He knew most every employee by name. Later, for others, he was a dependable employee. He was active in the Jaycees and Elks for years, giving of his time and energies. Jay Kirby never met a stranger. He always enjoyed being with people. His family is small, but his friends are many. To those who called Kirby 'friend', thank you for all your love and support, especially over this past year and a half.

"In June 2003, Daddy found out that he had an esophageal tumor. This began one of the hardest years of his life. Psalm 23 best describes this year to me. 'Yeah, though I walk through the valley of the shadow of death, I will fear no evil.' For a period of approximately six months, Daddy survived without solid food, underwent emergency surgery to repair a ruptured aortic aneurysm, suffered a heart attack, congestive heart failure, gastrointestinal infections, kidney failure, and pneumonia. He had lost more than 85 pounds. Daddy spent five weeks in the hospital in Athens where I work. He was sicker than he even knew, but even on his worst days he was still joking and good natured. The nurses loved him, but they also thought he would not make it out of there alive.

"Then in January 2004, a hospital chaplain prayed with Daddy in his hospital bed. Daddy believed he was healed. Not only did he believe he was healed, but he believed in the Healer, the Great Physician, Our Lord, and Savior Jesus Christ. Daddy almost immediately began to show signs of recovery. His heart grew stronger, and he began to eat again. He spent a month in rehab and lived with my brother for three months. And four months from that healing prayer, Daddy came home again to Douglas. Daddy walked through the valley of death, but he came out on the other side.

"Psalm 91 says, 'He who dwells in the shelter of the Most High will abide in the shadow of the Almighty.' Jay Kirby found his way to the shadow of the Almighty. He was a son, a brother, a husband, a father, a grandfather, and a friend, but most importantly, he is a child of God. He was the only one of his kind. Created with loving care—his days were numbered before there was even one of them.

"Like Jay Kirby, your life and relationships are unique. Science has proven what God has known all along. There is no other and never will be another you. You are not an accident. You may have been a surprise, but you are not an accident. Psalm 139 says, 'For You formed my inward parts; You wove me in my mother's womb. I will give thanks to You, for I am fearfully and wonderfully made; Wonderful are Your works, and my soul knows it very well. My frame was not hidden from You, When I was made in secret, and skillfully wrought in the depths of the earth; Your eyes have seen my unformed substance; And in Your book were all written the days that were ordained for me, when as yet there was not one of them.'

"You are a designer original—created and loved as God's precious child. Like Jay Kirby's life, your life is your story! You know the good and the bad. Your friends and family may know part of your story, the outside you, but

God knows all of you and He still loves you. Maybe you too received a bad report. You may have received that phone call late at night or even very early in the morning. You may have decided that death was near for you as well. You too may have walked through the valley of the shadow of death.

"The last six months were some of the best times of Daddy's life. He went back to the Elks bingo nights. He traveled several times to visit his parents and family in Alabama. He had a few dates and shared many good times with friends. He enjoyed and valued each day as never before.

"Daddy and I talked a lot. Just a few days ago he told me that he was spending a lot of time talking with Jesus. I am a nurse and I believe people know when their time is near. When someone dies, we think of them as gone, dead, buried in the ground. But only bodies die, people don't die. Jay Kirby's body is in this manmade box, but he is with Jesus in heaven in a place made especially for him. Psalm 23:6 'Surely goodness and mercy will follow me all the days of my life, And I will dwell in the house of the LORD forever.'

"Let us pray: Lord, we thank you for the life of Jay Kirby. As family and friends, we thank You for the opportunity to love him and share our lives with him. I thank you for his salvation and that he is with you in heaven. But Lord most of all, we thank you for Your son, Our Lord Jesus Christ and for the salvation He made available to us. We pray your will be done on earth as it is in heaven. In the precious name of Jesus. Amen."

Just three months later, on my 51st birthday, the man who helped bring me into this world, died. Daddy Jerry was my father, but he was never really my daddy. After he and mom divorced, he served in the Army and was stationed in Germany and when he returned, he married Betty, his second wife. They adopted a son, Greg, and then had a son, Kevin, and a daughter, Karen. Gary and I went to Atlanta to visit Daddy Jerry and Betty at Granny (Beatrice) Atkins' the year before we were married. Then Daddy Jerry came to visit me and my family most every year after that.

Later in life, Daddy Jerry suffered with many health conditions. He had several heart attacks and once suffered a cardiac arrest at the door of the Emergency Room. Thereafter, he lived with an erratic heart rhythm, which occasionally caused him to pass out. Somehow, he hurt his back and broke his tailbone. There was nothing the doctors could do but give him pain medication, which he took in copious amounts for intractable pain. Eventually he was diagnosed with Alzheimer's, from which he and all his family suffered greatly until he died.

Daddy was buried in the Masonic Cemetery in Atlanta. Within five years, Karen suffered a stroke and died. Kevin got a divorce and intestinal cancer. Then Betty died and I heard that Greg was doing drugs. In October 2017, I conducted the funeral for Howard Atkins, Daddy's brother and I still communicate with Aunt Marie, Daddy's sister, who is 86 years old.

Gary and Andy expanded our little family in a similar way to how Mike and I did years ago. Mike and Robbi had their firstborn son, Grant in June of 1978 and four years later Gary and I had our firstborn son, Gary II. Then Mike and Robbi had their second son, Adam and Gary and I had our second son, Andy. The names starting with G's and A's as well as the alternating birth order were not intentional, but interesting.

Then in 2010 my little family began to expand when Andy and Kimberly delivered our first grandchild, a beautiful baby girl named Kylie Brooke Huckaby. The next year Gary's firstborn, Walter Gunner Huckaby was born and just six months later Andy's son Andrew Garrett Huckaby was born. One year and one week later we welcomed Gary's second son Phillip Gray Huckaby into the family. To carry on the family tradition, they all call me Momma Bee and Gary is Poppa Bee.

After Gary's divorce in 2016, he and Gray and Gunner bought a house in Jackson County a couple of miles from the East Jackson elementary, middle, and high school. About that same time, Gary and Lauren, Gunner's preschool teacher, began to get better acquainted. They were married in a private family ceremony on December 8, 2018, and also had a beautiful spring wedding ceremony at the Thompson House on May 21, 2019. Our four doorstep grandchildren are now 11, 10, 9 and 8, and Gary and Lauren have given us our second granddaughter Maggie Beau Huckaby, who just turned eight months old.

Kylie Brooke has her daddy's smile and his twinkle in her eye, and she is every bit a daddy's girl. When she was younger, Kylie wore the lace and frills of the Disney princesses while picking up bugs and worms and snakes if she could. Kylie is also carrying on the Huckaby intelligence, becoming a Beta Club member in the fifth grade, but when she was just two or three, she was already skillfully using her smarts and her little girls' ways. I heard her talking to Poppa Bee one day, looking up at him with her big, beautiful eyes and in a sugary sweet voice saying, "But Poppa Bee. I need such and such" and, of course, whatever it was Kylie wanted, Poppa Bee gave her. I cautioned him. "One day when she is sixteen, she will bat those lashes and say, 'But Poppa Bee I need that car.'"

"Yeah," Gary said, "and I will probably get it for it for her too." I like to think that Kylie is taking after me in her love for gymnastics, cartwheels, and backflips. While I can't do any of that anymore, I will always be her biggest fan.

Andrew Garrett is a huge personality in a little package. He was always little for his age, even to the point of concern. I was so distraught by his small frame that I feared for his life or his ability to thrive and probably harassed Andy and Kimberly until they took him to a gastroenterologist and an endocrinologist. They began supplementing his poor appetite with protein growth drinks like Ensure, which helped his weight, but drinking it right before bed resulted in so many cavities they had to be filled under general anesthesia.

At times Garrett's personality would burst forth from small size into an external rage, which got him permanently excused from almost every daycare in Oconee County. One time, I was asked to pick him up when a day care complained. That was a hallmark day in Andrew Garrett's life, because that was the day he got to know Momma Bee in a whole new way. I have never been so mad at any human as I was at him that day, except once when his daddy was about that age and acted the same way. Let's just say Garrett now knows he better obey me, his parents, and his teachers immediately, or else and he doesn't want to find out what "or else" means.

To help him channel his pent up anger, which was often instigated by big sister Kylie, I convinced his parents to enroll him in karate and agreed to help get him there. So, Garrett and I started going to karate and I have totally enjoyed watching that young man transform before my very eyes. He excels in his routines and has won the hearts and admiration of his instructors. Today Garrett is a few months away from a first degree black belt. He is a fierce warrior in the execution of his form, with his weapons, and in competition, and his transformation is evident in his behavior at school as well. This year he was appointed class leader because of his apt attention and help in the classroom. Way to go, Garrett. I am so very proud of you, young man.

Walter Gunner Huckaby has always been a miniature replica of his daddy. I often look at Gunner and see my little Gary, and while there are similar personality traits, Gunner is definitely his own person. He is shy and quiet like his dad, but Gunner is a natural born leader, even though he tries to hide in the crowd. He is contemplative and analytical and a sharp thinker. He loves to build things and has an amazing sense of structural creativity, just like his dad. I believe Gunner can grow up to be whatever he wants to be. He has the internal fortitude to succeed with whatever he tries to accomplish.

If you have a ball, any kind of ball, Phillip Gray Huckaby wants to play. I have never known another child who loves to play ball as much as Gray. Physically, he looks like his big brother Gunner, same height, eyes, and hair, and sometimes he looks up to him as older and smarter, but mostly Gray goes his own way. He has had a strong and sometimes frustrating ability to focus when he gets engrossed in something and does not respond when you speak to him. He is interested in science, like dinosaurs, sharks, fish, and crystals, and he tells me such details that I know he has been thinking about them a lot. Best of all, Gray loves the UGA, Georgia Bull Dawgs. His room is red and black and decorated with his favorite Dawgs on the wall and pillows and everywhere you look. I wonder if one day Gray will be a UGA Bull Dawg. Seems like a perfect match for a young man who loves balls and UGA Dawgs.

Maggie Beau is our youngest Huckaby. At just eight months

old, already she is quite the center of attention. She has her mother's beautiful face and her daddy's gentle demeanor, but she is a motor mouth like me. She is shy and quiet until she gets comfortable with you and then she gets loud and proud. I can only imagine what this little lady will be like, but with her doting big brothers, Mommie, and Daddy I know she will be loved and protected every day of her life.

The littlest Huckaby is my four-legged fur baby. I wanted a little white Maltese puppy for decades, but traveling as much as I did, I just could not get one. Then in 2019, I realized that I was home most of the time, so I started praying and asking the Lord if it was the right time to get a puppy and for guidance in finding the one for me. I also needed the money since Maltese puppies can be quite expensive.

Before long, I found a breeder who just happened to live in Georgia and was expecting a litter in August, so I could have a puppy by October. Wow! I was so excited and understood this to mean that I would be staying home more than traveling, and that I could pursue getting one, but I was also a little nervous. I wanted to be a good puppy parent.

I visited my precious little fur baby when he was just two weeks old and brought him home when he was two months. What should I name him, I prayed? Then one night as I ended my day in prayer, I heard, "Bebee is his name," so his name is Bebee. I have learned so much about puppies and about myself. I learned that I loved to cuddle with this soft, furry mass of happiness, and I also know now how rough it is going out for his pee-pee poo breaks in cold, rainy, and windy weather. Still, he is worth it. Thank you, Lord.

The boys had Paco, the dachshund and I have Bebee, but Gary has always been a cat person. When we were first married and lived in the mobile home park, a beautiful white cat came to our house. Gary took to it immediately, but it was sick with feline leukemia and died a few weeks later. Soon, we got a female cat we called Momma Cat, who kept us abundantly supplied with cats around the house for decades. Once we had 25 cats, which was 25 too many for me. In 2010, Andy gave Gary a six-week old yellow kitty whose feet and head were so large, I named him Samson. He grew to be a very large and quite fierce cat. He lived on the screened porch and came and went through the cat door, but most often he could be found sitting on Gary's lap. On December 7, 2017, Samson didn't come home. In fact, he never came home again. We don't know what happened to him or where he went, but Gary searched for Samson and grieved for weeks and misses him still.

This year Gary and I will be legally married for 44 years, but, unfortunately, we have never had a real husband and wife relationship. I had gotten away from Christian friends and regular church attendance during my marriage to John. After my divorce, Gary and I dated a couple of times, but instead of taking time to get to know each other, we began spending every moment together and moved together to Athens. I didn't ask the Lord or pray about him, I just assumed that since Gary had grown up in the church, he and I would hold the same beliefs and values. I was wrong, so very wrong!

Our differences were not obvious at first. We both enjoyed the UGA football games and dancing afterwards at O'Malley's or the B&L Warehouse. We enjoyed our careers, a pharmacist and a nurse working the same shift, and going to the beach when we were off. When we sat on the porch late at night, I talked a lot about a home and a family. Gary talked about his love of golf and when he said that golf would always be his first love, I believed that would change, but when a home and a family became a reality and Gary's focus stayed on golf, our differences began to get in the way.

2 Corinthians 6:14-15 says, Do not be yoked together with unbelievers. For what do righteousness and wickedness have in common? Or what fellowship can light have with darkness? What harmony is there between Christ and Belial? Or what does a believer have in common with an unbeliever? Rev. Kent Reynolds explained it like this. When two oxen are yoked together, if one is small and the other is tall or if one is obedient and the other rebellious, there will be trouble. One ox will pull in one direction and the other will go in another. That is a great picture of what has happened to us.

Over time and with every choice we made along the way, the space between us widened. Our paths rarely coincided and only crossed when I needed or expected Gary to function as a husband, and of course, he didn't. It took me 40 years to understand. Seeing the man with the mustache and receiving the revelation of the word curse and the subsequent healing from a life of deception opened my eyes. I had seen in Gary who and what I was deceived into seeing. Our marriage had been a farce. I grieved for the 40 years of my life that were lost. I grieved for the years without love and companionship. Then I released it all to Jesus.

Now I am free of the pain and remorse and give thanks for so much. I have two wonderful sons who are good men, husbands, fathers, and best of all, my sons are Christians. I am thankful for their families, their loving companions, and precious children. I am thankful they too are Christians.

I am thankful to God for the house and lifestyle I have been afforded through Gary and for the many positions, degrees, and opportunities I have enjoyed. God has been with me every day, every step of the way, loving me more than any human ever could and for that I am eternally thankful.

Debbie Huckaby

The End is a Beginning

Santosh Kalwar said every beginning has an end and every end has a beginning and at 70 years old, I am closer to the end than the beginning, so I am looking back over my many years to find and share bits of the wisdom.

Through my studies and experiences, I have come to understand and appreciate stewardship of the body, mind, and spirit as a most excellent quality. This is founded in my understanding of who we are and how we are created in the image of God. Genesis 1 tells us that God created plants and animals that reproduce after their own kind and in Genesis 2 we read how God created man in God's own image. In Exodus 20, God commanded that we should not make an image or idol in the form of anything in heaven above or on the earth beneath. In other words, we are not to create an image of God. That is because we are to be the image or representation of God on earth and multiple New Testament verses tell us how. Hebrews 1:3 says Jesus Christ, the Son of God, God the Son is the exact representation of His being, therefore, we are to spend our lives becoming like Christ. Stewardship of our mind, body, and spirit is essential to becoming all God created us to be.

Being the steward of my body means that I must know what

my body needs, and I must do my best to provide for those needs. For example, I need to know what foods will give my body the strength to live life to its fullest capacity. Along with food, I must provide the needed sleep, water, exercise, clothes, and accessories like glasses, shoes, gloves, etc. to keep it safe and healthy. I must protect it from harmful things like sharp objects or UV rays, dirty water, loud noises, parasites, bacteria, chemicals, and excesses of any kind. This is not a one and done kind of action. Because I change and the world around me changes, I must constantly reassess the status and needs of my physical being. 1 Corinthians 6:19 says that my body is a temple of the Holy Spirit. It is the vehicle or tool God has given me to execute the purpose for which I am created. It is a gift from God, and I am accountable for its well-being. Therefore, I must do my best for it as long as I am in it.

My mind and emotions, sometimes called the soul, need care also. Like eating good food for my body, I must provide the best for my mind as well. What I see cannot be unseen. What I read is etched in my brain forever. My thoughts can be nurturing or damaging, so I must take responsibility for what I think. Paul tells me how in Philippians 4:8. "Brothers," Paul writes, "focus your thoughts on what is true, noble, righteous, pure, lovable, or admirable, on some virtue or on something praiseworthy." Every contrary thought must be apprehended and turned over to the Lord Jesus Christ for purification. Especially condemnation, which is not of the Lord and must be banished (Romans 8:1).

I have often said, "Pay attention to what gets your attention." Given the billions of distracting stimuli that I encounter each day, if something floats through my mind more than once, I need to pay attention. If it is a To Do item, then I put it on a list so my mind can be relieved from rehearsing it. If it is an event or words

I spoke or words spoken to me that keep replaying in my head, then I consider how it makes me feel. Am I sad, or hurt? Do I feel guilt or shame? Did it make me feel inadequate or rejected? Then, I take it to Jesus.

"Lord, what do you want me to know about this? What part of this is mine to own?" I pray for forgiveness for my part and to forgive others for theirs. I pray about next steps. Do I need to apologize or somehow make restitution? Was there another place or time that I felt like this? I pray and listen and wait. Years of practicing this healing prayer has given me more awareness of my thoughts, better communication with the Lord, and healing of many hurts along the way. Like the scar from a physical wound that has healed, the memory of the event or words remain, but where there was pain, now there is peace.

Stewardship of my body, mind, and emotions is synonymous with care of the spirit. My spirit is eternal. This world is not the end and when my physical body (vehicle) is dead, my spirit will live eternally with my Lord and Savior Jesus Christ. Until then, it is my responsibility to be a good steward of my spiritual well being. Jesus said, "Man does not live on bread alone, but on every word that comes from the mouth of GOD (Matthew 4:4)." Therefore, I must keep my spirit fed with the Word of God, which is a lamp for my feet and a light for my journey (Psalm 119:105).

These beliefs and practices of stewardship were founded in my view of the human person best described by Daniel Fountain in his book, Health, the Bible, and the Church, where he says the Biblical view of a human person is an inseparable, interdependent, and intermingled unified whole. Quite simply this means that my mind, body, and spirit are different aspects, not different parts, of my being and whatever affects one aspect affects all.

Whole person thinking leads to whole person living, and that facilitates holiness.

Wholeness is exemplified in integrity, which is defined as the state of being whole or united. I now understand that when I feel restless, conflicted, or generally discontented, one or more aspects of my being are out of sync. At times this has been divine discontentment or God's way of getting me ready to transition to another place or position. I say, God takes me a place out of me before He takes me out of it. In those times I could only wait on God whose timing is perfect.

The other times, however, were indications that something in my life needed to change. Those were times when I had become undisciplined or procrastinated or needed to deal with an interpersonal issue. Several times I was carrying a burden that I needed to place in Jesus' hands and leave with Him. For all those issues, prayer helped me understand and make the needed response. Then when my mind, emotions, spirit, and body were working in tandem, there was unity and there was peace.

Every child of God has been given gifts. These are often described as talents and abilities, which all people have, but the gifts I am referring to are gifts of the Spirit, the Holy Spirit. Found in Romans 12:6-8, 1 Corinthians 12:8-10, 1 Corinthians 12:28-30, Ephesians 4:11, and 1 Peter 4:11, God's gifts are given for the equipping of the church. My gifts include leadership, administration, words of wisdom, teacher, kinds of healing, and apostle. I have spent my life learning about the Holy Spirit, the gifts I have been given, and how they are to be used. I have noted that when I am in the center of God's will and operating in my gifts, I have a greater sense of God's presence and greater evidence of God's grace.

I remember my first sermon. It was Daddy Jay's funeral, and

the funeral home chapel, which seated about 200-250 people, didn't have a microphone. The singer offered her karaoke machine, but it quit working soon after she set it up. So, I prayed, and God's amazing grace gave me the ability to speak and project my voice so that all could hear. I also remember the incredible joy and peace of God's presence the first time I assisted Rev. Parker Benson in the Great Thanksgiving, which are the prayers that surround Holy Communion. When I was a candidate for ordained ministry in the UMC, my mentors acknowledged my giftings of leadership and administration, and tried to get me to become a candidate to an appointment of elder, but at the time, I didn't recognize those as ministry gifts, so I dismissed their leading. I had a lot to learn.

In fact, learning is the best gift I have ever received, and the most important gift I would like to pass on to others. Learning has been and still is a big part of my life. From the Dale Carnegie book I tried to read when I was six or seven, through the six degrees I have completed, learning from others has broadened my perspective and expanded my world. Learning from countless experiences has taught me what it means to love and hate, and every emotion in between. Learning freed me from years of deception in my personal life and prepared me to see the world for what it is.

Finally, learning has opened my eyes to who I am, but more importantly, learning has kept my heart searching for God the Father, God the Son, and God the Holy Spirit. I am a lifelong learner, so for me, the end will always be a beginning. I pray it may be so for you too.

Debbie Huckaby

About the Author

Debbie Huckaby has been a leader of "new beginnings" for more than four decades in the fields of healthcare, business, and ministry. Debbie ministers with a passion for whole person health (mind, body, spirit), to people from all walks of life by speaking and writing about God's word and by facilitating individual and group new beginnings.

She earned her Nursing degree from South Georgia College, and a Bachelor and Master of Business Administration from Brenau University. Following a call to the ministry, Debbie earned a Master of Theology from Wheaton College, a Master of Divinity, and a Doctor of Ministry in Preaching and Global Leadership Transformation from Asbury Theological Seminary. Additionally, Debbie completed a Post-Doctoral Fellowship in Israeli biblical, economic, political, and geographic history. Debbie is an ordained Wesleyan pastor, who has taught Theology and Bible classes for more than 20 years in her local church, community, and ministry settings.

She is a wife, mother, and grandmother to five and loves to walk with her Maltese puppy, Bebee.

www.ingramcontent.com/pod-product-compliance
Lightning Source LLC
Chambersburg PA
CBHW030315100526
44592CB00010B/443